Children in the House

CHILDREN
IN THE HOUSE

The Material Culture of Early Childhood, 1600–1900

KARIN CALVERT

NORTHEASTERN UNIVERSITY PRESS · BOSTON

Library of Congress Cataloging-in-Publication Data

Calvert, Karin Lee Fishbeck.
Children in the house : the material culture of early childhood, 1600–1900 / Karin Calvert.
p. cm.
Includes bibliographical references.
ISBN 1-55553-189-X
1. Children—United States—History. 2. Material culture—United States. 3. United States—Social life and customs. I. Title.
HQ792.U5C35 1992 92-14142
305.23′09—dc20

Designed by Christine Leonard Raquepaw

Composed in Simoncini Garamond by Coghill Composition Company in Richmond, Virginia.
Printed and bound by Thomson-Shore, Inc., in Dexter, Michigan.
The paper is Glatfelter, an acid-free sheet.

MANUFACTURED IN THE UNITED STATES OF AMERICA

96 95 94   5 4 3 2

To Braunda and Howard Fishbeck

and

To Ian David Calvert

Contents

CONTENTS

Figures

Acknowledgments

Many friends and colleagues have read various versions of this work and offered encouragement and thoughtful advice. Richard Bushman and Stefanie Wolf were a part of the project from the very start, and each offered invaluable suggestions and unflagging enthusiasm from beginning to end. Kenneth Ames and James Curtis originally taught me how to read artifacts and visual images, making this study possible. Murray Murphey read the final versions with meticulous care, which was as deeply appreciated as his constant support. Del Upton was equally generous with his time, and the final product benefits from his very thoughtful comments. Margaretta Lovell, Melvyn Hammarberg, Robert Schuyler, Michael Zuckerman, Joseph Illick, Wayne Craven, and Damie Stillman have given me encouragement, suggestions, and the example of their own work. While numerous libraries and museums were invaluable caches of documents and images, a special word of appreciation needs to be said to the staff of the libraries of the Henry Francis du Pont Winterthur Museum, whose expertise and enthusiasm were particularly valuable. Finally, my husband, Ian Calvert, was a steady center who offered both encouragement and a very necessary sense of perspective.

Children in the House

Introduction

Members of any society carry within themselves a working definition of childhood, its nature, limitations, and duration. They may not explicitly discuss this definition, write about it, or even consciously conceive of it as an issue, but they act upon their assumptions in all of their dealings with, fears for, and expectations of their children. Every culture defines what it means to be a child, how children should look and act, what is expected of them, and what is considered beyond their capabilities. Older children learn to adapt themselves to the personas encouraged by their society, to be feminine or masculine, obedient or mischievous, innocent or worldly as their society expects of them. Very young children, however, lack the necessary perception and skills to conform.

Parents deal with the disparity between the individual infant and the cultural ideal in numerous ways. They adopt the convention that their child is everything they believe it should be. Today we tell ourselves and each other that any baby girl is dainty, pretty, and a little coquette and that any baby boy is strong, brave, and quite the little man. We see promising signs of intelligence or talent in all sorts of infant gestures. Parents also physically control infants to encourage desired behavior. Modern parents, for example, are more likely to cuddle and comfort baby girls, and bounce and toss baby boys, to both affirm and encourage proper gender identification. Parents have further relied on clothing, furniture, and other material goods specifically designed to modify children's appearance or behavior to meet social and cultural expectations. For much of the twentieth century, for example, we have adhered to an amazingly rigid color code for infant clothing—pink (and recently lavender) for girls, blue for boys. The code goes much further. Only girls can wear ruffles on the shoulders of their overalls or lace edging on their play clothes; and while both baby boys and girls can wear their hair at a variety of lengths, only little girls can hold their hair in place with a barrette. In an age that stresses freedom, self-expression, and equality, such rigid and detailed rules seem quite curious, but they serve an important social function. Institutionalized sartorial differentiation informs everyone who comes in contact with a child of its gender, so that they will respond in socially accepted ways to this particular little person, thus reinforcing the gender role that will be expected of it in the future. Pink and blue baby clothes become evidence of the importance of early gender identification in a society where so little seems certain. It tells us something about our present fears, preoccupations, and priorities. The objects used in the raising of children have changed dramatically over time, but they have always met more than the simple physical needs of the children. They have also met the parents' need to mold their infants into the accepted cultural image of the time.

The link between artifacts and cultural constructs makes the study of material culture an important method for gaining access to cultural beliefs and assumptions so basic that they are rarely verbalized and to social fears too emotionally laden for direct discussion. Some parents of the past did write down their views concerning proper upbringing and their own children's behavior.[1] A few contemporary physicians or other recognized authorities wrote about the mechanics of childrearing and the treatment of childhood illnesses. Most parents, however, took the ordinary details of caring for young children too much for granted to bother to write about them, if they wrote at all.

Children described the substance of their lives even less frequently. Those under the age of seven, the group of primary interest here, were usually both illiterate and inarticulate. The rare children who did write most often did so with explicit instructions concerning what to say ("be sure to tell Aunt Harriet how much you liked her present"), or under supervision, or with the knowledge that their letters, essays, and diaries might be read by other family members at any time. Ten-year-old Caroline Richards of Canandaigua, New York, for example, wrote that since her elders had the right to read her diary she dare not confide everything to it.[2] The right to the privacy of one's own thoughts is a quite recent acquisition in the history of childhood, and parents of the past expected to be able to read their children's diaries and correspondence. Very few children broke through the constraints of convention and parental control to record everything they really felt. Because examples of young people determined and able to speak their own minds are so rare, we are that much more charmed with the forthrightness of one Maryland girl who, in 1800, carefully cross-stitched onto her sampler, "Patty Polk did this and she hated every stitch she did in it. She loves to read much more."[3] If few adults and fewer children wrote about the methods and goals of common childrearing practices, many more left behind artifacts used for the task. The objects, as it were, became a physical trail by which to track cultural change.

From the cradle brought over on the *Mayflower* for little Peregrine White, parents availed themselves of leading strings, walking stools, swaddling clothes, skeleton suits, cribs, jumpers, dolls, rocking horses, pantaloons, perambulators, high chairs, bassinets, and crawling blankets in the day-to-day task of raising a child. Virtually no child-related objects have remained continuously in use in America, however. Rather, a few types of children's artifacts flourish for a time and then disappear, to be replaced by a new and quite different constellation of goods considered necessary to properly bring up a baby. An analysis of such artifact constellations can help uncover the nature of the everyday lives of children and the assumptions and concerns foremost in parents' minds at any one point in history. Such parental preoccupations, in turn, relate directly to the society's perception of the fundamental nature of children.

The little world parents create for their children reveals a great deal about the accepted place of children in the larger world. The key is to seek out the assumptions underlying the popularity of specific styles and forms of childrearing artifacts. For example, did the costume of a particular time accentuate gender differences or focus on distinctions of age? Did forms of furniture for infants encourage autonomy and efficacy or concentrate on comfort or protection? Were children's artifacts plain and functional, or elaborate and status bearing? Were particular rooms within the house reserved for the use of children, and if so where were they located, how were they furnished, and how much time did children spend there? When did a young person graduate from a strictly childish costume or room to adult dress and quarters? What toys, if any, were commonly available, and what gender or age restrictions were attached to particular toys? What was life really like for the children at a particular moment in American history, and how did those experiences shape their perception of life? How did parents use clothes, toys, and furniture to create, enforce, or encourage socially correct behavior in their very young children?

Any one object may be capable of numerous functions or meanings, only some of which are valid to a given society at a particular time. A doll, for example, can simply be a child's toy; but at times it has also been a religious image or magical fetish, fashion mannequin, effigy, educational tool, collectible, investment, or objet d'art. On the other hand, a single object might fulfill several different functions simultaneously. A seventeenth-century coral and bells, made of a shaft of red coral set in a silver handle and surrounded by tiny silver bells, served as a pretty rattle, a teether, a magical charm to ward off evil, an investment (as did any silver object), and a tangible symbol of the parents' wealth and status, all at the same time.

Similarly, an object may function on any or all of three distinct planes. It may have one or more technomic or practical uses, or uses accepted as practical by a society. The coral of the baby's rattle, for example, offered a smooth surface to relieve the discomfort of teething, and parents considered it a potent charm to protect children from the evil eye. An object may also have a sociotechnic role by which it facilitates the interactions or relationships between people or conveys information about the owner. The intrinsic value of the silver coral and bells announced the comfortable status of the infant and the family. Finally, an object can fulfill an ideotechnic function as part of a symbolic vocabulary expressing or affirming cultural beliefs and values.[4] In the case of our example, as one of the few toys made expressly for young children in the seventeenth century the coral and bells became a standard symbol or icon for infancy.

While objects can have multiple meanings for the society that uses them, constellations of objects, in this case things intended for use in raising young children, can share common meanings and can therefore point to common concerns and perceptions of reality. As basic cultural assumptions change over time, the artifacts associated with those assumptions lose their usefulness and disappear or undergo modification, and new forms are introduced to meet new needs. Most children's furniture of the seventeenth century was designed to stand babies up and propel them forward, whereas most nineteenth-century furniture was meant to hold infants down and contain them in one spot. The different intentions suggest very different attitudes toward the needs and best interests of the child. The interrelatedness of artifacts also means that when one object is abandoned, others become untenable. When American parents renounced restrictive swaddling for primarily social reasons, for example, they eventually abandoned cradles for the very practical reason that cradles could not effectively contain active, unbound infants.

Before the middle of the eighteenth century very few objects existed in Western culture expressly for the benefit of children, and such forms as did exist changed very little and very slowly over time. Then, with comparative suddenness between 1750 and 1850, a significant number of middle-class parents twice repudiated, abandoned, and replaced all of the popular forms of children's furniture, clothing, and playthings. Such a unique rejection and re-creation of the everyday artifacts of childrearing indicated profound change in society's perception of the nature of childhood and in attitudes toward children.

American children born before the middle of the eighteenth century enjoyed very few objects designed expressly for their use. Those artifacts that did exist—the cradle, swaddling clothes, standing stools, walking stools, and leading strings—forced the young child to lie straight, stand straight, or walk erect. This concern with uprightness, both in a physical and in a moral sense, was one of the crucial preoccupations of that era, since, among other things, it marked one of the major distinctions separating mankind from the rest of the animal kingdom. Very young children tottered precariously between upright humanity and the beasts of the field. By itself, nature in the seventeenth century seemed inadequate to the task of transforming infants into civilized and functioning adults. Parents, therefore, used specially designed artifacts to impose specific patterns of behavior on their offspring—to create at least the semblance of adult appearance and behavior—and to assimilate the child rapidly into adult society.

By the middle of the nineteenth century, the traditional forms of children's artifacts had disappeared, along with fears about the animalistic nature of children, to be replaced by completely new and different artifacts. The crib, high chair, swing, and perambulator all served as barriers between the child and the adult world. Their function was to contain, restrain, and isolate young children who had not yet mastered self-control or sufficient caution. In place of direct participation in the activities of adults, many nineteenth-century parents fabricated a separate world for their offspring filled with special artifacts, activities, and rituals that emphasized the perceived differences between children and adults. Accepting the era's sentimental image of childish sweetness and innocence, parents sought physical barriers to protect their children from physical injury, temptation, and worldly contamination.

In the two centuries following European settlement, the common perception in America of children changed profoundly, having first held to an exaggerated fear of their inborn deficiencies, then expecting considerable self-sufficiency, and then, after 1830, endowing young people with an almost celestial goodness. In each era, children's artifacts mediated between social expectations concerning the nature of childhood and the realities of child-rearing; before 1750, they pushed children rapidly beyond the perceived perils of infancy, and by the nineteenth century they protected and prolonged the perceived joy and innocence of childhood. This book concludes with the end of the nineteenth century, since the complex and multilayered history of childhood in the twentieth century is a topic for a book by itself.

The evidence points to two periods of significant and widespread change before the beginning of the twentieth century. The first began about 1750 and gained momentum during the 1770s; the second occurred in the 1830s and 1840s. At each point the evidence indicates that virtually every aspect of the lives of young children changed. Old forms of dress disappeared to be replaced by radically new ones. Similarly, traditional furniture forms were rejected in favor of very different objects. Changes were made in where children slept, how they were cared for, what nicknames were popular, and what toys were available. A quantitative examination of nine hundred portraits of children, for example, charting the appearance of costume, toys, children's furniture, and representations of playfulness, indicated major shifts in the perception of young people and their roles occurring at about 1750 and 1830.[5] The findings were corroborated by changes in children's books, parental letters and journals, and childrearing manuals happening at about the same times. This does not mean that every parent abruptly dropped familiar methods of childrearing and embraced the new ideas. The process depended very much on where parents stood in their own family history (first-time parents have usually been more willing to try something new than parents who already have other children), on geographical location, since new ideas come first to urban populations, and on the whims and

predilections of individual parents. The dates, therefore, remain only an ap-
proximate guideline indicating the point at which change in social patterns
became evident. Older methods of childrearing continued among some families and communities long after they had been abandoned by others. The
periods suggested here indicate only a significant change in childrearing
practices in a substantial number of middle-class homes.

The normative methods of childrearing, and the attendant vision of the
nature of children, were influential, but by no means universal. Many working-class and immigrant families in America continued into the twentieth
century childrearing practices commonly abandoned here by 1750. This
book sets out some of the concerns and assumptions held by the normative
culture. Other studies are needed to examine the variety of childrearing
methods actually practiced at any one time in America.

While this is an examination of child-related artifacts made or used in this
country, there is little in the conclusions that is unique to America. For the
most part, immigrants made the transatlantic journey bringing with them the
social and cultural patterns of western Europe. Americans continued to purchase European-made goods, organize their living spaces in ways similar to
their European counterparts, and read European books and newspapers.
Lucy Larcom commented on the continued duality of identity still very
much alive in the first half of the nineteenth century for a child growing up
in New England:

> Our close relationship to Old England was sometimes a little misleading
> to us juveniles. The conditions of our life were entirely different, but
> we read her descriptive stories and sang her songs as if they were true
> for us too. One of the first things I learned to repeat—I think it was in
> the spelling book—began with the verse:
>
> > I thank the goodness and the grace
> > That on my birth has smiled,
> > And made me, in these latter days,
> > A Happy English child.[6]

Most of the changes that took place in the perception of the nature of
childhood in America also occurred in Europe. Each nation or ethnic group
there experienced change, but change at its own pace, reinterpreting general
trends to accommodate local traditions. German parents lavished more toys
and child-sized furniture on their children than did their English counter-

parts, for example, but clung to the custom of swaddling long after it had been abandoned elsewhere. Similarly, while American children of the nineteenth century remained a very real presence in the family, many English children gradually disappeared into the separate world of nursery, nanny, and boarding school. Although it is important to note those things that seem uniquely American in the development of the concept of childhood, the European theories, trends, books, fashions, and artifacts that made their way across the Atlantic and influenced American practices have been included here because they are as much a part of the American childrearing tradition as America is a part of Western culture.

The history of childhood has focused on two connected issues: first, whether Western culture had traditionally recognized a concept of childhood as inherently distinct from maturity; second, the nature of the emotional bond between parent and child. Philippe Ariès set the agenda for this debate in his highly influential book *Centuries of Childhood*, which first posited that the concept of childhood in the West did have a beginning and a consequent history. While Ariès drew most of his evidence from French sources, with occasional references to English society, he clearly saw his findings as applicable to all of Western culture. Ariès argues that medieval society did not recognize childhood as a distinct stage of human development with its own characteristics, needs, and limitations. Children were merely juvenile members of adult society. They participated in the same work as adults, wore the same styles of clothing, and enjoyed the same pastimes. Only in the seventeenth century, Ariès argues, did the concept of children as significantly different from, rather than merely smaller than, adults emerge. Once parents viewed their children as different from themselves, they began to limit children's access to adult activities and to offer more intense and specialized instruction and discipline. For Ariès, the seventeenth century was the great watershed, and the development of the concept of childhood has progressed apace ever since.[7]

Ariès bases many of his assumptions about medieval society on a lack of discernible distinctions between adults and children. Medieval children, for example, dressed like their parents and participated in many of the same activities as adults. Therefore, children were viewed as grown-ups in miniature. Unfortunately, the lack of manifest distinctions in any particular area is not evidence of a lack of recognized distinctions between different social groups. A society that has a special costume for children clearly sees them as in some way set apart from their elders, and has chosen to express that separateness visually. However, another society may have an equally well developed concept of the distinct nature of childhood, but not choose to give it sartorial expression. This should be very evident to a society in which members of both sexes, and persons of all ages and social classes, wear blue jeans and sneakers and yet remain very much aware of distinctions of age, class, and gender. That medieval children dressed like adults is not proof that there was no medieval concept of childhood. The absence of evidence is not evidence of absence.

Ariès argues that while some medieval parents had affection for their children, many were indifferent to their young. If the development of the notion of the specialness of children in the seventeenth century led to greater solicitude in their care, it also meant a significant loss of freedom, since special discipline and supervision were also seen as part of children's particular needs. Other scholars have been even more severe, viewing the history of childhood as a steady progress from a cold and brutal past to present enlightenment. Edward Shorter, in *The Making of the Modern Family*, argues that before the modern era parents were indifferent to their children at best. David Hunt, in *Parents and Children in History*, concentrates on Doctor Heroard's account of the upbringing of the future Louis XIII and extrapolates to the French population at large. If the infant Louis was treated as little more than a useful possession by the adults around him, Hunt reasons, how much worse must have been the lives of ordinary children. Lloyd deMause is by far the most pessimistic, describing a long, dark, and brutal story of the parent-child relationship. For him, the history of childhood is very nearly the history of child abuse. Only comparatively recently, deMause argues, has Western society developed a nurturing and loving environment for children.[8]

More recently, the absence of a notion of childhood has been challenged. Ross Beales, for example, cites convincing evidence that Puritans in seventeenth-century New England were well aware of developmental differences between infants, youths, and adults. Opposed to the view that most children were cruelly and callously treated before the modern era are scholars who have found evidence that parents in the past did love and care for their offspring. In *Inside the Great House*, Daniel Blake Smith examines letters written by Chesapeake planters and their wives in which they speak tenderly of their little children, fondly describing childish antics or accomplishments.

Smith paints an uncompromisingly cheerful picture of life among the planter elite. There are no bad or neglectful parents here; even slavery is a positive element since it provides these privileged children early experience with command and enhances their self-confidence.[9]

A major revision of accepted thinking is Linda Pollock's *Forgotten Children*, which combines a thorough historiography of the subject with an examination of several hundred diaries from 1500 to 1900. She finds considerable evidence that parents in every century studied had affection for their children, recognized various stages of development, disciplined but did not abuse, and worried about their offspring's present and future well-being. From this Pollock concludes that "there have been very few changes in parental care and child life from the 16th to the 19th century in the home, apart from social changes and technological improvements."[10]

The history of childhood has often been bedeviled with a presentist point of view. Those who see considerable difference between the childhood of the past and the present see yesterday as bad and today as good; progress has been made. Those who find the hopes and feelings of parents much the same across time argue that child life has changed very little. Long frocks or dungarees, hornbooks or computers, the lives of children remain relatively constant in each successive generation. Neither position is wholly accurate.

There should be enough evidence that there have always been loving parents, neglectful parents, and abusive parents to put that issue to rest. Whether the proportionate numbers of each type change over time depends on whether one employs a modern, or contemporary, view of what is deemed proper and in the best interests of the child. The nature of childhood has been defined very differently in different eras. What is regarded as good or bad for children at any one time can change tremendously, and loving parents of one era can behave in ways diametrically opposed to the accepted practices of another time.

The issue, then, becomes not a question of whether parents loved their children but of how they treated the children they loved. A given parental attitude does not presuppose a single mode of behavior. The concept of childhood has changed dramatically over time, with changes in the social structure, cultural assumptions, and technological innovations leading one generation of parents to reject the childrearing patterns of its predecessors. The course of change was not so much a progression from traditional to modern (meaning from bad to good) as a succession of alternative approaches. Each succeeding stage in the history of childhood has had both positive and negative features. What children gained in one area of their lives, they usually lost in another.

Parents are individuals. Most of them feel affection for their children even in the most difficult of circumstances, though not necessarily all of the time or equally for all of their children. And some parents can be abusive under any circumstances. Instead of attempting to read the minds and hearts of parents, it may be more informative to look at the nature of children's experiences in past centuries. How were they cared for? What habits were stressed and which neglected? How did they spend their days, and where their nights? A few scholars have already given close scrutiny to the processes of family life. John Demos examined the Puritan family in seventeenth-century New England, trying to determine from physical evidence something of what it felt like to live in that society. Michael Zuckerman examined the diary of William Byrd of eighteenth-century Virginia to reconstruct Byrd's level and pattern of involvement with his family, slaves, neighbors, and peers. Each study produced a rich, complex, sometimes contradictory and untidy picture of actual family life.[11]

Regardless of which side of the debate scholars favored, they have treated the concept of childhood as a single entity in history. Most investigators have given little consideration to class differences affecting attitudes or methods of childrearing. In fact, the evidence presented in most studies on childhood has been culled from documents and artifacts produced by or for the middle and elite classes of America and the middle class and aristocracies of Europe. Those scholars who described a long, brutal past in Western childrearing practices have usually assumed conditions were even harsher for working-class children. Those who have contended that parents have always been affectionate and caring have cited evidence that poor parents felt guilt and regret over the privations their children suffered or the harsh work load they were forced to bear. But little work has been done on a separate in-depth investigation of the lives of poor children: a study of working-class or immigrant children is badly needed and has yet to be written.

The purpose of this book is to get beyond the issues that have consumed much of the energy brought to the history of childhood in the last two decades, the issues of whether there was a concept of childhood in the past and whether parents felt affection for their little ones. I will assume that there was always some concept of childhood, although it may have been vastly different from the present one, and that many parents were genuinely fond of their offspring, though often in spite of, rather than because of, the accepted perception of children. The evidence used here includes letters, diaries, autobiographies, childrearing manuals, children's furniture, toys, and clothing, all of which were generated by or for the literate, fairly affluent middle class. These and other items constitute a rich resource of materials that can add significantly to our picture of child life in the past and that deserves careful study. Through these resources we can re-create detailed descriptions of everyday life and learn a great deal about children, parenting, families, and society in the process. The purpose of this work is not to look at previously unexamined groups within society, but to look at the same group once again, in a new way.

It is equally important that the middle class has had an influence in American society far beyond its real numbers. Working-class and immigrant parents tended to raise their children as they themselves had been raised, changing much more slowly and less radically; but they often did in fact change their childrearing methods over time, and those changes tended to follow the patterns established by the middle class. By the early twentieth century, photographs taken by Jacob Riis show tenements in New York City furnished with white metal cribs and wooden high chairs, objects only introduced into middle-class homes within the previous sixty years.

Even more neglected than class differences has been the significance of gender for concepts of childhood. Most scholars have simply mixed evidence about boys and girls or extrapolated from one to the other to produce a monolithic history of childhood for any given era. Scholars seem to assume that boys and girls were treated the same, loved (or neglected) to the same degree, and shared the same experiences of childhood. Ariès does acknowledge that childhood for French girls was very different from that of their brothers. In fact, while the primary thesis of *Centuries of Childhood* is that the concept of childhood was first recognized in the seventeenth century, making that the great watershed in the history of childhood, he rather casually mentions early on that, since virtually none of the changes he describes pertained to girls, then really only "boys were the first specialized children," and his conclusions would therefore be based on only their experiences. Since much of Ariès's argument focuses on the changing nature of the seventeenth-century French school system (from which girls were excluded), the book might better have been called *Centuries of Boyhood*. Similarly, Hunt focuses on the infancy of Louis XIII, generalizing to the public at large; but he is also studying the life of a young boy and extrapolating to children of both sexes. Would a baby girl, even a royal baby girl, have been given the same sort of childhood as Louis?[12]

In fact, life was often very different for boys and girls at any given time. Boys and girls in America were dressed differently, treated differently, given different amounts of time for play, work, and study, and taught to handle all three activities differently. The reality is that there has never been a single form of childhood in America, but two coexisting gender-specific paradigms. Any study of the history of childhood must be cognizant of the fact that gender is a crucial ingredient in a child's life experience and that change in the concept of childhood happened much more slowly and less decisively for girls than for boys.

The approach I take here is to describe the life of children as they experienced it in the past. The descriptions will focus on how youngsters were cared for, dressed, protected, trained, and amused to give some idea of what it was like to have been a child in 1660 or 1760 or 1860. Much of this method depends on the examination of surviving artifacts, the description of the use of artifacts in contemporary sources, and the opinions of parents and children concerning the prevailing customs of childrearing. The description will give us a sense of what daily life was like for the child based on accepted customs and conventions, rather than on perceived parental affection or indifference. Parents' preoccupations in the process of childrearing point to larger issues of the accepted perceptions of the nature of children in a society.

In both a material and a grammatical sense, children have usually been regarded as objects. Traditionally, they were the possessions of their parents, to be dealt with as parents thought best. From the early years of colonization to the end of the nineteenth century, children were the recipients of discipline or largesse, care or neglect. Adults designed, produced, and purchased the material goods used by children, structured their time and their environment, and defined the recognized stages of development and the appropriate image and behavior for each stage. Any study devoted to children has as much to say about the adults who made the decisions, formed or accepted the cultural assumptions, purchased and used the material goods, and determined what it meant to be a child (and what it meant to be an adult) as it has to say about the children involved. If children are the object of this book, their parents, to a large extent, are equally the subject.

PART I

THE INCHOATE ADULT: 1600 TO 1750

1

The Upright Child:
Swaddling Clothes and Walking Stools

SWADDLING

 To the seventeenth-century mind, human beings were quite literally made, not born. The physical development of children was too important and too uncertain to be left to the vagaries of nature. Newborn infants appeared as unpromising material, a shapeless "lump of flesh," "a round ball" that had to be molded into human form by the midwife.[1] Directly after cutting the umbilical cord, the midwife set to work on the baby to give it the human shape that she believed it could not attain without her help. She placed the child on her lap or in a shallow bath of warm water, supported the baby with her left hand, and with her right began molding the head, firmly pressing out any temporary misshapenness due to the trauma of birth. She smoothed the sightless eyes, shaped the nose, opened the mouth, and rubbed the jaw to make the features firm and regular. She then pulled the arms and legs to their full extension, rubbing and shaping each in turn so that the child would grow straight and tall. Finally the midwife carefully but firmly pressed the bones of the baby's skull toward the soft spot on its head, then bound the head with fillets of cloth to further draw the bones together. Every day during the weeks immediately after birth, the midwife or the mother continued to press her thumbs gently against the bones of the skull. When the soft spot finally closed, it was accepted as proof of the efficacy and necessity of the procedure.[2]

Once the midwife had molded the child's body into the best estimation of correct shape, she preserved her handiwork by firmly wrapping her charge in the traditional swaddling bands of yards of long, narrow linen bandages. Unfortunately, direct evidence from the seventeenth and early eighteenth centuries of swaddling in America remains virtually nonexistent, as does information on such other everyday activities as how to fold a diaper or where to place a cradle. Quite simply, no one considered the mundane physical care of young children a topic worthy of much attention. Most women learned the skills and techniques of caring for a baby while still young girls from watching and helping their mothers or other adult women care for their own infants. There was no need to write about such ordinary things. In fact, the very silence regarding swaddling suggests that the custom was simply taken for granted. Only when swaddling became controversial in America did it become worthy of discussion. Such references as do exist are often ambiguous. The term "clout," for example, referred to any form of rag or old piece of cloth, from a dish clout to a beggar's tattered clouts. Since the term was commonly used for both a baby's diapers and swaddling bands, the mention of an infant in clouts might or might not refer to a swaddled child.

The evidence is clear, however, that infants in Europe during the seventeenth century underwent swaddling for the first few months of life. Moreover, swaddling remained popular right into the twentieth century in areas with particularly cold winters or where living conditions were such that little attention could be spared to tend the baby. In fact, various forms of swaddling are still practiced in Russia and eastern Europe and in China. Swaddling simplified child care by keeping the baby warm, immobile, and out of harm's way. Its usefulness in the early years of the American colonies is apparent. Direct references to the practice of swaddling in America began to appear only after the practice started to lose favor with physicians and a growing number of middle-class mothers. For example, the self-styled "American Matron," author of *The Maternal Physician* (published in 1818), wrote disparagingly of "the skullcaps, forehead cloths, swaddling bands and stays, in which our great grandmammas used to imprison their hapless offspring."[3] If we know when most American families stopped swaddling their babies (during the last decades of the eighteenth century for most middle-class families), then we can presume that before that date swaddling was commonly practiced. In fact, swaddling continued in some rural areas and among many recent immigrants to America into the first decades of the twentieth century.[4] The evidence suggests, then, that swaddling was common in America until the middle of the eighteenth century and that it did not die out completely for another century and a half.

One group of men who did discuss swaddling before the middle of the eighteenth century were English and European physicians who wrote medical texts. Sometimes, along with recipes for colic and teething pain, they included descriptions of childrearing practices in the communities they served, frequently detailing both customs of which they approved and those they felt to be decidedly wrongheaded. Physicians on both sides of the Atlantic read each other's works, cited the same authorities, and borrowed extensively from their colleagues, with and without due credit.

Authorities writing before the 1750s accepted swaddling as essential to a child's health and development, though they often disagreed on the most effective way of applying the linen bandages. The traditional method had been described as early as the fifteenth century by the respected physician Paulus Bagellardus, and it changed very little over the next two hundred years. The midwife placed the infant facing her on her lap. She first drew the legs out straight and then proceeded to wind the swaddling securely around the feet, legs, and torso, stopping under the baby's arms. Then she drew the arms of the child straight down along the body, carefully smoothing and shaping them as she did so. With a second piece of linen, the midwife carefully wrapped the child from the fingertips to the shoulders. A third piece of cloth, a stay band, was secured at the forehead and shoulders with additional strips of cloth. The end result was an immobile little mummified package about the size and shape of a loaf of bread. Unable to stretch their arms or legs, wiggle their fingers, or turn their heads, swaddled babies were in danger of choking on their own saliva if left flat on their backs. Most physicians cautioned that babies should be unwrapped and changed once every twelve, or at the very least every twenty-four, hours.[5] Probably few children were actually changed that often. And, since water for washing had to be carried in (often from a good distance), heated, and then discarded, diapers that a baby had merely wet were not washed but simply hung in front of the fire to dry. Since most babies spent much of their first few months wrapped tightly in wet and soiled swaddling bands, it is hardly surprising that salves and potions for diaper rash and skin diseases were a staple part of medical texts dealing with infant disease.

To ensure accurate application of the swaddling bands, the seventeenth-century British physician Felix Wurtz favored placing the child on a table, as the flat surface would help the nurse correctly align the child before winding it in the linen bands. He also cautioned against binding the legs directly together, as this, he felt, would cause lameness later in life. Instead, he directed the midwife to extend the legs carefully, with extra padding between them to hold them in correct alignment when bound and to keep the ankles from chafing against each other. One of the greatest mistakes, Wurtz warned, was that mothers who "will have their children yet handsomer" bound them too tightly, "which maketh the child unquiet." A restless baby, in its struggle for relief, could twist itself about within the swaddling, disturbing the careful alignment of the skeleton within its linen cocoon. If this should occur, the child would grow crooked, "like a twigg, according as it was tyed." Looser bindings, Wurtz argued, would result in contented and quiet babies who would not attempt to change the position in which they were confined.[6] While firmly wrapping tiny babies often seems to soothe them, such warnings as Wurtz's suggest that at least some children, through carelessness, overzealousness, or indifference, were so tightly bound as to cause acute discomfort.

The British physician Francis Glisson, who pioneered the study of rickets in 1650, recommended the more drastic use of splints as well as swaddling to hold the limbs fully extended.[7] Instead of splints, some mothers put their babies in tiny padded corsets that held the spine straight. Additional discomfort for the child frequently resulted, since swaddling bands and clouts were held in place with straight pins (the safety pin being an invention of the nineteenth century), which, if incorrectly inserted, could cause anything from minor irritation to severe injury. In a 1709 issue of the *Tatler*, Sir Richard Steele imagined the pain inflicted by pins from the child's perspective:

> The girl [employed to care for the child] was very proud of the womanly employment of a nurse and took upon her to strip and dress me anew, because I made a noise, to see what ailed me; she did so and stuck a pin in every joint about me. I still cried; upon which she lays me on my face in her lap; and, to quiet me, fell a-nailing in all the pins, by clapping me on the back.[8]

Infants remained completely swaddled for at least the first three months. After that, if the weather was not too cold, their arms were freed, but their legs remained bound. At anywhere from six to nine months of age, swaddling stopped and children went into their first long petticoats. Exactly when a mother decided to modify or give up swaddling depended on the health and physical shape of the child, the work schedule of the mother, and the time of the year, since physicians urged that swaddling be continued through the winter months and that any change wait for warmer weather.

Swaddling was popularly practiced because it served several useful functions. By making it impossible for a child to kick off the bedclothes, it kept a baby warm when the bitterly cold winter air seeped into ill-heated or unheated rooms. It eliminated the risk of chilblains or cracked and bleeding skin that occurred when a child's hands became wet in the normal course of sucking its fingers or thumbs. There was no need to get up in the night to check on babies; they remained covered in the morning precisely as they had been when put to bed the night before. Of course, very tightly bound swaddling could interfere with the child's circulation and cause considerable suffering.

Swaddling bands also made an infant easily and safely portable. The primary responsibilities of seventeenth-century women were managing the household and childbearing, not childrearing. It was their task to effectively and smoothly preserve, conserve, and manage all of the family resources, and it was their lot, as the Daughters of Eve, to bear the risks and pain of childbirth, producing on average a new baby approximately every two years over a span of about twenty years.[9] Since most women continued to bear children until menopause, many still had young children at home when they died. An industrious and thrifty wife was essential for a family's comfort and survival. With so many other priorities, many women had little time or attention to spare for their infants, whose care had to be turned over to others, often servants or older siblings who may have given rather perfunctory attention to the task. But, since infants were considered insensible creatures, who "seem only to live and grow, as plants," needing only rudimentary servicing, not much was actually expected of a caretaker.[10] In such a situation, swaddling helped protect the child. Virtually anyone could safely tend or carry a swaddled baby, since, regardless of how it was held, the child would remain straight, secure, and fully supported within its wrappings. Physicians, in fact, recommended picking up an infant by placing one hand on its chest and another on its back.[11] There was no need to give special support to the head or neck, for the necessary bracing came from the costume, not the attendant. A swaddled baby, like a little turtle in its shell, could be looked after by another, only slightly older child without too much fear of injury, since the practice of swaddling made basic child care virtually idiot proof. Little harm could come to the infant, barring actually dropping it, of course. Unfortunately, dropping did occur all too frequently, since tossing the baby up in the air or from one person to another was a common form of amusement, and accidents happened.[12] Whether through a false confidence in the invulnerability of the child encouraged by swaddling or through common indifference, babies often met with cavalier treatment from those around them. Swaddling, therefore, offered them some useful protection. And when there was no time or person to spare to watch the child, the swaddled baby could be laid anywhere—on a bed, table, or shelf, on the ground in the fields, or even hung from a peg for safekeeping—and be just as comfortable as a native American baby fastened to its cradle board.

A very important rationale for swaddling was to ensure that a child would grow straight and tall, that the dubious lump of infant flesh would be properly molded into the shape of an erect adult. One of the primary justifications for swaddling was the pervasive fear that without such external aid children would never learn to stand erect, would, so the French physician François Mauriceau warned in 1675, "crawl on all fours like little animals for the rest of their lives."[13] Swaddling was considered imperative to form the bent limbs of the newborn into the straight limbs of the adult. Sleeping in the bent fetal position was routinely blamed as a major cause of rickets. A very common and much-feared disease of children in the seventeenth century, rickets was actually due to a calcium deficiency from lack of sufficient milk and sunshine that left young bones too soft to support the weight of the child without bending. Unaware of the real cause of the malady, parents focused on stretching and straightening tiny limbs. Without swaddling, parents and physicians believed, a child might grow bent and misshapen, would certainly never learn to walk, and could never become a whole human being.

While supposedly training the tiny bones in the direction they were to grow, swaddling served a more immediate cosmetic function. The cloth bands and the long mantle that usually covered them actually extended some distance below the infant's feet, visually elongating the tiny figure to more adult proportions. In "The Birth Feast," for example, painted by Jan Steen in 1664, the young mother lies in state in childbed while friends and relatives who have come to admire the new baby and to offer congratulations mill about the room. Near the center of the painting the new father holds up the swaddled child, its body held erect and straight, visually elongated by the linen bands and red mantle. Newborn and newly bound, the child "stands" encircled by the proud father's arm, a tiny upright man. Swaddling not only ensured the future form of infants but endowed them with the desired mature posture right from birth, making them more attractive to contemporary eyes.

This need to express the adult potentiality of the infant suggests an underlying ambivalence about the actual position of the young child in the universal scheme of things. The seventeenth- and early eighteenth-century conceptualization of the organization of life was of a great, unchanging, and perfect chain of being extending from the lowliest organism through the increasingly complex species of the animal kingdom to mankind. Humanity was further ordered by race, from the Hottentot, inevitably placed at the bottom, to European man, inevitably placed at the top. Above the various races stood a multitude of celestial beings, rising upward toward the ultimate perfection of the Holy Trinity. In all of this, mankind stood at a crucial point on the chain—at once the lowest form of thinking creatures, and yet also the finest achievement of earthly creation.[14] Humanity's claim to earthly supremacy rested primarily on its possession of a soul and three characteristics that set it apart from the animal kingdom: the ability to reason, to speak, and to stand and walk erect. An individual's proficiency in these activities further indicated his relative position within the hierarchy of mankind. A European gentleman was admired for the soundness of his reason, the artistry of his conversation, and the grace and dignity of his bearing. On the other hand, the French naturalist Buffon assured his readers that a Hottentot, when pressed, would take to all fours for greater speed of escape or pursuit.[15] Each subspecies of humankind had its allotted place in the scheme of creation. It was all very satisfying to a society that found itself so coincidentally well placed in the grand scheme of things.

The issue of the defining characteristics of humanity found popular expression in European folklore in the guise of tales of the wild men who roamed the more distant forests. According to legend, they were hairy, manlike creatures, brutish and violent, often victims of their own passions. As Edmund Spenser described them in The Faerie Queene, they differed from men in their inability to think logically, to speak in more than "confused sound of senseless words," and in their preference, when pressed, for travelling on all fours.[16] Lacking the power of speech, the wild men were unable to communicate with each other, and so could never develop mutual trust, reach agreements among themselves, set up communities of their own, or establish governments. Instead, each led a solitary existence, protecting his territory from his neighbors. Lacking reason, the wild men could never know God, and thus were denied eternal salvation. Through legends and visual images the wild men served as a dialectical antithesis to mankind; a definition of humanity through negative example. Wild men, for all their superficial similarities with mankind, were irrevocably excluded from the ranks of men.[17]

Unfortunately, the very criteria that excluded wild men from human status just as reasonably excluded human infants. Like wild men, babies lacked the power to reason, speak, or stand and walk erect. Babies could also be nasty, brutish, and dirty, communicating in wordless cries, grunts, and screams, and were given to crawling on all fours before they could be made to walk like men. While babies might be loved, and loved deeply, in seventeenth-century eyes they were themselves unlovely. If man was a logical creature, then he had to logically conclude from the evidence that his own offspring were born in a subhuman state. The child, in Thomas Hooker's opinion, lived "the life of a beast."[18] Such deep and worrisome misgivings about what sort of creatures children really were motivated common tales in which fairies or the women of the wild men stole human babies from their cradles, replacing them with fairy children or with wildlings. Since the replacements were indistinguishable from human babies, the human mother could remain unaware of the switch for many months. Only gradually, as her child failed to acquire human shape and virtue, would she realize the awful truth.[19] The fear that their sleeping babies might really be changelings permitted mothers to express their fears that their infants really were "little strangers," alien and unpredictable.

In his *History of the World*, Sir Walter Raleigh associated each age of man with one of the planets: Mercury with the second age of schooling and soldiering, Venus with the third age of love and desire, and so forth. Infancy, the first age, which he considered categorically different from the rest, he compared to the moon.[20] The moon was a celestial body, but not actually one of the planets, just as an infant was more of a potential than an actual human being.

Swaddling served to quiet parental fears by permitting mothers and fathers to do something actively to ensure that their children would acquire the uniquely human characteristic of standing and walking upright. It also altered the physical appearance of their babies, giving the infants a more reassuringly adult form. The simple device of swaddling helped to bring the unknown under control; parents were assured of the ultimate humanity of their offspring, and their children were assured the opportunity to grow in stature and take their rightful place in a civilized society.

FURNITURE

Once the mother or nurse had thoroughly and firmly swaddled the infant, she laid it in a cradle upon a mattress of folded cloth, "hard and pricking straw, feather, or dried oak leaves." While cradles had existed since the time of ancient Greece and Rome, seventeenth-century authorities distinguished between "purposely made" cradles and other, presumably improvised beds for young children, suggesting that a specially made baby's bed was still considered a comparative luxury.[21]

Very few cradles have survived from the seventeenth and early eighteenth centuries; but then, very few adult-sized beds survive from the eighteenth century, and virtually none from the seventeenth. Occasionally, probate inventories include a cradle listed among the household effects. That they appear less often than many other common forms of home furnishings is not all that surprising, considering that most inventories represented the estates of mature men or women whose children had already outgrown the need of a cradle. Any baby furniture that might have existed in such households could have worn out over long years of use or could have already been passed on to grandchildren. To further complicate the issue, written references to "cradles" do not necessarily specify whether the term is being used to refer to a specifically constructed infant's bed on rockers or to a baby's bed fashioned from whatever came to hand. The term "cradle" commonly meant any of a large number of possible containers or supports found about the farm and in the house—from a cradle scythe to an iron grate to numerous types of baskets. An infant's cradle referred to the baby's place of lodging, whether in a wicker basket, old box, old chest, or specially designed bed. What really mattered was that any sort of separate bed was better for an infant than being put to sleep with its mother, nurse, or some other older person. Adults, drugged by exhausting physical work, or perhaps by the common daily consumption of ale, all too often rolled over on an infant in the night and smothered it. "Laying over" was a common and worrisome cause of infant mortality, and (to what extent we cannot know) at least sometimes a convenient cover for infanticide.[22] The baby who slept alone slept most safely.

Traditionally, a "purposely made" cradle was a piece of furniture of board construction or wicker, affixed to wooden rockers, and often hooded at one end. Regularly spaced holes or pegs along the upper edge of the sides of many cradles were used to lace a swaddled infant securely in place. Other cradles were made deep enough that the baby could be restrained by firmly tucking the bedclothes under the mattress. The physician Felix Wurtz, writing in the middle of the seventeenth century, describes caretakers who bound their charges with tapes laced "from hole to hole in the Cradle which they tie very hard; for should they not do so, they believe their Child would not stay in the Cradle . . . whereby the inlaid Child is packed up like a pack of Wares." Attendants placed the cradle near the fireplace, both to keep the baby warm and to keep an eye on the child while the daily work of the house progressed. If loosely tied, the restraints kept babies safe from any accidental bump against their rocking beds that might tip them out onto the floor among the bustling activity around them. As in everything else concerning infant care, attendants worried more about immediate safety and future growth than about the child's comfort. Overzealous or indifferent attendants could easily lash the child down far too tightly. Felix Wurtz had observed many such cases during his practice; he concluded, "I am assured that by such hard binding, great and anguishing pain is caused."[23]

Parents and medical authorities believed that if children habitually slept lying very straight they would develop good posture and walk sooner. Cradles made before the middle of the eighteenth century were often long and narrow, the ideal shape to accommodate a tightly swaddled infant and a configuration that would discourage slightly older, unswaddled babies from turning on their sides and drawing their knees up into the typical modified fetal position that is so natural for children. Dr. Glisson, for one, further advised that the bedding should be soft enough to partially enfold the children on all sides, essentially packing them in place. This additional precaution "may contribute very much to correct the Crookning of the BacBone and the whole Body . . . so that they may be compelled as it were to straightness."[24] The cradle provided secure containment for an infant and, as an adjunct to swaddling, offered a physical means of shaping babies into the likeness of upstanding adults. Here, as frequently happens when an issue is considered vitally important, society often seeks to assure the desired results by incorporating redundancy into the system. Colonial parents hoped to ensure that their infants would grow strong and straight by encasing their children in stiffened corsets, winding them firmly with linen bandages, and then immobilizing them in deep or narrow cradles, all in the hopes of controlling their physical development.

The cradle served functions other than being a secondary form of swaddling. Its hood and sides protected the infant from the cold drafts that circulated through poorly heated and poorly insulated houses. Traditionally, a dark green cloth covered the cradle to keep out drafts and because it was commonly believed that green was a soothing color that protected and strengthened the eyes. Parents considered this particularly important for young children, since they believed all infants were born with very weak eyesight. They attributed most later vision problems to exposure to bright light during the first months of infancy. The entire cradle was compact enough to fit within the bed hangings of a full-sized bed at night for additional warmth and protection. The heavy bed hangings provided a bit of privacy to the occupants of the bed and held in the body heat they generated, creating a slightly warmer miniature room within a room. Living in houses that barely stayed above freezing during northern winters made the hazards and discomforts of cold a serious problem in childrearing. Keeping a baby warm was a constant struggle. Swaddling bands might help, if not too tightly applied, as did the one to three caps traditionally worn by infants. For further protection, mothers covered their infants with piles of rugs or blankets, covered the cradle itself with additional drapery to keep out any draft, and set it and its occupant to toast by the fire whenever possible. Warmth, mothers believed, protected children from contracting rickets, a common affliction that could destroy the fine upright posture so greatly desired.[25]

Infants were most vulnerable to catching cold at bathtime, and so the mother or attendant sought a protected area before the fire and prewarmed the bathwater to reduce the risk of chill as much as possible. Physicians and common practice agreed that babies should be bathed daily for the first six months. After that, the attendant usually increased the length of time between baths, since even doctors believed that "one should not bathe children too much as is generally done as it is not necessary." A bath once a week was quite sufficient.[26] Some attendants were so concerned with keeping the baby warm that they tended to overcompensate and make the bathwater too hot for comfort or safety, too hot even for an adult to tolerate comfortably.[27] Medical texts commonly included accounts of babies inadvertently scalded; popular logic seems to have assumed that it was better to err on the side of overheating than to risk disease, deformity, or death from a chill. Through all of the accounts of the misadventures of little children, attendants (whether mother, sibling, or servant) seem to have fairly commonly disregarded the issue of an infant's comfort or, rather, remained oblivious to the possibility that a baby could suffer real discomfort. People assumed that children were as insensible as plants, having neither reason nor feeling. Perceiving infants as inherently different from themselves, as decidedly and disturbingly other, some parents lacked the ability to feel much empathy with the child's condition. And since adults believed that infants were incapable of recognizing what was in their own best interest, their protests were irrelevant. In general, their attendants seem to have done things, not for babies, but to them.

Directly after the bath, when the child's body was relaxed from the warmth of the water and the fire and from the freedom from swaddling, was the best time for exercise. Parents regarded such exercise as important if the infant was to acquire the strength necessary to get up on its feet and begin walking as early as possible. In the seventeenth-century cosmos, such things did not happen by themselves; they had to be made to happen, and one could not start too early preparing the child. One recommended exercise consisted of laying the baby on its back, then bending the legs first backward and then up toward the head, followed by stretching and rubbing the limbs. Finally, the arms and legs would be pulled back down in alignment with the body before swaddling. Physicians considered this particular procedure especially important for baby boys to keep their joints and muscles supple. Other popular forms of infant exercise included standing babies up in a lap, tossing them up and down, and holding them suspended first by the hands and then by the ankles to stretch the body and make it limber.[28] Procedures considered equally beneficial were "the drawing of the Children backward and forward upon a Bed or a Table between two Nurses, the one holding it by a Hand, the other by a Foot" and the "rouling of the Child, . . . upon a Bed or Table. This exercise being rightly practiced doth help much to straighten the body."[29]

Children showing signs of rickets or any other deformation received more radical forms of treatment. The nurse wrapped a length of linen about the baby's chest and under the arms and a second piece under the chin, then suspended the child from the bands "so that it is a pleasure to see the Child hanging pendulous in the Air, and moved to and fro by the Spectators." If this form of traction was not enough to achieve the desired results, parents could "hang leaden Shoes upon the Feet, and fasten weights to the Body, that the parts may be more easily extended to an equal length." "But," Glisson warned, "this exercise is only proper for those that are strong." Hanging the child up, with or without extra weights, was meant "to restore the crooked Bones, to erect the bended Joynts, and to lengthen the short Stature of the Body."[30] Babies were regularly tossed, rolled, molded, stretched, dandled, and dangled to prepare them to stand on their own two feet as soon as possible so that they might become independent of their nurses. Walking was the beginning of self-sufficiency, and walking with grace and bearing was the mark of gentility.

When infants finally gained their freedom from swaddling bands, their first clothes consisted of a bodice and long petticoats very similar to the costume of their mothers, except that the "long coats" of infancy extended a foot or so longer than the child. The portrait of Mrs. Freake and her daughter Mary painted in Massachusetts in 1674 depicts Mary at about the age of six months dressed in the long coats of infancy (Figure 1). Her stiff, doll-like pose was not the result of an inexperienced or ill-trained artist's inability to adequately portray a lifelike baby. Mary's little figure looks hard and rigid because, like most children her age, she was probably wearing a stiff corset under her bodice. A young child's corset or stays closely resembled those worn by adult women, except children's stays were corded or quilted for stiffness, rather than boned. Some children wore stays in conjunction with swaddling; others received their first corset when they were long-coated.[31] The stays held Mary's body straight and stiff, giving her the desirable appearance of an erect and mature posture while training her body to grow straight and tall. The artist, however, may have depicted Mary as stiff and upright whether she actually was or not in order to present her with the dignity befitting any civilized person. To make Mary suitably appealing to his seventeenth-century audience, the artist eliminated or glossed over most of her babyish characteristics, which were commonly perceived as the shortcomings and inadequacies of infancy. In an age that considered children by nature disconcertingly animalistic, the artist would have attempted to make Mary look as adult as possible in order to make her image pleasing to his patrons, who in this case were the child's parents—no small consideration.

Long petticoats, however, served more than the cosmetic function of creating the illusion that a baby was proportioned like an adult. The long, entangling skirts helped to keep the child covered and warm, and, most important, utterly foiled any attempt the infant made to move about by crawling. Parents and physicians alike viewed crawling, not as a natural stage in the process of learning to walk, but as a bad habit that, if not suppressed, would remain the child's primary form of locomotion for the rest of its life. The seventeenth-century physician Mauriceau warned that, if not properly swaddled or gowned, children would never learn to walk, but would forever "crawl on all fours like little animals."[32] In the eighteenth century, Dr. William Buchan in his books on childrearing pointed out to mothers the long-term risks of letting their babies creep. He cited evidence from the narratives of the French naturalist Buffon, who observed that unrestrained African babies readily learned to "shuffle along on their hands and knees; an exercise that gives them ever after a facility of running almost as swift in that manner as on their feet."[33] As late as 1839, when babyish behavior had gained considerable acceptance, the American childrearing authority William Alcott complained that American mothers who wanted their infants to be admired decked them out in excessive finery, forced them to sit up straight, and still prohibited their creeping.[34] As a form of locomotion connected with animals, crawling raised too many fears and negative associations in parents. It further emphasized the differences between children and adults, and it seemed to be development in decidedly the wrong direction. Parents wanted their children to become more like them, not less. Most babies born into middle-class homes before 1800 did not learn to crawl before they learned to walk. It simply was not allowed, or at least was actively discouraged.

American colonists regarded crawling as a demeaning, animalistic form of locomotion beneath the dignity of any human being. Moving about on all fours was fit only for beasts, savages, wild men, the insane, and the subjugated as a token of their subjection. Stories and illustrations abounded of madmen who, when they lost their reason, lost the other distinctly human characteristics of speech and erect posture as well. Examples of the popular association of insanity and crawling extended from the mad Nebuchadnezzar becoming one with the beasts of the field to William Hogarth's rake who ended his days grovelling on the floor of Bedlam. The defeated crawled before the conqueror, as the serpent was doomed to crawl in the dust of the earth as punishment for his mischief in Eden. In fact, a common iconographic expression of the natural order of the universe overturned was a depiction of the learned Aristotle, made mad by love, submitting to the degrading whims of the enchantress Phyllis by sinking to his hands and knees to willingly become her beast of burden. Western culture inculcated a very powerful symbolic language of the hierarchy of things, from Hell below to Heaven above, from the crawling of beasts to the marching of kings. Children, if they were to assume their rightful place in the divine order, had to do so on their feet, not on their hands and knees. Crawling was too distasteful and unsettling to be accepted, even in the very young.

Not surprisingly then, most of the handful of traditional furniture forms designed expressly for children encouraged early standing or walking and prevented crawling. Parents pushed children to stand at as early an age as possible, partly to strengthen their leg muscles to ensure early walking and partly from the common belief that it was unlucky for a child to learn to speak before it had begun to walk. At about the same time that mothers freed their children completely from swaddling bands, they began to make use of the standing stool. Essentially, it looked like any normal wooden stool, with somewhat shorter legs and a round hole in the top into which the child was placed. The device, which fitted rather snugly around the child's waist, supported babies just finding their feet, but did not allow them the respite of sitting or crawling.[35] Unlike somewhat similar products of today, the seventeenth-century standing stool had no attached seat. A child could not get out of the stool or sit down in it. The simplest, and probably most common, versions of the standing stool were homemade. Parents fashioned them of willow rods, narrow wooden boxes, or simply a floor-to-ceiling wooden pole with an attached willow ring that fastened about the little waist and kept the child on its feet. Even simpler was a hollowed-out tree trunk: "The inside and upper edge are smoothed, and a child just able to stand is put into it, while its mother is at work by its side, or going after the business of the house."[36]

Standing stools of whatever configuration kept infants off the cold and dirty floors and out of harm's way. Colonial parents did not attempt to make their homes safe for young children by screening fireplaces, covering wells, or blocking stairways, but instead stressed safety through obedience and self-reliance. Any baby creeping or toddling about untended faced the possibility of serious injury from simple household accidents. Standing stools offered some protection.

Because standing stools were convenient and accepted as beneficial to the development of their young children, harried mothers sometimes abused their use. It was all too easy to leave a baby standing in the contraption for long periods, freeing the mother to concentrate on her many other chores. Doctors complained of children being left for hours on weak and shaky legs, some until they fainted from fatigue.[37] The too-common abuse of what Wurtz regarded as "mere . . . stocks for poor infants" so incensed him that, in the middle of an otherwise detached medical treatise, he lashed out against the device, wishing "that such standing stools were burn'd, and that never any were made, by reason of the great misery that Children endure from such standing."[38] Nonetheless, when children gained their release from swaddling bands they soon found themselves encased in some form of standing stool. If left too long, they undoubtedly cried, but, by and large, most people did not take the cries of babies very seriously. Many parents loved their children dearly, but fewer seemed able to empathize with the pain or discomfort infants endured. Traditional wisdom held that babies cried to exercise their lungs and when their wants were frustrated. Infants were parasitic and selfish creatures, greedily absorbing the vitality and the milk of the woman they suckled and quite incapable of feeling any sort of affection for those who cared for them.[39] Left to their own devices, they would remain selfish, animalistic, and savage. Parents believed they had to coerce their babies into growing up, and they expected protests and resistance.

Once children could stand, they were ready to walk. Here again, parents and physicians believed that children needed to be pushed, and the earlier the better. They had no faith that children would come to walking of their own accord. Even Dr. William Cadogan, a progressive and caring physician writing in the middle of the eighteenth century, favored early parental initiative, arguing that "a child, therefore, should be pushed forwards, and taught to walk as soon as possible. An healthy child a year old will be able to walk alone." Cadogan urged that "weakly children" be put "upon their legs" as early as the others, since "crooked legs will grow in time strong and straight by frequent walking."[40]

To get the child walking was the major goal of the year-long battle with swaddling, corsets, special exercise, and hours spent in standing stools. The walking child had taken the first step toward claiming its place in the human community. The parents were also thereby reassured that their child was progressing normally, that their offspring was no changeling. For the children themselves, walking marked the beginning of their independence. As Cadogan explained, "this we may call the era of their deliverance; for this great difficulty surmounted, they generally do well, by getting out of the nurse's hands to shift for themselves."[41] During their first year infants endured the neglect of insensitive, inattentive servants, siblings, even mothers, and tedious and painful confinement in assorted manmade contraptions. After such rigorous restriction and discomfort, walking represented a wonderful new freedom. Of course, parents, as could be expected, did not leave their children to learn to walk on their own, but again employed a variety of specially designed artifacts to hasten the process. Particularly popular were leading strings and walking stools.

Leading strings consisted of stout ribbon or cord fastened to toddlers' clothing or passed around their chest and under their arms. Any adult holding the strings guided the child's steps, protected the youngster from falls, and prevented any attempts the child might make to drop down to a crawling position. Leading strings should not be confused with hanging sleeves, which were broad, decorative ribbons attached at the shoulders of the bodice and extending to the floor. These were vestigial sleeves left over from the fashions of the sixteenth century, abandoned by adults but still commonly worn by children. Leading strings, on the other hand, were a utilitarian device that functioned as a combination guy rope and reins to control and protect youngsters. Since parents put children on their feet while still so young, falls were common. Thickly padded headgear called puddings offered some protection from hard knocks. Essentially a pudding resembled a stuffed sausage of cloth that encircled the baby's head like a hat brim and was held in place by a strap that went over the top of the head and tied under the chin.[42] Puddings served as very necessary bumperguards during the precarious process of learning to walk. The small child in a pudding literally tottering on the brink between infancy and childhood was a very powerful image, so much so that an affectionate name for any young child was puddin' head.

When no one was available to guide the toddler, a walking stool offered both protection and control. Walking stools, also called walking cages, running stools, go-gins, or go-carts, came in a variety of shapes. Some looked like a standing stool with wooden wheels attached (Figure 2). Others resembled a hoop skirt made of wicker and with attached wheels. All types of go-carts fastened securely about the waists of tottering babies to offer additional support as they pushed themselves along. Unlike twentieth-century baby tenders, the earlier versions lacked any sort of seat. Children tired of walking had no means of sitting down so that they might shift their weight off their untried and shaky legs. Nonetheless, there was no discernible opposition to the use of walking stools. Even Felix Wurtz, who so vehemently disapproved of standing stools, believed that the addition of wheels made all the difference, since "in these stools the children can hold out longer, because they can stir and move in them."[43] Unlike standing stools, go-carts did not protect youngsters from accidents. Children in walking stools, if unattended, could and did walk into open fires or down stairwells.[44] This drawback does not seem to have particularly concerned anyone; accidents, though regrettable, were an inevitable part of raising children.

Walking stools were popular because they served several useful purposes. They permitted a child to practice walking without adult aid. They made it impossible for a child to drop down and sit on cold and dirty floors and, thereby also, discouraged any lingering urge to crawl instead of walk. And, in a limited way, they gave the baby a first taste of autonomy and independence. With the aid of the go-cart, little children could go where they wanted to go, follow around the person of their choice, and participate in the activities of the household. They could travel on their own, at least as far as uneven floorboards, raised door sills, and cluttered rooms would permit. Equally important, the corseted, gowned, and walking baby acquired the rudiments of standard civilized behavior and appearance. Such a pleasing and reassuring sight to contemporary eyes was worth the risks involved. The year-old child on wheels was literally in step with the adult world around him.

Cradles, along with standing and walking stools, were the most common forms of children's furniture in colonial America. The seventeenth- and early eighteenth-century home functioned around the needs and activities of adults. There was little time or interest in catering to children; to do so, parents believed, would merely prolong the inadequacies of infancy. Parents expected children, once they were walking on their own, to accommodate themselves to the family's routine. Learning to walk was the dividing line between the uncertainties and vulnerabilities of the first year of life, when even the very nature of the child was suspect and disquieting, and the youngster's entry into the family as a functioning junior member. After that achievement, the child was simply expected to blend into the everyday life of the family as best it could. The age of special needs was over. In all of their future activities, children would deal with an adult-sized world.

In fact, even before their children learned to walk, parents expected them to accommodate themselves to the family's routine. During their first year, infants slept in cradles located amid the bustle and noise of daily life. Children any older than a year or so slept in trundle beds pulled out from under full-sized ones, in regular beds, or on straw pallets on the floor. Youngsters were not clustered together but dispersed throughout the house to sleep with parents, siblings, or servants—wherever there was space. There were no children's rooms, as such, or even much sense of a private or personal space. Virtually all beds accommodated more than one person, and sleeping arrangements changed as needs changed. Children might be moved to another bed or to another room in order to squeeze in an extra guest or to provide a separate sickroom, for example.[45] In the typically small colonial house, children rarely found themselves completely alone.

The home of Col. Walter Smith in Calvert County, Maryland, was the exception that proves the rule, since the room-by-room probate inventory made upon his death does refer to one small room as "the children's room." When Colonel Smith died in 1711, he left a comfortable estate in land, slaves, and livestock, and counted among his personal property all the accoutrements of a gentleman, including a fine sword, a watch, a powdered wig, and a snuffbox. He had furnished his home with the luxury of leather-covered chairs, looking glasses, and an ample supply of costly textiles. A small closet contained a dozen books, a lap desk, and a spice box. The best bed and a daybed stood in the parlor, while upstairs the parlor chamber contained one, the kitchen chamber two, and the hall chamber three additional beds. Between the hall and the parlor on the ground floor was a small closet designated as the children's room. This tiny space contained only a quilt, some blankets, a warming pan, a chair, and two carpets. If seven beds proved insufficient for all the members of this prosperous household, it is possible that a couple of the younger children were put down at night on the rugs and blankets of this little extra room. This remains virtually the only reference to a children's room in early America.[46]

The use of high chairs in America remained very rare until well into the nineteenth century. A few seventeenth-century high chairs have survived, probably precisely because they were so unusual and therefore considered worthy of saving—it is the common artifact that is used up and discarded. Most little children took their meals seated on whatever was handy that would give them sufficient height to reach their plates, including an obliging lap, or else simply ate standing at the table. Children were expected to address their parents as "sir" and "madam" and to stand as a sign of respect whenever their elders entered the room, and so standing at the table demonstrated a proper sense of deference, as well as being practical.

Child-sized chairs were extremely rare in America, though a few did exist. The widow of Capt. Adam Thoroughgood retained a wicker child's chair among her possessions in 1640.[47] There were no little beds, dressers, or tables made for children. Colonial parents were not concerned with providing furniture that would make their children's lives more comfortable. In a society of limited resources, parents concentrated almost exclusively on those objects they deemed necessary to accomplish the formidable task of turning an unformed infant into an ambulatory child. The purpose of children's furniture was to get the child up and functioning independently within the family as quickly as possible. After that, no further material aid was deemed necessary. The belief that infants would never become civilized adults if left to their own devices meant that parents had to find ways to push their children forward. Failure to do so would irrevocably damage the child. The importance of the task encouraged parents to seek insurance through a redundancy of artifacts. Adults swaddled, corseted, stretched, and laced their babies into cradles, and then stood them up by means of leading strings, standing stools, and walking stools. If one object failed to accomplish its purpose, another was already in place. Colonial parents adopted only those objects designed to turn their unformed infants, in the course of the crucial first year of life, into passably functioning members of society.

2

Dependency:
Petticoats and Playthings

PETTICOATS

 In 1670 three children of the Mason family, David, Joanna, and Abigail, posed for an unknown painter in Massachusetts (Figure 3). As artists had always done, the painter emphasized those things that his patrons considered most important. In order to achieve a recognizable representation of the individuals before him and of their comfortable status in life, he focused on the faces and intricate costumes of the children. He reduced the setting to a suggestion of a tiled floor and a black void and positioned his subjects across the very front of the canvas. Their rigid full-length and nearly full-frontal positions overlap one another so slightly that no detail of costume or expensive white linen, lace, ribbons, and jewelry is lost. Eight-year-old David, the oldest of the three children, wore the voluminous petticoat breeches, slashed sleeves, and shoulder-length hair that were the height of adult fashion at the time, and he carried the kid gloves and silver-handled walking stick of a young gentleman. Painters commonly employed his hand-on-hip pose for adult men to suggest presence, authority, and elegance. David's younger sisters displayed the costumes, hairstyles, and accessories popular with all women of their station. Altogether, the portrait emphatically presents the likenesses, gender, and social status of its subjects. Their stiff postures, solemn expressions, and adult accoutrements make the young Masons seem the very image of the seventeenth-century miniature adult. They suggest a social system in which the sexes and

39

the social classes were clearly differentiated, but age was not. The contemporary perception of the social position of children was not as simple as it first might appear, however. The main issue was neither age nor gender, but autonomy.

To unravel the sartorial code, we must turn to a different form of evidence. In dealing with infants, we have both surviving artifacts (cradles, walking stools, and puddings) and a body of prescriptive literature discussing the use of those artifacts by the society. When we turn to older children, we find a very different situation. Colonial households did not contain any form of children's furniture for youngsters already old enough to walk. Parents of the seventeenth and early eighteenth centuries did devise a special physical environment to meet the very particular needs of their infants, but they assumed older children could cope quite well in the adult world without special aids.

Some examples of children's costume and personal possessions have survived, but they were not often discussed in any of the written material of the period. From such sources we can get only brief and fragmentary glimpses into the daily lives of young people. However, we do have a significant number of portraits of children painted in America before 1750 that offer a rich body of evidence concerning society's perceptions of the nature of children and of childhood. A great deal of information is encoded in the costumes, hairstyles, choice of pose, and types of artifacts typically included with children and in the arrangement of the subjects in sibling groups. By comparing the visual treatment of boys with girls, for example, or children over the age of seven with younger children, we can better understand what distinctions and divisions within childhood, or between childhood and maturity, were recognized in early American society.

Unfortunately, a painting is not a photograph. A photograph captures a real moment in time, for a photographer has only a limited ability to edit either when he is shooting or developing a picture. A painting, however, is the creation of an artist who has nearly unlimited ability to alter or invent — to change the color of a gown to better complement the composition, or to alter the style of an old coat to bring it up to fashion. He could remove the unsightly wrinkles from baggy stockings, include a nonexistent fan in a lady's hand, or add a fawn as a charming (though fanciful) pet. Artists of the seventeenth and early eighteenth centuries usually attempted to render a good likeness of the face of each subject, but felt free to improve on costume, setting, and other details.

Furthermore, since originality was not considered essential to a successful painting, artists matter-of-factly borrowed from each other and from the recognized Continental masters. European prints based on popular paintings were common sources for the settings, props, costumes, and poses painted into American art.[1] A particular gown or hairstyle, depicted on a particular American child, may or may not have been what that child was actually wearing at the time. However, regardless of whatever borrowings or improvements an artist employed, a portrait had to conform to the type of presentation considered appropriate for each sitter's age, sex, and social station. Since the American artist worked on commission, his portraits had to fit his patrons' perception of themselves and their children. The painter had to present his young subjects in a way that met social expectations about the nature and appearance of, for example, girls, or older children, or younger brothers. A portrait served as a visual representation of society's expectations for a given segment of the population, even if the image of the particular sitter was tidied up a bit for public viewing.

Costume carried meaning in paintings because it carried meaning in the real world. Before the technological innovations of the nineteenth century made cloth and clothing abundant and relatively inexpensive, the considerable and infrequent investment in a new suit of clothes made the purchase an act of major importance. Clothing was valuable enough to be listed in inventories and willed to heirs. Advertisements for lost or stolen clothing appeared in colonial newspapers.[2] The importance attached to clothing made it an obvious vehicle by which to announce socially relevant information about one's status, age, or occupation; and the outward trappings of rank were taken quite seriously, as seventeenth-century sumptuary laws clearly indicated. Contemporaries could read a person's relative position in society in the particular choice of fabrics and the cut of a suit of clothes.

As the portrait of the Mason children demonstrates, only two basic forms of costume were available in the seventeenth century. One form consisted of knee breeches and frock coat, the other of ankle-length petticoats. Each type of costume had its own separate constellation of artifacts and conventions. An individual who wore knee breeches also wore a waistcoat, a frock coat (which, after 1680, fastened with buttons), a white linen shirt, and carefully oiled hair that fell long and curled onto the shoulders. The artist usually portrayed breeched individuals in a broad pose, such as with an arm out-stretched or with the elbow out and one hand resting on a hip, as in the case of young David Mason. Someone who wore petticoats, pinafore, and bodice fastened those garments with ties and laces and also wore a white linen cap to cover the hair, which was piled tightly atop the head. The artist positioned this second type of figure in a narrower pose, with the arms held close to the body. They appeared less imposing on the canvas and in the world.

What is particularly noteworthy, however, is that this distinction of cos-tume was not based merely on the gender of the wearer. Its meaning was more complicated than that. Two-and-a-half-year-old Henry Gibbs posed for his portrait in the same year as did the Mason children, wearing a cos-tume similar in nearly every detail to that of Joanna and Abigail Mason. Henry appears in his portrait in petticoats, pinafore, and a little white cap, or biggin. He wore a red coral necklace and carried a bird (a typically femi-nine prop in paintings) in a hand held tight against the front of his body. The edge of one of a pair of hanging sleeves is just visible behind his skirts. Beneath the noticeably straight lines of his bodice, Henry probably wore a padded corset to ensure proper posture and genteel bearing. Underneath the corset, he would have also worn a white linen shift next to his skin and a number of underpetticoats, depending on the time of the year and the degree of chill in the air. Underwear as we know it was a much later inno-vation, and only nonambulatory infants wore diapers. Henry would have worn nothing under his shift and petticoats, making it very easy for him to relieve himself when the need arose. Unlike their attention to learning to walk, parents showed little concern with speedy toilet training in an age given to rather ad hoc toilet habits, even among adults. The one major dif-ference between Henry's costume and that of the Mason girls was his falling band, a broad, square collar worn only by men and boys. The presence of that collar immediately identified Henry as a boy to his contemporaries, just as a pink barrette identifies a toddler in jeans and T-shirt as a little girl today. Boys in the seventeenth century, however, did not always wear a falling band; while its presence indicated the wearer was male, its absence was no assur-ance that the child in question was a girl. What we in the twentieth century must keep in mind—particularly as it goes against the powerful modern convention of reserving skirts exclusively for girls—is that, to members of his society, Henry looked like a fine, sturdy little boy appropriately dressed in the petticoats commonly worn by all little boys.

The classification of family members based on the distribution of petticoats and breeches suggests that the allocation of power and independence
was a prominent criterion for understanding distinctions within the family
group. The breeches of the men and older boys, who went out into the world
to work or to school, marked them as separate from a subordinate group of
women and young children in petticoats who remained within the confines
of the home. Before 1750, portraits presented the family as having two com-
plementary components, one dominant over the other. This social significance of dress was well understood in a deferential society and a hierarchical
culture. Nicholas Noyes, for example, argued in 1712 against the new fashion of men wearing periwigs because most such wigs were made of women's
hair. "Women's hair," he reasoned, "when on their own heads, is a token of
subjection—how comes it to cease to be a token of subjection when men
wear it?" He went on to argue that a wig of women's hair could no more be
a "token of superiority" if worn by a man than could breeches become a
"token of subjection" if worn by a woman. To the early eighteenth-century
mind, the symbolic value of an object was apparent, intrinsic, and immutable. A man's hair was his pride and crowning glory, to be displayed and
admired. A woman's hair was a very private thing, modestly hidden under
her cap from all eyes but those of intimate relations. Convention required
especially that she cover her head in church. The petticoats and caps of
women and children signified their subjection, as the breeches of men and
boys were emblems of their dominant social roles. Men wore frock (that is,
dress or formal) coats, and women wore petti (that is, petty or informal or
unimportant) coats. Nor was the system subject to change. "The words in
Deuteronomy 22:5 are very plain and very terrible," warned Noyes. "The
woman shall not wear that which pertaineth to man; neither shall a man put
on a woman's garment; for all that do so are an abomination to the Lord thy
God."[3] Men should not dress like women, nor women in men's clothing.
Little boys like Henry Gibbs, however, dressed like their mothers and sisters
precisely because they were not yet men. This does not mean that little boys
were seen as feminine. Men and boys had worn long skirts, or robes, for
centuries. Breeches were the sartorial newcomers, having first appeared only
in the sixteenth century. Men adopted breeches as a costume that gave them
a great deal of physical freedom and set them apart from less active elderly
men, as well as from women and children. Boys merely went on wearing the
long skirts they had always worn. A little boy in petticoats in the seventeenth

century looked no more feminine in contemporary eyes than a girl in overalls looks masculine to twentieth-century Americans. He was simply dressed the way all children had dressed for centuries. His costume merely indicated that he was not old enough to enter into the world of grown men.

Through the first half of the eighteenth century, women and children continued to dress as members of the same undifferentiated subordinate group within the family. Fashions changed over time, but the social implications of costume remained constant. In 1766, for example, Catherine Beekman sat for a portrait wearing the fashionable petticoat, bodice, and corset of the time (Figure 4).[4]

Catherine's costume, however, did more than merely identify her position within the family circle. It also helped control her natural childish exuberance and restricted her to the more dignified and sedate deportment of an adult. The long, cumbersome skirts discouraged climbing and crawling, while the stays made bending or turning at the waist extremely difficult. The set of the sleeves was such that Catherine would not have been able to raise her arms straight above her shoulders. Taken altogether, a child dressed in this fashion would be unable to do much hard running or playing. By tightly restricting and encumbering her movements, Catherine's dress not only made her look like a small adult but also forced her to act like one.

Significantly, throughout the seventeenth and the first half of the eighteenth century, the costume of female family members underwent only very modest alterations from the first petticoats of the toddler to those of the mature woman. A girl, whether Joanna Mason or Catherine Beekman, would never rise above the subordinate position into which she was born. As a young maid, she was subject to the will of her father, as a wife to her husband, and as a widow to her grown son. All females dressed more or less alike because the social position of an adult woman was not so very different from that of a child. Development from girl to woman was only subtly reflected in changes in dress. A little girl wore a bodice that laced up the back. Only when she reached adolescence was she usually allowed to wear a gown open down the front to reveal a stomacher and fancy petticoat. She might also continue to wear a pair of hanging sleeves for several years after learning to walk as a symbol of her youth. The costume of a young girl was essentially the same as the costume of a grown woman. In her portrait, a girl carried the same types of objects (flowers, fan, needlework), adopted the same hairstyles, and assumed the same poses as an adult. However, if a girl could be viewed as a miniature woman, the grown woman could also be viewed as simply a more advanced child. In terms of acceptable human development, the female passed rapidly from a short infancy to a long period of relative stasis. She would grow up, but she would never move beyond the subordinate role into which she had been born. The concepts of subordination, femininity, and childishness shared a common visual and sartorial vocabulary, and they were tightly intertwined in the colonial mind.[5] It was impossible to signify one of the three linked characteristics without also alluding to the other two.

A boy, by contrast, would outgrow his subordinate position and take his place among the adult men in the family, and, therefore, his development was important enough to the society to be emphasized by periodic changes of costume that marked his progress. Change was a part of being male. The metamorphosis of boy into man occurred as he gradually gave up childish and feminine artifacts and adopted dominant, masculine ones. The concepts of masculinity, maturity, and authority also shared a visual vocabulary. Robert Gibbs, though not yet five, had already begun the transformation when he posed for his portrait in 1670 (Figure 5). Like his younger brother Henry, Robert still wore petticoats, pinafore, and hanging sleeves, but he had already given up his white cap in order to display his long, dark hair, which fell in curls to his shoulders, a clear symbol, as Noyes argued, of masculine superiority. Robert also carried a pair of gloves, a common masculine accessory, and stood for his portrait (probably at the suggestion of the artist) in the conventional hand-on-hip pose of masculine self-assurance. Robert, as any contemporary viewing the portrait would have recognized, was clearly growing up, but his petticoats and hanging sleeves still marked him as a member of the dependent world of women and children confined to the home.[6]

A young son of the DePeyster family of New York had progressed a step beyond Robert Gibbs when he posed for his portrait in the early 1730s (Figure 6). Master DePeyster, at the age of five or six, had graduated to a robe, which closely resembled a frock coat in cut but extended clear to the ankles.[7] As Philippe Ariès has pointed out, the robe was the costume worn by all men in the middle ages.[8] When they abandoned it for the new fashion of breeches in the sixteenth century, it was retained for boys and the students of academies and signified their junior status. The seventeenth-century boy's robe had the buttons, cuffs, and cut of a fashionable frock coat. It was more masculine, and therefore more mature, than the strictly feminine gowns of early childhood. Nevertheless, the robe was still a skirt and still marked a boy's immaturity and dependency.

A boy was breeched at the age of six or seven. On that momentous occasion he gave up petticoats and dressed, like David Mason, in a little replica of an adult man's frock coat, waistcoat, breeches, and hat. However, any display of childish temper could put the boy back into petticoats until he promised to behave.[9] Considering the importance attached to breeching, the threatened humiliation of being returned to baby clothes was a powerful inducement to proper behavior.

For all of the symbolism attached to his new suit of clothes, the breeched boy was not a miniature adult. Rather, he was a boy learning to become a man. His breeches did not signify his maturity, but did mean that he was now out in the world among men and no longer sequestered at home with the women and little children. A boy in breeches was old enough to work in the fields, in the shop, or at school, to venture into the world and begin preparing himself to make his own way. The junior status of adolescent boys could be clearly read in their portraits. Although they were dressed like adults, they still posed with artifacts associated with women or children. Artists never depicted boys of this age with such standard male artifacts as an account ledger, military baton, spyglass, or Bible, all of which alluded to occupation or achievement. Boys did carry objects that represented masculinity and gentility, such as gloves, walking stick, or sword. More boys, however, posed for their portraits with objects associated exclusively with women and children, such as fruit, flowers, or pets, all of which suggested the cultivation and leisure activities of women and children in affluent homes. A sprig of cherries or a pet flying squirrel in the portrait of a teenage boy might be the last visual tie to the subordinate class from which he was emerging.[10] The costume declared that the boy was on his way in the world; the frivolous object he held, that he had not yet arrived.

Sibling portraits can tell us even more about familial relationships among children in colonial America. In the portrait of the brothers and sisters of Christopher Gore by John Singleton Copley, the images of four children share the canvas, with the two girls on the left and their brothers on the right (Figure 7). Copley gave the boys, however, two-thirds of the canvas. The older boy wears a frock coat and knee breeches and stands virtually in the center of the painting, a full head taller than any of his siblings. With his arms extended he controls a significant portion of the available space and dominates the portrait. He stands at the center of the painting, the tallest and broadest figure, the first-born male. His younger brother, in childish dress, sits by his side in a clearly subordinate position. His robe, however, is a bright pink, the brightest color on the canvas, designed to quickly draw the viewer's eye to the little boy. Pressed tightly together on the remaining one-third of the canvas sit the two sisters, dressed in very similar costumes with nearly identical hairstyles. We can determine which is the elder only by their relative size. In fact, the elder sister is actually the largest child depicted in the portrait; her brother dominates the picture only because Copley painted the older girl sitting down. The same sort of positioning is evident in other group portraits. David Mason commands attention over his younger, virtually undifferentiated sisters. The dominance of the male figures is not absolute across colonial portraiture, but it occurs with enough consistency to suggest a social preference at work.

Colonial costume reveals a society particularly concerned with issues of power, autonomy, and independence. Gender lines were not clearly drawn in costume; very young males wore the same costumes as females. Age distinctions were not always clear. All females dressed more or less alike, as did all males over the age of seven or eight. But the lines between the dominant members of the family and their dependents were very clear. Two quite distinct costumes existed to differentiate between men and their women and children. Age only became noteworthy in the case of small boys as they progressed to greater and greater independence.

Gender and power were so tightly linked that the society used a single visual vocabulary to express both subordination and femininity, and a second system to represent both masculinity and domination. So meshed were these pairs of qualities that the only time a woman wore a frock coat and tricorn hat above her petticoats was as part of a riding costume. Adopting a masculine form of dress was the only way she could visually express her role as master of the horse. Similarly, the only way to indicate the subordinate social position of a little boy was to dress him in petticoats and pinafore. Age and gender mattered only as they affected the degree of autonomy within the family hierarchy.

PLAYTHINGS

Probably the most significant fact about toys in the seventeenth and early eighteenth centuries was their rarity. Very few playthings have survived from that era and very few are mentioned in any of the written sources. While portraits made of children before 1750 portray them with fruit, flowers, pets, fans, gloves, and walking sticks, they included virtually no toys. Nor did they depict their young subjects in the act of play, or in playful or informal poses. Children in portraits stood or sat as primly and seriously as their elders. Artists sought to capture a sense of human dignity in each painting, regardless of the age of the subject.

Traditionally, a child's task was to become an adult, and any activities considered suitable for adults were equally acceptable for children. Young people and their elders enjoyed the same jokes and amusements and played the same games in those European and American societies where play was acceptable; communities that discouraged play for adults (on religious grounds, as in Puritan New England), discouraged it for children as well.

Actually, neither playing games nor possessing toys was considered inherently childish by definition. On the contrary, the most expensive European toys—such as intricate automatons and elaborate baby houses with miniature furnishings and doll occupants—were made exclusively for an adult market.[11] In fact, in the seventeenth century the word "toy" referred to virtually anything of a frivolous or inconsequential nature. Shakespeare used "toy" to refer to a funny story; John Milton used it to mean an amorous dalliance; Robert Sanderson, in reference to a lively tune; and Captain John Smith, to describe any inexpensive trifle.[12] A toy was anything that amused a child or an adult. No one viewed toys as a separate category of artifacts designed for the delight of children, or children's play as all that different from adults'.

Some objects defined as toys by modern standards actually had more serious purposes. One example was the infant's coral and bells. This rattle was made of silver (sometimes even of gold) or less costly materials, with a smooth piece of red coral fastened in the silver handle, which was hung with tiny silver bells. The bells amused their young owners, enticing them to hang on to the rattle and make use of it. The coral, however, was the really important element in the device, for the coral, parents believed, protected children from disease. Just as nature could not be trusted with the process of closing the soft spot on a baby's skull or forming straight limbs, it could not be trusted with the process of teething. Parents feared teething the way they feared diphtheria and whooping cough. Doctors also viewed its perils with considerable alarm. They cautioned that difficulties with teething could lead to "fevers, cramps, palsies, fluxes, rheumes and other infirmities," even "fall-ing-sickness, and sometimes death thereby."[13] Physicians agreed that serious complications could be averted by rubbing the gums with a suitable potion, though they agreed less on the most effective ingredients—recipes for such salves included everything from the brains of a hare to mouse dung. If noth-ing else worked, an attendant or a doctor cut the child's gums to release the teeth.[14] A less drastic approach was to give the child something smooth and hard to bite in order to ease the discomfort and hasten the process of teeth-ing. Physicians variously suggested a colt's or wolf's tooth or a piece of ivory, crystal, or silver as suitable teethers, but the most common recommendation was to give the baby a piece of red coral.[15] The smooth surface of the coral made a good teething device and had the added benefits, acknowledged "by consent of all authors," that it resisted the forces of lightning, warded off evil, and, if ground into a powder and drunk, would stop a nosebleed.[16] A baby's rattle was not just a childish amusement, but a serious weapon against pain, disease, and even death. Like other objects specifically designed for infants, its main function was to protect and hasten the development of young children, not to amuse them. Even Puritan households that frowned on other playthings accepted the rattle as a tool, though not as a toy.

In the Middle and Southern colonies, play, sports, and amusements were acceptable releases for all ages. Children and youths played tag and blind-man's bluff, wrestled, raced, and enjoyed stilts, skittles, hoops, tops, and kites, all of which could be made at home.[17] Such activities were not re-garded as strictly children's games, but simply common amusements, similar to playing baseball today. Tops were a traditional emblem of childhood, not because they were exclusively childish toys, but because it could be said of both the schoolboy and the top that "the more you whip it the faster it goes."[18] Both children and adults enjoyed such whimsies as wooden whistles, pinwheels, and ball-and-cup, which could be purchased for a few pennies or whittled with a pocketknife.

Especially in the South, where gentlemen enjoyed horse racing, gaming, and hunting, boys named their hoops for imaginary steeds, played at cards, and practiced marksmanship with a bow and arrows.[19] No one deemed it advisable or necessary to shield children from any adult activities. Quite the opposite was true. As young people were meant to become adults, engaging in work and play with grown-ups would teach them more about the world they would enter. Whatever was an accepted pastime for adults was therefore acceptable for children as well.

Children and their elders were able to enjoy the same amusements for a number of reasons. Adults of colonial America were less jaded than later generations; what we would call children's games they enjoyed with relish and enthusiasm. And since games of blindman's bluff and hunt-the-bean had not yet been designated as children's activities, there was no stigma attached to playing them. Like modern carnival games and prizes, colonial play and playthings were not age specific.

Little girls probably participated in at least some of the active games pursued by boys. Some very little girls also enjoyed the company of rag babies, or poppets, and a handful of European-made dolls found their way into the American colonies. One fine example was brought to Pennsylvania by a member of William Penn's family as a present for a friend in 1699. A gift to a young lady in her late teens, the doll was more of what might now be called a collectible than a plaything.[20] Seventeenth- and eighteenth-century dolls were made of wood in the image of mature women of fashion. Many of them were sent abroad from Paris to display the latest styles of the season and were purchased by milliners to keep themselves and their clients abreast of changing fashions. Other dolls were merely expensive toys or trifles, more often a woman's possession than a child's plaything, especially when new. Regardless of their intended purpose, such extravagant toys were very rare.

Such playthings as did exist were most likely made by the children who used them. Unfortunately, it is usually adults who are responsible for saving toys, and they rarely find value in the simple improvisations of children. Only the finest and least typical toys survive. Adults most often preserve toys made by adults for other adults.[21]

Play was less acceptable in Puritan New England than in the Middle colonies or the South. When Thomas Shepard castigated his congregation in 1649 for spending the Sabbath "in rioting and wantonness, in sports and foolishness," both adults and children had probably been guilty of indulging in the popular games of the age.[22] To the orderly Puritan mind, playthings were unproductive and wasteful, distracting the child (and the adult, for that matter) from the important tasks one faced in life. Toys were temptations to idleness, reverie, and fantasy. The connection between toys and evil was most apparent in the fact that dolls, or poppets, were the possessions not only of little girls but also of witches, who used "pictures, poppets, and other hellish compositions" in the practice of their craft.[23] Most dolls were simple rag babies handmade by mothers or other women for very young children's play. Nonetheless, a poppet was as dangerous as a loaded gun, and, in the wrong hands, it could be just as deadly. If childish play and the devil's work employed the same objects, it is hardly surprising that such objects were suspect.

It would be a mistake to assume that children in New England pined after toys that they did not have. Today's Amish children in Pennsylvania receive very little in the way of toys beyond the rattle and teethers of infancy. From a very early age, their parents instead give them a sample of their future legacy: a new lamb or calf with which to start their own herd, a special plot in the garden, or the first of a set of dishes or linens. These objects have real importance, partly because they are real goods with value. They connect the children with the adult world around them and make them a part of it by giving them a stake in it. Amish children look pityingly at the plastic make-believe toys of "English" children that seem so foolish and shallow compared to their own possessions. Their material connection to the adult world gives them dignity, purpose, and responsibility, as well as pleasure. The motivation is similar to any mainstream American youth's preference for a battered secondhand jalopy over the finest Matchbox miniature model. Reality offers satisfactions that fantasy cannot equal.

It is quite likely that something similar occurred with the children of colonial New England, who took pride and pleasure in the acquisition of useful possessions. They may not have felt the loss of forbidden trifles as much as we tend to assume. Prescribed play and the desire for toys, versus playfulness and delight in trifling things, is a culturally generated phenomenon.

Except for the bows and arrows of young Southern gentlemen and an occasional infant's rattle (neither of which was actually considered a toy), playthings did not appear in American portraits of children before 1750. The stock poses were solemn, dignified, and formal, without any suggestion of childish playfulness. Not only toys but also cradles, go-carts, puddings, swaddling clothes, and all other child-related artifacts were also absent from children's portraits. Except for the inclusion of a pair of hanging sleeves just visible behind a child's shoulder, and the little boy's long retardetaire robe, all articles of dress and all props (fruit, flowers, fans, gloves, etc.) were just as suitable for adults as for children.

Childhood in the seventeenth and early eighteenth centuries simply had no positive attributes of its own considered worthy of expression. In fact, childhood as modernly defined did not exist, or did not have meaning. Children passed through a hurried infancy, fraught with risks. The first year of life was a particularly vulnerable age. Parents were anxious to get their children through it safely and successfully, to be assured that their children were healthy, normal, and had a fair chance of survival. Since the recognized ideal was adulthood, society defined children as adults in the making and preferred not to draw attention to the perceived shortcomings of their extreme youth. Childlike was childish, foolish, degrading, and animalistic. David Mason in 1670, for all the stylishness of his long, curled hair, petticoat breeches, and silver-handled walking stick, was neither a child nor a miniature adult, but rather a junior member of society, an understudy for the grown-up role he would one day assume. Society defined children as inchoate adults, and childhood as a period of inadequacy. Maturity was both a goal and a reward, and no one looked back with much regret.

Figure 1. MRS. FREAKE AND BABY MARY. Artist unknown; Massachusetts, 1674. (Gift of Mr. and Mrs. Albert W. Rice, Courtesy of the Worcester Art Museum, Worcester, Massachusetts)

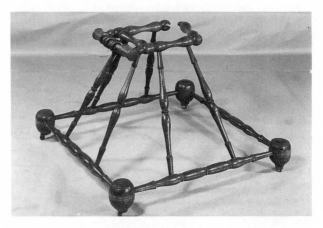

Figure 2. WALKING STOOL. American, seventeenth century. (Courtesy of Bernard & S. Dean Levy, Inc., New York City)

Figure 3. DAVID, JOANNA, AND ABIGAIL MASON. Artist unknown; Massachusetts, 1670. (Courtesy of the M. H. de Young Memorial Museum of the Fine Arts Museum of San Francisco)

Figure 4. CATHERINE BEEKMAN. John Durand; New York, c. 1766. (Courtesy of the New-York Historical Society, New York City)

Figure 5. ROBERT GIBBS. Artist unknown; Massachusetts, 1670. (Courtesy of the Museum of Fine Arts, Boston)

Figure 6. DePeyster Boy with a Deer. Attributed to Gerardus Duyckinck; New York, c. 1730-1735. (Courtesy of the New-York Historical Society, New York City)

Figure 7. The Brothers and Sisters of Christopher Gore. John Singleton Copley; Massachusetts, 1753. (Courtesy of the Henry Francis du Pont Winterthur Museum, Winterthur, Delaware)

Figure 8. COLONEL BENJAMIN TALLMADGE AND SON WILLIAM. Ralph Earl; Connecticut, c. 1790. (Courtesy of the Litchfield Historical Society, Litchfield, Connecticut; Budney Photograph)

Figure 9. Mrs. Benjamin Tallmadge and Children Henry (age 3) and Maria (age 1). Ralph Earl; Connecticut, c. 1790. (Courtesy of the Litchfield Historical Society, Litchfield, Connecticut; Budney Photograph)

Figure 10. MAPLE HIGH CHAIR. New England, c. 1700-1730. (Courtesy of Bernard & S. Dean Levy, Inc., New York City)

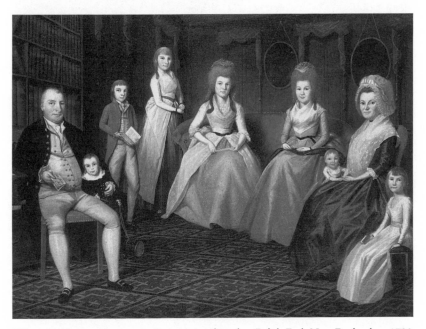

Figure 11. ANGUS NICKELSON FAMILY. Attributed to Ralph Earl; New England, c. 1790. (Courtesy of the Museum of Fine Arts, Springfield, Massachusetts)

Figure 12. MANN PAGE AND HIS SISTER ELIZABETH. John Wollaston; Virginia, c. 1757. (Courtesy of the Virginia Historical Society, Richmond)

PART II

THE NATURAL CHILD: 1750 TO 1830

3

Science, Cold Water, Fresh Air, and Soothing Syrup

CHILDHOOD AND SCIENCE

About 1790 the family of Col. Benjamin Tallmadge posed for the artist Ralph Earl at their home in Connecticut (Figures 8 and 9). On one canvas, Earl depicted Colonel Tallmadge sitting at his desk with his older son, William, a boy of about six, by his side. William posed for his portrait dressed quite differently than had been boys of his age in previous generations. He wore neither long skirts nor a miniature version of his father's coat and breeches, but a suit consisting of a pair of long trousers and a short jacket. In the companion portrait, Mrs. Tallmadge held her baby daughter, Maria, while the middle child, young Henry, sat on the floor at her feet. Mrs. Tallmadge wore a fashionable blue gown and lace fichu; her hair was elaborately teased, oiled, powdered, and dressed with ostrich plumes and flowers in the equally stylish mode of the day, a flagrantly assertive display in an age of revolutionary rhetoric. On her lap she held her unswaddled baby daughter dressed in a very long, delicate gown. In front of her sat her younger son, wearing an ankle-length gown similar to what little boys had always worn. Unlike the costumes of earlier generations of little boys, however, Henry's simple white muslin frock over a pastel slip in no way resembled the dress worn by his mother. The hair of the brothers William and Henry was also simply dressed in a style free of the complex formality displayed by both of their parents. In keeping with this new image of childish simplicity, Earl posed Henry sitting quite informally on the floor,

55

casually toying with a little blue carriage. Clearly neither the boy's parents nor the artist they had commissioned viewed Henry as primarily an adult in the making. Instead, the portraits of Henry, William, and Maria Tallmadge clearly present children as quite distinct from adults, with their own dress, hairstyles, activities, characteristics, and artifacts. The portraits of Henry Tallmadge and Robert Gibbs represent not only two different centuries, but two quite different perceptions of the nature of childhood.

More had changed in a century than just the physical appearance of children. By 1770, parents had, for the most part, given up the use of swaddling, standing stools, walking stools, corsets, leading strings, and puddings. They had changed their attitudes toward the effects of cold on children, and they had made significant alterations to the one piece of furniture that survived the revolution in childrearing, the infant's cradle. Virtually all of the rest of the traditional childrearing paraphernalia had been tossed out. Gone were all the forms of confinement that forced a child to grow straight and walk early. New and very different costumes, toys, and furniture forms appeared and prevailed. This across-the-board rejection of traditional childrearing methods suggests a very significant divergence from traditional assumptions about the nature and needs of young children.

Parents of the new republic had very different ideas about how a baby developed and matured and about how to avoid the risks of illness during the first vulnerable years. They had new theories concerning the proper way to raise their children and the nature of their own roles as parents. The power and pervasiveness of the new perceptions of children are evident in the dramatic shift in the artifacts of childrearing used in the home. From the point of view of the children, the change was one from physical coercion and restriction to considerable freedom, but with a price.

The shift in the perception of the nature of childhood occurred primarily during the second half of the eighteenth century as a result of a far broader reinterpretation of the nature of the universe, a reinterpretation that actually began among scholars of the seventeenth century, but took another hundred years to be assimilated into common thought. Philosophers and scientists had gradually turned from the conception of a static but precarious world caught between divine and satanic whim, where man was powerless to anticipate events and therefore powerless to prepare for them, to a dynamic model of the world. In the new conception, all things, whether individual organisms, whole species, or even human cultures, progressed through observable and predictable stages of development. Scholars had begun to view the physical world as functioning within a framework of immutable laws, and life as developing according to predictable patterns. Nature gained new respect as a complex but orderly system based on observable physical and biological laws that functioned very well without the interference of man.[1] Perhaps the most compelling image of seventeenth- and eighteenth-century scientific thought was the orrery, the endlessly fascinating machine that explained the universe through complex, programmed clockwork. It represented a cosmos designed to function predictably and automatically, a world that was ultimately understandable.

All of this meant that not only were the course of the heavens and the stages of development in butterflies clear, predictable, and constant, but that the developmental stages of man were equally predictable. For many scholars, the prospect of deciphering the mechanics and laws of nature brought with it the exciting possibility of using knowledge to improve humanity itself. The Marquis de Condorcet, for example, argued that man, as part of the physical world, was subject to the same laws of nature, and that his development could be observed, predicted, and eventually manipulated. Human perfectibility seemed a real possibility.[2]

For centuries, Western civilization had accepted the theory that a child inherited both congenital and acquired characteristics from its parents; that is, parents passed on to their children both genetic factors (hair color or bone structure) and distinctive features acquired by the parents during the course of their lives. This was an old idea; scholars from Aristotle to Roger Bacon had described children born with birthmarks that resembled a father's scar or the strawberries a mother had longed for during pregnancy.[3] The acquisition of such characteristics had seemed highly capricious and unpredictable. One never knew what could affect the unborn child, what physical mark or unexpected sight or even what unguarded thought would be stamped onto the infant. It all seemed further evidence of the incomprehensible will of God acting on the lives of men.

The optimism and confidence in the predictability of nature and the perfectibility of man evident in the thought of the second half of the eighteenth century led scholars to turn the theory of acquired characteristics completely on its head. Now the theory seemed to offer ways for mankind to control its own development, to program into future generations desirable attributes. The doctrine of acquired characteristics gained the interest of a surprisingly wide range of the populace, and discussions of it found their way into biological, anthropological, and medical volumes, travellers' accounts, and popular histories.[4] Oliver Goldsmith, for example, asserted in *The History of the Earth and Animal Nature* of 1774 that "nations who have considered some artificial deformity as beautiful, who have industriously lessened the feet or flattened the nose," after many generations of the practice consistently produced infants born with the desired shape. Within this manmade evolutionary process, Goldsmith and his contemporaries found a plausible explanation for "the small eyes and long ears of the Tartars" and "the flat noses of the blacks."[5] This evolutionary twist to contemporary theories of heredity was possible because eighteenth-century scholars viewed the world as developmental, predictable, and, to a large extent, controllable. They took the theory of acquired characteristics, which had traditionally concentrated on isolated transmission from parent to child, and broadened it into an explanation for the development of national and racial features, involving a controllable, cumulative process spanning centuries. The evidence suggested to them that man himself could, and in fact did, control the acquisition of his own physical characteristics. Man had the power to instigate change in his own species.

Some scholars took the theory one step further and hypothesized the possibility of consciously manipulating heredity to shape the minds, as well as the bodies, of generations to come. "May not our parents," asked Condorcet, "who transmit to us the advantages of their conformation . . . transmit to us also . . . intellect . . . understanding, energy of soul or moral sensibility?"[6] If so, then education becomes all important, for it would "have an influence upon, modify and improve" the future generations of mankind, affording a possibility "to enlarge the boundary of our hopes."[7] A theory once offered to explain capricious and isolated events had become an all-encompassing tool with which to manipulate the future development of mankind. It offered a new sense of optimism and confidence based on the belief that intellectual and physical accomplishments could be made cumulative from generation to generation.

Where parents of earlier times had looked at their new infants and seen the terrifying physical and moral perils to be overcome, parents of the late eighteenth century saw in their children infinite possibilities to be channelled and nurtured. Where seventeenth- and early eighteenth-century authorities had assumed that children had to be made to progress to each stage of development, and that without parental intervention no progress would be made at all, later physicians assumed that it was as natural for children to learn to stand, walk, and talk as it was for fish to swim. Walking and talking were, they reasoned, acquired characteristics passed from generation to generation. The parents' responsibility, therefore, was to guide and encourage their child's natural progress, and to gently discourage any bad habits before they took root. True education, they argued, could not be based on fear of children's incapacities, but on faith in their innate ability to develop. Understanding, reason, and a quiet confidence became the hallmarks of the ideal parent.

Children became a serious subject of study. "We know nothing of childhood," cautioned Jean-Jacques Rousseau in 1762. "The wisest writers devote themselves to what a man ought to know, without asking what a child is capable of learning. They are always looking for the man in the child, without considering what he is before he becomes a man."[8] Rousseau argued that parents needed to give their children enough freedom to develop at their own pace, without, however, letting freedom become license. Youngsters learned better and progressed faster if given the opportunity to experiment and experience for themselves within the guidelines established by their parents. They developed quite naturally on their own, without coercion, because the development of their parents before them was a part of their heredity.

A variety of physicians and self-styled authorities set themselves the task of providing numerous systematic programs for rearing children based on the laws of natural science. While many European scholars wrote books on the subject, only a select few received considerable attention in America. One of the earliest, and the most respected authority, was John Locke, whose book *Some Thoughts Concerning Education* appeared in 1693 but attracted little notice for nearly a century. Only then did Locke's ideas strike a chord with most parents. Locke became the standard authority in America in the last half of the eighteenth century, and references to his theories dot the works of American physicians, child-care authorities, and novelists, even appearing in the private correspondence of concerned parents. Many more authors borrowed extensively from his theories, sometimes copying principles and examples without crediting the source.[9]

Locke's ideas deeply influenced Dr. William Cadogan, whose volumes on childrearing first appeared in London in the 1740s. Benjamin Franklin introduced him to the American public when he ran a lengthy excerpt from Cadogan's *Essay Upon Nursing and the Management of Children* in the *Pennsylvania Gazette* in 1749.[10] Cadogan, in turn, influenced the childrearing theories of Dr. William Buchan, whose own books on the subject were first published in the 1760s. In America, Buchan became an authority nearly equal to Locke. His books went through a score of American editions, and authors in this country frequently cited or borrowed from his works.[11]

Jean-Jacques Rousseau did not publish *Emile* until 1762, after the writings of Locke, Cadogan, and Buchan were in print. With the exception of the novelist D. D. Hitchcock, few Americans writing about childrearing made direct reference to Rousseau. His emphasis on almost total freedom for the child, with no formal schooling until adolescence, conflicted with the popular emphasis in America on early education for children. His influence tended to be indirect and often undeclared, coming via English authors who had incorporated Rousseau's theories into their own writing.

The new generation of childrearing experts essentially agreed that children needed more freedom and less restriction and protection. Locke was the first to reassure parents that children would naturally outgrow many of the ordinary deficiencies of early childhood without parental intervention or the use of physical restraints. Since youngsters would inevitably learn to stand erect and walk, Locke urged parents never to "trouble yourself about those faults in [children], which you know age to cure." He assured parents that, as he delicately put it, the "want of well-fashioned civility in the carriage . . . should be the parents' least care, whilst [their offspring] are young."[12] He is referring here to crawling; although he was obviously not concerned about its lingering effects, he still (writing late in the seventeenth century) could not bring himself to use the term. Locke and later experts agreed that children would grow straight and tall if left unbound, would learn to walk if not forced to do so too early, and would remain altogether healthier if not protected so assiduously from the cold and damp.

The perception of childhood had changed from one of a period of vulnerability and deficiency, through which fearful parents pushed their children as quickly as possible, to that of a vital preparatory stage, in which children needed only freedom and guidance to develop their natural talents and inherent moral nature so that they might one day raise even finer offspring to still greater heights of achievement. Education needed time to take hold, and an extended childhood provided that time. Children needed to postpone their assimilation into adult society until they had finished the business of education. As the American author D. D. Hitchcock explained in 1790, "The first seven years of life are a period of greater importance, in the business of education, than is generally imagined."[13]

The Tallmadges were parents of the new school. Their baby Maria was free of the restrictions of swaddling. Their sons enjoyed less restrictive clothing, which permitted more active play. And their oldest son, William, in his special suit, was still quite visibly a boy, with none of the solemnity and enforced dignity imposed on David Mason in his portrait of 1670. David had to do his best to overcome his immaturity and imitate the adult mien expected of him. The society into which William Tallmadge had been born expected him to look, dress, and act like a boy. Extreme youth was no longer an unfortunate or embarrassing condition. A prolonged childhood was the key to man's ability to improve himself. "We lament the helplessness of infancy," wrote Rousseau, yet "we fail to realize that the race would have perished had not man begun by being a child."[14]

SWADDLING ABANDONED

By the last half of the eighteenth century, all of the traditional artifacts of childrearing—swaddling bands, stays, walking stools and standing stools, and even cradles—had come under the scrutiny of a new generation of physicians and parents and been found unnecessary at best and, at worst, harmful to children. In fact, there had been steadily increasing criticism of the traditional devices even before Locke published his theories. A number of mothers by the late seventeenth century had already begun to modify the age-old tradition of swaddling. This might mean binding infants' chest and legs, but leaving their arms at liberty. Some mothers abandoned swaddling when the child was only a few weeks old, and still others rejected it altogether, relying instead on cradle laces or stays as sufficient to hold a child straight and secure.[15] Locke himself disapproved of swaddling of any sort and encouraged parents to trust to nature's ability to produce well-formed and healthy children. Infants, he argued, needed lighter and looser clothing than they had traditionally worn.[16] Samuel Richardson made the heroine of his 1740 novel *Pamela* a strong advocate of Locke's theories. Upon reading his *Thoughts Concerning Education*, Pamela contemplates the wisdom of Locke's advice:

How has my heart ached many and many a time when I have seen poor babies rolled and swathed, ten or a dozen times around; then blanket upon blanket, mantle upon that; its little neck pinned down to one posture; its head more than it frequently needs, triple crowned like a young pope, with covering upon covering; its legs and arms as if to prevent that kindly stretching which we rather ought to promote . . . the former bundled up, the latter pinned down; how the poor thing lies on the nurse's lap, a miserable little pinioned captive.[17]

Childrearing authorities after 1750 seem to have picked up an already growing sentiment, expanded and systematized it, and returned it to a public clearly predisposed to accept what they read. By the 1770s many American mothers had forsaken swaddling altogether, and most younger physicians were completely opposed to the practice. Doctor Buchan declared that "dwarfishness, deformity, diseases, or death" often resulted from swaddling a child like "an Egyptian mummy." He placed blame for the continuance of the practice on "mercenary nurses," who found swaddled babes less work than unswaddled ones, on "ignorant, busy, or self-centered" mothers, whose main concern was pretty children, and on conservative physicians stubbornly resisting change. In 1809, looking back on a long and successful career, Buchan noted that no endeavor had given him more pleasure "than my exertions in early life to rescue infants from the cruel tortures of swathing."[18] To the satisfaction of men like Buchan, much of the English and American middle class, as well as some urban families in France, had abandoned the centuries-old practice of swaddling by the end of the eighteenth century. The growing conviction that a child's development was natural and predictable assured parents that they did not have to rely on coercive devices to force their children into shape.

In 1818 the anonymous author of *The Maternal Physician* noted with satisfaction that "the skull caps, forehead cloths, swaddling bands and stays, in which our great grandmammas used to imprison their hapless offspring" had been "consigned to complete oblivion."[19] The continued influx of immigrants from Germany, Italy, Russia, and other European nations where the majority of the population still practiced time-honored methods of child care meant that the custom of swaddling continued within some pockets of the American population well into the first decades of the twentieth century. For most American babies, however, the only remnant of the practice that remained after 1800 was "a piece of flannel round the navel" to protect it and to support the back and abdomen. Other than this bellyband, most infants born around the turn of the nineteenth century wore "a linen or cotton shirt, a flannel petticoat, and a linen or cotton gown," all fastened with cloth tape.[20] The new cotton ties on baby clothes were a safety feature advocated by physicians. Doctor Buchan warned mothers against "the dangerous use of [straight] pins," recalling one case when he found pins "sticking about one half inch into the body of the child, after it had died of convulsion fits, which in all probability proceeded from that cause."[21] Old ways passed slowly, however. In 1849, Ann E. Porter wrote a short article for *Godey's Lady's Magazine* describing the birth of a cousin's baby in 1834. Her cousin had read all the new books on child care, but she had hired an old nurse loyal to the traditional methods of bringing up a baby. Upon being shown the new layette, the nurse exclaimed:

> Lawful sake, ma'am! do you expect me to use these ere strings and loops? I never did before, and you can't expect me to begin now; besides, what kind er shape suppose your baby'll be if I don't pin it up snug and tight now?[22]

Warnings about working-class nurses who remained loyal to traditional ways appeared often enough in middle-class women's magazines in the early nineteenth century to suggest that not all babies escaped the restrictions of swaddling and the danger of straight pins.

What babies gained in freedom from restrictive clothing, they lost in protection from the cold. "The first thing to be taken care of," warned Locke, "is that children be not too warmly clad or cover'd, winter or summer."[23] Borrowing an analogy from the ancient Greeks, he presented an argument that would be repeated by nearly every childrearing authority for the following 150 years. "The face when we are born," he argued, "is no less tender than any other part of the body. 'Tis use alone hardens it, and makes it more able to endure cold."[24] Where parents of Locke's generation had done everything in their power to keep their babies as warm as possible, late eighteenth-century parents believed that children accustomed to cold from an early age would grow up hardened to it, and remain far healthier and more comfortable than their overprotected ancestors. Some physicians condemned traditional swaddling not so much for restricting children's freedom as for overheating them. "The first great mistake" of parents, complained

Cadogan in the decade preceding the American Revolution, "is that they think a new-born infant cannot be kept too warm; from this prejudice they load it and bind it in flannels, wrappers, swathes, stays, etc. . . . by which means a healthy child in a month's time is made so tender and chilly, it cannot bear the exterior air."[25] Cadogan believed that infants were not more delicate than adults, but actually stronger. Since children were natural creatures, he argued, not yet softened and corrupted by luxury, they were able to withstand the rigors of nature better than their elders. "The truth is, a new-born infant cannot be too cool and loose in its dress." A baby actually required less clothing and fewer covers at night, "because it is naturally warmer, and would bear the cold of a winter's night much better than any adult person whatever."[26] The society that had once viewed children as extremely delicate, with unformed natures and only a tenuous hold on life, now believed them fitter specimens of humanity than their elders, who had grown weak under the seductions of such luxuries as soft beds, rich food, and overly warm clothing. For the first time, Americans entertained the possibility that the attainment of maturity actually entailed some compromises and lost opportunities. Concern over these new and unsettling possibilities grew until, after about 1830, intimations of individual and national degeneration became a major concern and a recurring theme in America and Europe.

If children needed to be hardened against cold so that it could have no ill effects on them, then the daily bath offered a perfect opportunity. Locke recommended that a baby's first bath should be tepid, with each successive bath being slightly cooler until the child habitually bathed only in cold water, winter and summer. Buchan, writing in the 1760s, agreed with this procedure, but by 1818 the author of *The Maternal Physician* saw no value in putting off the inevitable, and favored bathing babies in cold water from the day of birth.[27]

While traditional wisdom had held that babies could not be bound too firmly, nor kept too warm if they were to become strong and healthy children, the advocates of a new reliance on nature believed just as strongly that loose clothing and exposure to cold made children more resistant to disease and deformity. Infants, they insisted, should be lightly clad, lightly covered, bathed in cold water, and exposed to the brisk air on daily outings. While babies raised under the earlier system may have felt stifled under their pile of blankets as they toasted by the fire, infants who grew up under the later regimen as often gasped at the shock of sudden immersion in cold water. Popular childrearing practices literally ran first hot, then cold.

While cold baths were certainly hard on little ones, they stemmed from the development of a more positive and optimistic attitude toward children. People had come to accept nature as benevolent. They believed things left to nature tended to turn out well—it was civilization that could corrupt. And since children were less affected by civilization than were adults, children were more natural, that is, more wholesome, creatures than were their elders, at least in some ways. For the first time, parents saw their offspring as in some ways superior to themselves, endowed with strength, sense, and fortitude. The perception of childhood began to include positive features.

FURNITURE ABANDONED

With the growing preference for keeping an infant cool, the traditional board-construction cradle lost popularity in favor of new forms whose slatted or spindled sides permitted a free flow of air over and around the baby. "Everyone knows that the air has not so free access to a child in the cradle as elsewhere," noted William Alcott, a respected American childrearing authority, in 1839, "especially if it has a kind of covering or hood to it, as we often see."[28] The increasingly popular Windsor cradles, made of bent wood and spindles, exposed their occupants to the healthful effects of fresh air and cool breezes. Thin pallets or folded blankets substituted for the old-fashioned feather beds that curled up around the child to keep it warm. Mothers no longer laced their babies into cradles, but left them free to kick and move about. If they dislodged their blankets in the process, it would do them no harm.

Although parents no longer forced their children to lie perfectly straight, many, particularly in the middle of the eighteenth century, still encouraged their children to do so. Doctor Cadogan, for example, felt that one of the "little niceties" involved in raising children successfully was "making them lie straight in bed. I do not mean extended like a corpse," he hastened to explain, "but that their limbs may be free and easy. I have sometimes seen children a year or two old lie doubled up in bed as in the womb, especially in cold weather."[29] Old habits and fears died slowly.

Many babies continued to sleep in traditional board cradles well into the nineteenth century, since families that already owned older cradles often went right on using them. More were made because their construction was uncomplicated and inexpensive and because virtually anyone could make one. The very end of the nineteenth century saw a resurgence in the production of traditional cradles as part of the colonial-revival movement and the new interest in the colonial past. Board cradles never died out completely, but, since the last quarter of the eighteenth century, they have never been the most popular form of infant bed in America.

The chief identifying characteristic of a cradle was not its size or construction, but the obvious fact that a cradle was meant to rock. Originally, rocking was thought to imitate the gentle motion of the womb. Seventeenth- and eighteenth-century physicians assumed that the fetus hung suspended from the umbilical cord within the womb; as the mother moved, the baby swayed gently back and forth. Babies enjoyed rocking in a cradle, people believed, because it reminded them of their in utero experiences. Mothers were assured that "even the worst tempered children are soothed by this motion, and at last sink into sweet sleep."[30]

Gentle rocking could in fact soothe a fussy infant, and certainly seemed harmless enough, but there were ways of abusing the intentions of the cradle. Physicians defended the efficacy of gentle rocking and assured parents that "no evil could arise" from the use of cradles (but with the caveat "while in the hands of careful and affectionate mothers"). The problems occurred when infants were left to the management of "impatient nurses or of giddy boys and girls" who "in the excess of folly and brutality" rocked the cradle so violently that the tiny occupant became insensible from the prolonged vertigo and sensory bombardment. Extended violent rocking could leave the infant catatonic for several hours. Books of advice on childrearing never accused mothers of abusing the cradle—they were, after all, the people who bought the books. Probably more than one harried mother, however, had found it expedient to resort to hard rocking to quiet a difficult child.[31] In early America the cradle had originally been promoted as a welcome reform, one that would protect infants from the all-too-common tragedy of being smothered while sharing a bed with adults. By the late eighteenth century, the cradle had become subject to abuses of its own.

Many doctors and mothers remained unwilling to give up the cradle and the attendant soothing effects of rocking. They preferred trying to eliminate the abusive behavior rather than abandon the familiar object. In order "to guard against this evil," Buchan insisted that "the transition from rocking-cradle to fixed bedsteads was not necessary." If an alternative to the traditional cradle had to be found, he preferred "the ease and safety" of "little baskets suspended on cords," which could still sway gently while suspended in the air.[32] William Alcott, writing in 1839, also advocated hanging cradles that could be "swung, rather than rocked."[33] While childrearing authorities argued strenuously in favor of swinging cradles, laypeople remained unenthusiastic. A few cradles that hung suspended from a frame and pivoted back and forth were made and sold in America in the nineteenth century, but they never commanded a major share of the market. Americans preferred all or nothing—either a traditional cradle on rockers or a stationary bed for their infants.

By the end of the eighteenth century, most American houses had grown larger and more comfortable and contained more rooms. A cradle rarely remained downstairs amid the bustle of work in the kitchen, or in the increasingly formal public rooms. More frequently it moved upstairs to either the parents' chamber or, more rarely, a separate nursery. A room designated as a nursery in the late eighteenth century could refer to one in which both the mother and baby slept for some weeks or even months after the birth, or to a room an infant shared with a nurse or older siblings.[34] By 1832, Dr. William Dewees of Philadelphia noted that "everybody almost in easy circumstances, has a part of the house appropriated to what is called the 'Nursery.'" Parents usually selected a room at the back of the house or on the third floor—as far removed from the rest of the family's activities as possible. They considered a nursery to be a strictly utilitarian space. It was not thought worthy of much expense or effort, since, like a sickroom, it was devoted to efficient care. Families, therefore, usually selected an unprepossessing room, not much wanted for anything else, to serve as a nursery. As guests never saw the nursery, there was not much pressure to select an attractive space. They reserved for other family members and guests the rooms that offered the best accommodation, the finest view, or the most comfortable quarters. After all, a nursery was only wanted as long as there was a baby in the house. After that, the space would be given over to something else anyway. Dewees and other reformers complained that the nursery "is usually selected because it is handy," or "because it is the only one that can be spared; without the smallest attention being paid to its fitness for the purpose for which it is designed."[35] Actually, even a very small and unprepossessing nursery was in the vanguard of change in the decades around 1800. Most families simply did not bother with one.

These earliest American nurseries remained very simple sleeping rooms for a tiny infant and its attendant. Alcott recommended that "no furniture should be admissable, except the beds of the mother and child, a table and a few chairs."[36] Americans for the most part never followed the English fashion of reserving a series of rooms for their children's use, which included a day room, a sleeping room, and sometimes also a school room, and then confining nearly all of the children's daily activities to their allotted apartments. Some American children slept in a sparsely furnished nursery at night, but virtually all children spent their days in the company of the rest of the family.

Separate sleeping quarters for young children did not necessarily indicate a new concern for the needs or comfort of infants. It was much more likely merely a part of the trend of the time to expand the size of most homes, incorporating into them more rooms designed for specialized functions. In other words, the nursery became an acceptable feature in American houses at about the same time that master bedrooms, dining rooms, and libraries did. Of these new features, nurseries remained by far the least common.

Once children outgrew their cradles, they had outgrown the need for a nursery. Then they were sent to sleep with other siblings, servants, or even their parents. George Washington's young grandson, John Parke Custis, shared a third-floor room at Mount Vernon with Washington's secretary. In 1774 at Nomini Hall, a very fine Virginia plantation, Robert Carter's four daughters shared a large sleeping chamber with some of the female domestic servants; his son Benjamin shared a room over the schoolroom with Philip Fithian, the tutor; and his nephew Harry and son Robert slept in the same room with Carter's secretary.[37] Most parents still believed that it was best to separate children and to put each under the watchful eye and steady influence of a trusted adult.

Dr. William Buchan complained in the middle of the eighteenth century of "making children sleep in small apartments or crowding two or three beds into one chamber." He also commented on a patient of his in the 1770s, one Edward Watkinson, who, at the age of eighteen, still slept with his parents as he had done since birth.[38] A young Philadelphia girl, Harriet Manigault, noted in her diary in 1814 that she was "seated very comfortably by a nice fire in Mama's room (where I sleep) and quite *sans ceremonie* in my *habit de nuit.*"[39] Her two younger sisters shared a room with a maid on the third floor. When her sister Emma was taken ill, she was moved into her mother's room, and Harriet moved to another chamber. Harriet, then eighteen years old, disconsolately confided to her diary, "I now sleep entirely alone, which never being used to, I do not relish much."[40] Between 1750 and 1850 children continued to sleep wherever seemed most convenient for the family. Sharing a room (and probably a bed) with someone else was so common and accepted that children and even adults found it decidedly disturbing to sleep in a room alone at night.

Children generally outgrew their cradles at about the time they were ready to learn to walk. Both parents and physicians saw no reason to push a child to begin walking early. Parents were much more willing to let nature take its course and to let the child walk when it was ready. Doctors assured parents that infants "require no exercise for the first and second month after their birth." After that age, babies, given the free use of their limbs, would exercise themselves, growing in strength and dexterity at their own pace.[41] Crawling, however, remained a highly suspect and most unsuitable activity. Physicians no longer warned of the evil effects of creeping; they simply ignored the practice altogether. Descriptions of the stages of a baby's initial year typically included, first, kicking while lying in the cradle, followed by learning to sit up, learning to stand, and taking the first step. As late as 1839, William Alcott lamented the large number of parents who still frustrated their babies' attempt to creep.[42] Only the author of *The Maternal Physician* admitted that her children learned to crawl before they learned to walk. She justified the activity as a useful form of exercise that strengthened the legs and hastened the advent of actual walking. "Children who are permitted to creep about the room as much as they please," she argued, "will usually prove more elegant in their forms, and strong in their constitutions, than those who are forced upon their feet too early."[43] In prints and paintings produced before 1830, artists depicted children standing, skipping, kneeling to play, sitting on the ground, and lying on cushions on the floor, but never a baby crawling on all fours. Society did not view creeping with quite the horror the practice had once elicited, but it was still not considered a form of locomotion suitable for human beings of any age.

On the subject of walking stools, however, nobody remained silent. All of the childrearing experts writing around the turn of the nineteenth century were adamant that children "should never be enticed to go by artificial means."[44] Once society was convinced that children could and would learn to walk on their own, go-carts, standing stools, and leading strings became obsolete. If walking was the natural and inevitable destiny of every normal child, then:

> Nothing can be more ridiculous than the numberless contrivances of mothers to teach their young to walk, as if it was a thing to be learned by their instruction; and to keep them propped up by wooden machines, or suspended by back-strings, as if their lives were to be endangered by the least tumble.[45]

Not only were such contrivances unnecessary, but they were actually quite "pernicious inventions" that interfered with the learning process they were intended to promote. "Go-carts and leading strings," wrote Buchan in 1809, "not only retard . . . a child's activity, and produce an awkwardness of gait" that was difficult to correct, but they could lead to illnesses of the chest, lungs, and bowels.[46] While the use of go-carts and the like may or may not have led to physical complaints, it certainly did lead to serious accidents. "I have heard my grandmother relate," wrote one mother, "that one of her sons walked down cellar in a walking stool and almost killed himself."[47] Other children in go-carts fell down "dark and winding stair-cases," scalded themselves on hot liquids while playing in the kitchen, or suffered severe burns when their clothing caught fire as they wheeled too close to an unguarded fireplace.[48]

Leading strings, standing stools, and go-carts disappeared from American homes. William Alcott reported a few still in use at the end of the 1830s, but they were the last remains of an abandoned system. What had once been the essential tools of childrearing were rejected out of hand. So complete was their disappearance that, in 1867 when *Godey's Lady's Magazine* reported on the French use of "support straps" (leading strings), and in 1885 when the children's periodical *Babyland* described the Italian use of go-carts, both publications approached the artifacts as products of strange foreign customs totally unfamiliar to their American readers.[49]

Parents of the late eighteenth and early nineteenth centuries abandoned the use of swaddling bands, standing stools, go-carts, and leading strings. They did not, however, replace these devices with new forms of furniture for children. Since they essentially believed that youngsters were quite capable of developing on their own, special furniture forms were unnecessary, and probably harmful, since they could interfere with the natural process of maturation. Americans did not reject all forms of children's furniture, however. There were in fact somewhat more high chairs and children's chairs available near the end of the eighteenth century than there had been in earlier generations. Nonetheless, children's furniture remained rare until the middle of the nineteenth century because no one saw such things as particularly necessary.

Comparatively more high chairs were made in the late eighteenth century than ever before, but they still remained a luxury. Typically, high chairs of the era were no more than their name implied — tall seating furniture to raise up little people (Figure 10). They were essentially dining chairs with slightly smaller seats and extra-long legs that usually lacked the amenities of a footrest and a safety belt or bar across the front; many lacked arms as well. As late as 1839, William Alcott complained that high chairs were both uncommon and uncomfortable. No adult, he argued, would be willing to sit at the table with his legs dangling well above the floor.[50] Actually, few children of the period ever had the opportunity to learn to dislike the high chair. Most continued to sit on whatever lap or other object raised them to table height.

Children's little chairs appeared more frequently after about 1770. Various small versions of the newly popular Windsor chairs, fancily painted chairs, and rocking chairs appeared in shop and probate inventories, newspaper ads, and portraits of young children. However, little chairs always appeared in portraits of girls under the age of seven, never with boys or older children. Of a sample of ninety-seven portraits of little girls painted between 1770 and 1830, nineteen paintings, or 20 percent, included a little chair. One or two baby boys posed for their portraits in high chairs, but never in a little child's chair. In the seventeenth century, chairs had traditionally been reserved for important members of the household or honored guests; everyone else sat on stools or benches. Over the course of the eighteenth century, chairs became more common, and easy chairs were considered especially appropriate for the delicate and infirm. Women and the elderly, in particular, were frequently portrayed enjoying the comfort of an easy chair, while healthy men and boys apparently had no need for them. The production of children's chairs suggests both the levelling of what had once been a prestigious furniture form and the assumption that females of all ages were delicate creatures who needed the extra comfort and support that chairs afforded. The association of little chairs with little girls also suggests that society expected or encouraged girls to engage in sedentary pastimes—reading or sewing or tending their dolls—while their brothers' active play left them no time for sitting still.

Beyond chairs and cradles, American parents purchased virtually no furniture expressly for their children's use. Freedom to grow up naturally meant freedom from the restrictions imposed by manmade items. The rejection of those artifacts was an end in itself. Most children simply learned to improvise to meet their everyday needs as earlier generations of children had always done, making the best use of whatever objects came their way. Probably the most common piece of furniture regularly appropriated for children's use was the ordinary cricket, or footstool. A cricket doubled easily as a child-sized seat, or gave the youngster enough extra height to stand comfortably at the table. Children in 1800 had become free to be children, but they still inhabited a world designed for adults.

SERVANTS AND SOOTHING SYRUP

In the decades immediately following the American Revolution, society's perception of childhood changed faster and more radically than society's attitude toward very young children. Middle-class families gradually came to accept childhood as a legitimate and necessary stage of life. They continued, however, to view infants as rather selfish, unlovely, and uninteresting creatures. Harriet Manigault of Philadelphia noted in her diary in 1815 that one William Morris, a visitor to her home, had entertained the family for an evening with a "charming acount" of his visit with a sister. When asked how many children she had, the astonished Morris replied, "Why really, I did not ask her," explaining that "he did not think young children had half the interest of puppies or little kittens."[51] On another occasion, upon learning that "poor Aunt Claudia intends to present her beloved with a tender pledge in four or five months," Manigault herself noted dryly, "I should not suppose that the prospect would delight him much, for his family is sufficiently large."[52]

That most people considered infancy a tedious preliminary to more promising stages of development was clearly evident in the vast majority of biographies and autobiographies written in the early decades of the nineteenth century. Typically, they began with a survey of family connections and ancestry and then moved directly to an account of the productive years.

Edward Channing's 1836 account of the life of William Ellery was a model of such compression, beginning: "William, his second son, was born in Newport, December 22, 1727, and with his elder brother, was entered at Harvard College, probably in 1743."[53] In one sentence, the author has taken care of what he considered the uninteresting, unimportant early years of childhood and has launched on to meatier matters.

Many who wrote about childrearing or motherhood praised mothers precisely because they shouldered the tedious and thankless task of child care. "Who but a mother," asked the author of *The Maternal Physician* in 1818, "can possibly feel interest in a helpless newborn babe to pay it the unwearied, uninterrupted attention" necessary for its survival.[54] D. D. Hitchcock in 1790, commending a mother, observes that "what she does now for her child, who does not so much as know her, proves what she will be capable of doing one day for him" when he has gained sense and feeling.[55] Hitchcock, so progressive in many aspects of child care, still viewed infants as totally incapable of any emotions beyond the animal craving for satisfaction of their physical needs. Like most of his generation, he still viewed the care of infants as parental duty, not pleasure.

Many mothers who sought some help with or release from their duty turned to the handy resources of servants and drugs to ease the burdens of child care. Traditionally, seventeenth- and early eighteenth-century mothers had relied on the assistance of servants or older children to care for infants. Since parents and physicians of the time believed babies were uncomplicated creatures, it followed that any "reasonable servant" could meet their basic needs and keep them out of danger.[56] The mother was then free to tend to her many other household tasks. Often the servant was merely the young mother's adolescent sister or the teenaged daughter of a neighbor. While still in her teens, Lucy Larcom went to help an older sister with two baby boys. Larcom described a close working relationship between a young girl who went into service for a few years before entering a marriage of her own and the woman who employed her. "A girl came into a family as one of the home-group, to share its burdens, to feel that they were her own. The woman who employed her, if her nature was at all generous, could not feel that money alone was an equivalent for a heart's service; she added to it her friendship, her gratitude and esteem."[57] With the tremendous amount of physical labor that fell to her lot, a young mother needed and sought some help with a new baby. The young servant, for her part, received practical experience and the opportunity to save some money toward her own future home.

Not surprisingly, later reformers were far less comfortable with the idea of leaving the important task of childrearing to youngsters and servants. It accomplished little to educate mothers in the new philosophies of scientific childrearing if the actual work was left to uninformed servants. As a rule, childrearing authorities placed the blame for the excesses of tight lacing, misplaced pins, go-cart accidents, and violent rocking on ignorant or ill-tempered servants who put their own ease above the child's health and comfort. If authorities thought that some mothers could be negligent, they kept their suspicions to themselves. As society in the late eighteenth century came to believe that careful attention to childrearing would improve not only the present generation but, through the inheriting of acquired characteristics, future generations as well, the care of children became too important to leave just in the hands of servants.

Locke, as usual, was the first to caution parents against the potentially unwholesome influence of servants whose actions and conversations could adversely influence young children. In fact, he argued that impressionable youngsters should be kept strictly away from contact with the servants, whose lack of "civility and virtue" could "horribly infect" their charges. Youngsters too "frequently learned from unbred or debauch'd servants such language, untowardly tricks and vices, as otherwise they possibly would be ignorant of all their lives."[58] The fictional Bloomsgrove family of Boston carefully observed Locke's warning in D. D. Hitchcock's didactic novel, *Memories of the Bloomsgrove Family*. "Mr. Bloomsgrove was a man of sufficient property to have kept a servant to attend each of his children; but apprised of the dangerous effects of such a measure," he placed the development and education of his children under his own immediate supervision.[59] The task of forming a child's character in the vital early years had become an important responsibility requiring direct parental involvement.

A mother who found it convenient to employ servants to attend her children opened herself to disquieting doubts about the possible damage such contact could have on the impressionably young. Unwisely selected servants could teach children bad habits and crude behavior, weaken their mental and moral fiber, and coarsen their character and physical appearance. Growing class consciousness and distrust only increased parental apprehensions. As households contracted and neighborhoods developed along class lines, the baby's nurse became less likely to be a neighbor's daughter and more likely to be a young immigrant or working-class girl, increasing the sense of risk.[60]

Some mothers still followed the practice of sending the newborn off to live with a wet nurse until it was old enough to be weaned. The system had the double attraction of supplying the child with necessary nourishment without inconvenience to the mother and of keeping it out of the way until it had reached the age of reason. As in previous generations, many women still showed little interest in their infants, leaving them completely in the care of the wet nurse for the first few months. "Many mothers seldom see their infants until brought home from nurse," complained the author of The Maternal Physician in 1818, "by which time they have probably acquired many bad habits."[61] The wealthy Virginia planter Landon Carter approved wholeheartedly of wet nursing, had used it for his own children, advocated it for his grandchildren, and noted with satisfaction that others among his wealthy neighbors also accepted the practice. His daughter-in-law, however, an advocate of the new methods of childrearing, fought vigorously in 1770 to retain the right to nurse her own child.[62] By 1800 more and more mothers chose to keep their babies home and nurse them personally in order to retain control of the child from the very first days of life. The increasingly common image of the "unnatural" mother who failed to nurse her child "from a love of ease, or a fancied superiority to the drudgery of giving sustenance to her helpless offspring" began to take its toll.[63] Although some of the wealthier families still hired live-in wet nurses, even this practice gradually died out in middle-class homes during the nineteenth century as more and more mothers nursed their own babies.

Where colonial parents had feared the animalistic tendencies of their infants, mothers and fathers in the decades around the turn of the nineteenth century were far more inclined to attribute any undesirable behavior by their children to the influence of improper supervision. Where earlier generations had seen the trouble stemming from children's natural frailties and vices, later parents saw the threat to their children as coming from not only outside the child but outside the family. Traditionally, parents had met the problem by enforcing correct behavior. Informed and conscientious parents after 1770 sought to protect their children from contact with the outside world. The nature of babies had not changed, but the cultural interpretation of their nature had.

Having been cautioned against using servants, and having jettisoned swaddling and standing stools, many mothers turned to alcohol, opium, or other drugs to soothe a restless baby. For centuries, Europeans and Americans had regarded the consumption of alcohol as beneficial for people of all ages. Meat and ale gave man strength, and ale was certainly safer to drink than frequently contaminated water and milk supplies. Beginning at the time of weaning, parents had given their babies beer or wine, both to strengthen and to quiet them. Locke believed the best drink for little children was small beer (a relatively weak brew), and felt that they should "seldom, if ever, taste any wine or strong drink," unless it was prescribed by a doctor. He sadly conceded, however, that "there is nothing so ordinarily given children in England [as strong drink], and nothing so destructive to them."[64] The consensus in the eighteenth century favored the use of alcohol in moderation for young children. Actual practice may have relied on it a good deal more than that.

Not until the temperance movement gained wide support in the first half of the nineteenth century did the practice of giving alcohol to young children come under attack. And not everyone agreed that a little beer or wine was bad for babies even then. One elderly woman in 1834 grumbled at "the injury that these temperance societies have done." Things had been better when her children were born. "Babies didn't cry so when I was young," she remembered, "and I never thought when I had a baby that I could do without a decanter of gin. There's nothing like it for the colic."[65] Given a little gin, beer, or wine, with or without water, any baby slept long and soundly, if not well. And, as many mothers continued to believe that alcohol strengthened their children, it seemed the perfect solution, since it offered substantial benefits for both mother and child.

"There are many mothers and nurses," William Alcott noted in 1839, "who not only rejoice that the infant inclines to sleep a great deal, since it gives them more liberty, but who take pains to prolong those hours . . . by artificial means. I refer not only to the use of the cradle," he went on to explain, "but to more artificial means—the use of cordials and opiates."[66] During the first decades of the nineteenth century many mothers rejected the use of alcohol to quiet their babies. As more and more middle-class women joined the popular temperance movement and its fight against the evils of demon rum, they and their friends were less likely to accept alcohol as suitable for use in the nursery. In their search for a substitute, they turned to the patent soothing syrups that were advertised extensively and sold under a bewildering variety of brand names, including Mogg's Mixture, Godfrey's Cordial, and Graham's Soothing Syrup. Virtually all of the formulas included a high percentage of alcohol. Many of them also contained opiates.

Soothing syrups were popular because they worked. The makers claimed that they quieted fussy children, and most of them certainly did that. Parents remained unaware of the actual ingredients in the medicines they so confidently used, and, even had they known, were unaware that such drugs could be harmful to their infants. Many child-care experts actually encouraged the use of addictive drugs to quiet children, thereby assuring parents of the efficacy and safety of the syrups. Lydia Child in the 1830s recommended the use of paregoric—an opiate—for emergencies, and *The Maternal Physician*, whose advice was usually very sound, defended a mother's right to stock a small home pharmacy of drugs useful in child care. She preferred a "gentle anodyne of paregoric, or syrup of white poppies" to soothe a baby during teething or while being weaned, and "a grain of opium mixed with three or four grains of ipecacuanha into pills, with syrup of white poppy heads" to dose sick children at bedtime. For fevers, she relied on saffron tea, although she admitted that "some physicians ridicule the practice as an old woman's notion, and say it intoxicates and inflames the blood." She defended her pharmacopeia on the grounds that "everything may be carried to excess," contending that it would be "absurd" to "forbid the use of opium entirely, because it will occasion death when taken to excess."[67] Other home remedies for restless babies included catnip tea, pine-root tea, morphine, camphor sling, soot tea (which actually was made of chimney soot), and sugared tobacco water. Some of these substances and concoctions were relatively harmless, others were quite dangerous. Not all produced the desired results of a quiet baby. Camphor, for example, the main ingredient in mothballs, is both an irritant and a stimulant—hardly a drug likely to soothe a fussy infant. Babies were dosed and doctored with a wide variety (and bizarre combinations) of depressants, stimulants, and poisons. Ironically, in an effort to protect their infants from the pernicious effects of swaddling, go-carts, and ignorant servants, parents had turned to an even more deadly and damaging alternative.

4

Childhood, Boyhood, and Youth

SKELETON SUITS AND MUSLIN FROCKS

 In 1757, Mann Page and his sister Elizabeth posed for the artist John Wollaston at their home in Virginia (Figure 12). As one would expect of a boy of ten, Mann wore a fashionable frock coat, waist coat, and knee breeches; his younger sister wore a stylish silk gown over a pair of stays. Unlike David Mason of an earlier generation, however, Mann did not look exactly like a small version of an adult male in every regard. A grown man of fashion in 1757 powdered his hair, or wore a powdered wig, and swaddled his neck in a long white linen cravat. Mann wore his hair simply and without powder; instead of a cravat, only the loosely gathered neck of his shirt, fastened with a black ribbon, showed beneath his coat. These simple modifications of standard male attire were less restrictive and more comfortable than the formal cravat and the hot, itchy, and cumbersome wig expected of mature gentlemen.

From about 1750, boys old enough to wear breeches were spared some of the more uncomfortable aspects of adult dress. The relaxation of the accepted dress code for boys between about the ages of seven and ten accompanied the development of more positive attitudes toward childhood in general. Mann Page would one day be a mature member of his society, but that society no longer felt the need to push the issue. Between the skirts of infancy and the breeches and wig of maturity, Americans accepted a slight modification of dress as a gentler entry into the business of growing up. In

Wollaston's painting the image of young Page incorporates the developing man (in breeches) and the playful child (holding a pet bird). Americans had created a separate and special stage of life for their growing sons. They no longer sought to maintain the fiction of maturity that had made eight-year-old David Mason seem pleasing in the eyes of his contemporaries of 1670. Childishness and playfulness were no longer shortcomings, but accepted characteristics of childhood—accepted enough, in fact, to be included in an expensive, formal portrait that would be displayed by generations of the Page family.

The young Mann Page dressed in the distinctive costume of youth for his portrait, but the development of his sister, Elizabeth, still held too little significance to their society to be marked by a special costume. Like Joanna and Abigail Mason, Elizabeth Page dressed in a fashion suitable for females at any age. However, instead of giving her the typical feminine attributes of a fan or a flower, Wollaston portrayed Elizabeth cradling a doll on her lap. She still dressed as a little woman, but Wollaston portrayed her as a child at play. Young girls were accepted as children, but society still viewed their development as limited, not worthy of particular attention. Women and girls were perceived as still much the same. Put simply, males changed; females didn't.

Between 1750 and 1770, only a small percentage of portraits of children suggest the newly accepted playfulness of childhood by including toys or a playful pose in the composition. Nonetheless, these portraits mark the beginning of a new acceptance of play as a natural and acceptable part of childhood.[1] Particularly after 1770, children's portraits frequently included toys: with girls, dolls, doll furniture and dishes, grace hoops, and dominoes; with boys, balls, rolling hoops, toy wagons and sleds, toy horses, and tin soldiers. All of these toys definitely signalled a new attitude toward play. In the first place, they clearly suggested that it was acceptable for children. Locke had pronounced play a learning process necessary for young people's development, believing that playthings were the natural tools of childhood and arguing that "recreation is as necessary as labour or food."[2] A century later, American families tended to agree with him. After reading Locke, Eliza Pinckney of South Carolina went out and bought her son a set of alphabet blocks so that he might "play himself into learning," noting that she began early "for he is not yet four months old."[3]

When play became not only acceptable but even encouraged for children, it also became closely associated with them. Instead of youngsters joining in with the games of adults as they had in earlier generations, they now were engaged in games considered suitable for their age. Society had created and defined childhood as a separate stage of development, with its own needs and virtues, and provided it with its own activities. Play and toys became the province of childhood. Young people now engaged in socially defined and approved children's games, while adults pursued other forms of recreation. Children no longer gambled at cards, and adults stopped playing hunt-the-bean. The generations increasingly inhabited different worlds.[4]

Play was also strictly segregated by gender in the eighteenth and early nineteenth centuries. Girls played with girls; "we were seldom permitted to play with any boys except our brothers," noted Lucy Larcom.[5] And girls played with dolls. John Mason's shop in Philadelphia, like many others, advertised "drest dolls, naked ditto and Lilliputian dolls" for sale.[6] Whatever the size of the doll, it was carved of wood to represent a lady of fashion. As such, it gave the child the opportunity to practice the graces and skills she would need as a woman. "She can dress and undress her doll; and carry it through all those ceremonies of giving and receiving visits," and she can make "those things" for the doll "for which women are usually dependent upon milliners." The doll also served as a baby that the little girl "nurses, instructs, and corrects."[7] Even without formal toys, girls' imaginary games centered on imitating the activities of adult women. Philip Fithian described the young daughters of Robert Carter "tying strings to a chair" and then walking back and forth pretending to spin yarn, "getting rags and washing them without water," scrubbing the floor, and "knitting with straws." Little Fanny and Harriet Carter also played at the "womanish Fribble" of "stuffing rags . . . under their Gowns just below their Apron-strings" and were "prodigiously charmed at their resemblance to Pregnant Women."[8] Girls' play was pointedly preparatory to their future roles in society.

Boys' playthings were meant for more active games. They rode in wheelbarrows and sleds, walked on stilts, jumped rope (strictly a boys' game until about 1830), rolled a hoop, and played cricket, marbles, ball, and battledore.[9] The games for boys were far more diverse than those for girls; no one activity summed up the socializing and training process for boys the way the doll did for their sisters. Whatever the game, play had merit as a way of refreshing the mind and exercising the body, so that children could return to their studies invigorated and able to absorb the more serious lessons of growing up. Play was not an end in itself so much as a tool to facilitate the child's development.

Children could not indulge in much active play in the costumes fashionable before 1770; to inhibit childish exuberance was, in fact, their function. With changing attitudes, radical modifications in the clothing of toddlers began to appear during the 1770s. Those old enough to walk gave up their long baby dresses for ankle-length frocks. Unlike earlier generations, they did not wear stiff corsets, tight bodices, high-heeled shoes, or tight sleeves. Instead, little children like Henry Tallmadge wore relatively loose muslin frocks and soft flat slippers.[10] As one might expect, Locke had been among the first to rail against the restrictive clothing children had habitually worn. "Narrow breasts, short and stinking breath, ill lungs, and crookedness" were the natural results of "hard bodices and clothes that pinch," he argued late in the seventeenth century.[11] The actual application of dress reform for young children only began about one hundred years later. The new style of frock was only lightly belted with a ribbon sash and was usually short-sleeved to permit considerably more freedom of movement than had been possible with earlier fashions. The very thin fabric and short sleeves were also in accordance with Locke's recommendations against dressing children too warmly. Following Locke's advice, Mrs. Bloomsgrove, in Hitchcock's 1790 novel, made certain that her children were "temperately clad both summer and winter, varying their dress but little" according to the seasons. "The idea," Hitchcock explained, "she probably received from Mr. Locke, who tells of persons in England who wear the same clothes summer and winter, without any inconvenience, or more sense of cold than others."[12] Like the cold bath and the lightly covered bed, the cotton gown was in keeping with the new conception of the naturalness of children. Adults had grown soft and weak from pampering themselves with luxuries, but they could protect their children from a similar fate by trusting to the strength of the natural constitution of the child. Parents were convinced that exposure to the cold would make their offspring less mindful of it and less likely to take sick. The new cotton frock offered little children greater freedom for active play, and greater need for such increased activity in chilly weather.

The white muslin frock that young children wore after 1770 represented a dramatic break with previous conventions of dress in America because it was strikingly different from the costume worn by adult women. Simpler, lighter, and looser than a mature woman's gown, it offered children greater freedom and (at least in warm weather) comfort. The frock visually distinguished children from women, while still setting them apart from men and boys in knee breeches. Both women and children still held subordinate positions within the family, but by visually dividing them into two separate groups the frock broke the long-accepted link between femininity and childishness. It had become possible to be one without being the other.

The changes in clothing styles after 1770 were particularly important in the lives of little girls. The new childish frock signified a greater emphasis on the development of a young girl, for she now wore a costume quite different from the one she would assume as an adult. From the time she began walking until her early teens, a girl wore her simple muslin frock; she then graduated to the far more complex gowns of silk or muslin, stays, and heels of a grown woman. The transition from one style of dress to the other served to mark her passage from childhood to maturity. For the first time, society visually recognized significant differences between girls and women. And also for the first time, the process of growing older for a little girl was also the process of growing up.

The distinctions between women and children were further accentuated by the popularity of a new hairstyle, worn by boys and girls but not by men or women. Until this time, children had adopted the adult hairstyle appropriate to their sex as soon as their hair grew long enough to dress. The most vivid image of the custom occurs in the sixteenth-century portrait Hans Holbein painted of his own family. In the painting, the artist's two-year-old daughter Katherina sits on her mother's lap, her wispy baby-fine hair plaited into thin little braids that are not long enough to encircle her head in the style typical of women of that time. Instead, a piece of string tied to the end of each braid bridges the gap to complete the coronet in the prescribed fashion. When nature fell short, parents resorted to artifice to bring their children in line with social expectation. In America, boys had worn their hair in long curls, cascading over their shoulders, in the seventeenth and early eighteenth centuries, then tied back in a queue around midcentury. Girls had piled their hair on top of their heads and covered it with a cap that became progressively smaller as the eighteenth century advanced.

By contrast, during the last quarter of the century children of both sexes no longer adopted adult hairstyles as soon as physically possible. Instead, they wore their hair straight and loose to the shoulder and cut in bangs across the forehead. The new style did not identify the gender of the wearer, but it did draw on the old gender-based vocabulary. The new childish hairstyle was similar in its essentials to the outmoded style once worn by men (and young David Mason) in the seventeenth century. Then the display of hair had been a male prerogative. After 1750, women and girls exposed more and more of their hair to public view until, by 1770, women's hairstyles had become huge, teased, and marvelously bedecked creations. At the same time, little girls wore what was virtually a retardetaire men's hairstyle. Quite obviously, women's hair no longer signified their subjugation to men and before God. It had become a rather defiant visible declaration of emancipation, perhaps more symbolic than real.

The breaking of the link between femininity and childishness meant that society could permit boys a greater display of culturally defined masculinity at an earlier age. When the only way of expressing independence and authority was with a masculine vocabulary of goods, little boys were consigned to feminine petticoats; there was simply no other way of expressing their dependency. Once the double connection between feminine and childish, on the one hand, and masculine and dominant, on the other, no longer held true, society was free to devise a costume for boys that simultaneously expressed both masculinity and their subordinate status vis-à-vis adult men. Boys between the ages of three and nine (the precise ages were up to the individual family) began wearing a new costume that was quite unlike anything worn before by either men or women of the middle and upper classes. Originally called a hussar suit, and later more commonly known as a skeleton suit, it consisted of long trousers and a short jacket worn over a shirt with a large, square collar. William Smith Tallmadge was depicted in the new style in his portrait of 1790, while his father, in the same portrait, posed in the traditional gentlemanly attire of knee breeches and frock coat. The hussar suit was not an American innovation, by any means. English, European, and American boys began wearing the same style at about the same time. It was not related to either the American or French revolution, as has been sometimes assumed, but was already the growing fashion in the early 1770s.

The hussar suit was not adapted for children from the styles worn by their elders. Trousers were, however, a common convention among the laboring classes, European peasants, soldiers, and sailors—the classes *sans culotte*, or without breeches. The name itself is a reference to the uniform of the hussars, the Hungarian cavalry. In the popular English children's story *Little Goody Twoshoes*, published in 1765, Goody's little brother had worn the petticoats of a young child until the sudden death of their parents. A kindly gentleman decided that he "would take Tommy and make him a little sailor; and accordingly had a jacket and trousers made for him," trousers being appropriate for both sailors and little boys.[13] Now that the link between femininity and subordination had been broken, society adopted a class-based vocabulary to express the social status of little boys. A costume modeled after the uniforms of soldiers and sailors expressed both a culturally recognized masculinity and the child's subordination to the adult men and older boys of his station. The vocabulary of submission was now borrowed from the dress of lower-class men rather than from that of middle-class women.

The skeleton suit separated boys from the mass of girls (and toddlers of both sexes) who still wore frocks, on the one hand, and from the upper echelon of youths and men in breeches, on the other. The result was the visual recognition of a new middle ground between infancy and youth, which in essence established a recognized stage of boyhood. By the last quarter of the eighteenth century, male children passed through three distinct stages—three or four years of infancy in skirts, another three to five years of boyhood in trousers, and two or three years of youth in a slightly relaxed version of man's dress—before finally attaining the full adult costume.

It was an important day in the life of a boy when he gave up his baby clothes for masculine trousers and jacket. John Neal recalled the day in about 1795, at the age of three or four, when he was breeched. "About this time," he wrote, "they put me into jacket-and-trousers; whereupon, they say I gathered up my petticoats and flung them to my sister saying, 'Sis may have these: they're too good for me.' " The significance of the event was not lost on Neal. "Here was a touch of human nature," he went on. "Being twins, we had always been dressed alike, till then; but from that time forward, I was the man-child and she—poor thing! only 'Sissy,' and obliged to wear petticoats."[14] The English writer Charles Lamb captured much the same sentiments in verse:

> Joy to Philip, he this day
> Has his long coats cast away,
> And (the childish season gone)
> Put the manly breeches on.
>
> Sashes, frocks, to those who need 'em
> Philip's limbs have got their freedom.[15]

For boys, the ritual of breeching was still a moment of pride and importance, the point when the baby became a boy. And, no matter how much less restrictive the new frocks were compared to earlier petticoats, trousers permitted much more freedom, a fact lost on neither little boys nor their sisters.

The development of a girl between 1770 and 1830 was less dramatic, and it was anticipated with much less enthusiasm. For girls, growing up meant losing, not gaining, freedom. Girls wore their muslin frocks from the time they began to toddle until sometime between the ages of ten and fourteen, when their mothers or older sisters piled up their hair and they stood for fittings for their first pair of stays. Elizabeth Ham vividly remembered her own transformation in 1793, years after the event. "The first reformation in my appearance," she wrote, "was effected by a stay-maker. I was stood on the window seat whilst a man measured me for the machine, which in consideration of my youth, was to be what was called half-boned." (This meant that instead of the corset being tightly fitted with whalebone stays, a slight gap was left between each stay, theoretically making the device more comfortable.) "Notwithstanding, the first day of wearing them was very nearly purgatory, and I question if I was sufficiently aware of the advantage of a fine shape to reconcile me to the punishment."[16] By 1800, adult women had adopted the new light and flowing Empire style of dress, very similar, in fact, to the muslin frocks of their own girlhoods, but they continued to lace in their adolescent daughters to ensure that the girls would attain a ladylike bearing. In 1809 Dr. William Buchan saw little if any improvement in the dress of girls. "It is true," he wrote, that "we no longer see the once familiar spectacle of a mother laying her daughter upon a carpet, then putting her foot up on the girl's back, and breaking half a dozen laces in tightening her stays, to give her a slender waist. But the absurdity of the contrivance" had only changed to include a brace that pulled the shoulders back, creating "a frightful indentation behind, and a weary stiffness in the motions of the pinioned arms. Yet," he noted sadly, "this is called grace and elegance."[17] Girls in their delicate, often sheer dresses of the early 1800s looked light and free as butterflies, but under their thin gowns they continued to wear a variety of restrictive harnesses designed to improve upon nature.

Even when the transformation from child to woman avoided the excesses of fashion, it remained an often unhappy affair. Lucy Larcom described her girlhood in Massachusetts with almost unflagging optimism, glossing lightly over every family hardship and tragedy, yet she wrote of facing her own approaching womanhood with something close to dread. "I was a tall girl at thirteen," in 1837, she remembered,

> and my older sisters insisted upon lengthening my dresses, and putting up my mop of hair with combs. I felt injured and almost outraged because my protestations against this treatment were unheeded, and when the transformation in my visible appearance was effected, I went away by myself and had a good cry.[18]

Elizabeth Ham and Lucy Larcom were well aware that they paid for the increased status of womanhood with the loss of much of the freedom they had known in childhood; for the most part, they found it an uneven bargain. The transformation was far more than just one involving appearance or restrictive clothing. It meant becoming a different kind of person. As Larcom explained:

> And the greatest pity about it was that I too soon became accustomed to the situation. I felt like a child, but considered it my duty to think and behave like a woman. I began to look upon it as a very serious thing to live.[19]

Boys revelled in both enhanced status and more freedom when they first donned trousers. Their sisters were forced to trade one for the other.

Between 1750 and 1830, society defined and created a new stage in human development, located between the helplessness of infancy and the advent of responsibility and increasing independence, and called it childhood. The development of a separate age of childhood and a separate sphere for children included the introduction or redefinition of particular activities, artifacts, hairstyles, and clothing as unique to and characteristic of this newly recognized condition. The stage was more fully developed for boys, however, than for their sisters.

FAMILY IMAGES

The portraits of children after 1770 document many changes in the socially accepted image of young people. They portray childhood as a separate age, complete with its own clothing, hairstyles, furniture, toys, activities, and mannerisms. By placing the activities of children in the forefront of the compositions, they suggest a society that not only accepted children as different from adults but could take delight in those differences. And after 1770 Americans began commissioning portraits of parents and children together in a realistic interior setting. Not only had the concept of the child been redrawn, but so had the roles of adults and the family unit.

Americans had commissioned portraits of individuals, married couples, sibling groups, and mothers with children since the middle of the seventeenth century. Nuclear-family portraits, however, were another matter. No depictions of both parents and their children are known to have been painted in America before 1730. After that date, a very small number of paintings was commissioned that included the members of a nuclear family within a larger group. John Smibert's "Dean Berkeley and His Entourage" of 1730, for example, included the dean, his wife and infant son, and the other members of his proposed college. The artist's and patron's intention was to mark the significance of the larger professional group. Berkeley appears as the leader of an important academic mission, not primarily as a husband and father. The inclusion of his family in the painting was secondary.

By contrast, portraits of nuclear families became relatively common after 1770. In many cases the artist portrayed the entire family on a single canvas. Other patrons commissioned one painting of the father and sons and a second of the mother, youngest children, and daughters (as in the case of the Tallmadge family), the pair to be hung side by side. A third alternative involved a portrait of the mother and children, and a companion piece of the father, alone. Unfortunately, over the years many such companion portraits have been separated and are no longer recognized as part of a pair.

Whatever the form, nuclear-family portraits became increasingly popular as middle-class families became more private, insular, and self-absorbed. One spur to this trend was the growing availability of painters capable of executing complex compositions. Many ambitious young artists followed Benjamin West to England, where they were exposed to the expertly executed domestic scenes of such painters as Sir Joshua Reynolds, George Romney, Arthur Devis, and George Stubbs. From the time of John Smibert's arrival in Newport, Rhode Island, in 1729, there had always been a few artists in America capable of the more complex compositions required for group portraiture.[20] That they were rarely called on for large compositions suggests a decided lack of interest in that type of presentation. After 1770, nuclear-family portraits were commissioned not only from professionally trained artists but from provincial limners as well. More and more families sought to preserve their image as a family, and painters of all degrees of skill were willing to comply.

Very rarely do American family portraits painted before 1830 include members of the extended family; one finds few examples of the large multi-generational families far more popular in Victorian portraits.[21] The typical family portrait painted in the decades around the turn of the nineteenth century included only one married couple and their offspring. Typically, families commissioned a portrait while the children were still young, and the paintings usually included infants and small children. Though a handful of paintings contained as many as six or seven children, most portray the parents in the company of two to four of their offspring. This, however, is not an accurate indication of family size, for a portrait was often painted before the birth of the youngest children or after older siblings went away to school. Typically, the portraits were of young, not yet completed families in the process of raising their children.

The 1790 portrait of the Angus Nickelson family by Ralph Earl includes an unusually large number of children, which makes it particularly useful for analysis since it contains examples of youngsters at all stages of development (Figure 11). The scene for the family gathering is a comfortably appointed parlor, quite possibly a fairly accurate representation of the family's own. In earlier generations, the artist usually placed the subject close to the front of the canvas so that he or she filled and dominated the composition. Artists and patrons of the time had preferred more grandiose, less realistic settings, usually involving a column, massive draperies, and a baroque garden vista borrowed from European prints. In any case, the setting really did not matter; the figure was all important. Beginning about 1770, a growing preference for more realistic interior settings, locating the family in its natural habitat, as it were, suggests changing priorities within the American family. Portraits placed the members of a family in surroundings recognizable and familiar to them and portrayed them in the process of interacting with each other. These were not solely paintings of individuals, but portraits of families—of the family members, the relationships between them, and the familiar surroundings of their home. Ralph Earl's painting of 1790 was not just a group portrait, but a depiction of a functioning family.

In Earl's painting the family head, Angus Nickelson, sits with his arm protectively around a younger son.[22] For more than a century, artists had conventionally portrayed the head of the house as the household provider, and the shelves of account ledgers, the desk, and the letter in hand attest to Angus Nickelson's standing as a prosperous businessman. Portraits of men had traditionally concentrated on their occupation and standing in the community. Men posed holding legal or account books, correspondence, a military baton, or a spyglass or compass; at other times a ship, farm, or business appeared in the background. In colonial America, men defined themselves by their occupation. What was new after 1770 was that painters began to dramatize the paternal role as well by depicting the father of the family in his own home actively nurturing and protecting his children. In fact, Earl's composition did not place Nickelson with his eldest son and heir, but with one of the younger children leaning against his knee. Earl alludes to the public Nickelson, but he concentrates on the private man, surrounded by his family within the sanctuary of his own home. His role as father is stressed more than his role as businessman. Not surprisingly, Earl portrayed Mrs. Nickelson in the more traditional maternal role with the youngest of her children, a little child in the white frock of infancy.

Family portraits after 1770 conventionally portrayed the mother with the youngest child, male or female. The father was depicted with the youngest or (if the youngest was still an infant) the second-youngest son. Fathers rarely posed embracing a daughter, unless the family had only girls. In the Nickelson family, Angus posed with one young son, while his wife sat between her toddler and a young daughter. In the arrangement of family members, artists conventionally grouped the males on one side of the composition and the females on the other.

The Nickelson family displays an intricate pattern of subclassifications based on age and gender. Had a portrait of a family painted in, say 1690, ever existed, it would contain no more than two visually distinct groups, one consisting of men and boys in knee breeches, the other of women and children in petticoats. The Nickelson family contained a far more complex network of relationships. The most obvious division is one of gender. All the females (and the infant) wear gowns; all the males wear pants. Hairstyles, on the other hand, divide the family by age. All the children have bangs and shoulder-length loose hair, while the adults wear more complicated styles. The major dichotomies of child/adult and male/female are clearly articu-

lated visually. By mixing the two sets of elements, costumes precisely classi-
fied any individual's age, sex, and position within the family.

The sartorial vocabulary of 1790 was complex and subtle enough that six
distinct positions within the family hierarchy are clearly expressed within the
Nickelson portrait. The most subordinate group consisted of the baby and
the little daughter, dressed in the sexless white frocks of infancy. Both children cluster closest to their mother. The youngest might be either a boy or a
girl; only boys this young were still visually linked with the world of women
and girls. The baby is also the least individualized and the least visible figure
in the portrait; clearly, at least to Earl, the least interesting. The little girl
holds an open book, an allusion to childhood as a time of learning and a
reference to reading as a suitably quiet activity for girls. The small boy leaning against his father's knee, on the other hand, was younger than his sister
holding the book. The boy's sex, however, gave him the right to abandon
the white frock at an earlier age in favor of a skeleton suit. While his sister
sits and reads, he is free to play with the toy drum he holds. The drum is a
suitably masculine toy, engendering martial enthusiasms, vigorous activity,
and loud noise. The wide white collar of his shirt was modeled after both
the collar of a sailor's uniform and the fashionable white kerchiefs, or fichu,
worn by most women, including his mother. Nothing else about his dress,
pose, or placement visually connects him with the world of women. His
older brother wears a transitional costume that combines the frock and waist
coats of manhood with the long trousers and loose hair of childhood.[23] Like
his younger sister, he holds an open book, but we can see from the exposed
pages that his was printed in Latin. The costume, hairstyle, and text identify
this older son as a young scholar. A daughter some years older stands next
to her brother; like him, she wears a transitional costume.[24] Her gown is
quite grown-up, but her hair still falls loosely onto her shoulders. The two
oldest daughters wear the formal gowns and pomaded, teased, powdered,
and bedecked hairstyles popular with adult women at the end of the century,
but without the matronly mob cap and wide kerchief that symbolize their
mother's age and position. At the pinnacle of the family hierarchy, Angus
Nickelson himself appears in the frock coat and knee breeches of a gentleman of property and standing.

The eighteenth century was an age interested in the classification and
ordering of things. This urge is clearly evident in the portrait of the Nickelson family. As the American middle class invested more time, attention, and

emotion in their families and in their own familial roles, they found the earlier gross distinction of subordinate and dominant subgroups inadequate. The development of new subclassifications of children required a more subtle range of distinctions to visually represent the redefined roles, enabling an artist like Earl to distinguish clearly and accurately between little children, little boys, youths, older girls, young women, and mature men and women.

Portraits document at least four major changes occurring in the classification of children and the perception of the family during the last half of the eighteenth century. First, the length of visually expressed childhood doubled. In the seventeenth and the first half of the eighteenth centuries, a boy wore petticoats and a long robe for six or seven years before receiving his first frock coat and breeches. From then on, he dressed in a style exactly like adult men of his social station. Breeching did not mean that a seven-year-old boy was accepted as an adult or even a miniature adult, but that society recognized him to be ready to begin the process of learning the skills and responsibilities of manhood. The boy at that age had entered his apprenticeship to the adult community. A girl of the same period passed almost imperceptibly from infancy into the world of adult women. Since she would never outgrow her subordinate status, but only advance within it, only very slight alterations to her gown at the age of six or seven marked the beginning of her training in the duties of a woman of her station. After 1770 boys exchanged their baby frocks first for long trousers and then for a modified adult costume over a childhood that now lasted nearly fourteen years and was clearly divided into periods of infancy, boyhood, and youth. Girls also exchanged their childish frock for a modified adult costume after 1770. Childhood for them, however, lasted about twelve years and was divided into only the two stages of infancy and youth, suggesting that girls were still seen as developing within a narrower range, their limitations set by nature.

Second, the number and composition of visually distinctive groups within the family changed twice during the second half of the eighteenth century. Until midcentury, portraiture recognized only a dominant group of men and boys, who literally wore the pants in the family, and a subordinate group of women and children in petticoats. Between 1750 and 1770 the dominant group split in two, as adolescent boys (like Mann Page) adopted a modified costume that distinguished them from their elders. After 1770, the original subordinate group of women and children splintered into a range of new subgroups, each with its own recognizable costume. Family relationships were more subtly and precisely defined. The father still stood atop the family hierarchy, but the hierarchy itself had become more complex. The new interest in defining and redefining family relationships suggests a growing interest and emotional investment in the nuclear family.

Third, a separate vocabulary of childhood developed by the last quarter of the eighteenth century, breaking the link between femininity and childishness. The perception of childhood, as portrayed in portraiture, became increasingly distinct and positive, with virtues, activities, and artifacts of its own. Society created or re-created the concept of childhood, and defined and expressed its characteristics through a wide range of material goods. Art portrayed the new position and the new freedom accorded children and suggested a new fondness for socially defined childlike behavior. Children often took center stage in the art of the period, which portrayed them gamboling about their more sedate elders. There is a new sense of delight in the young and their antics.

Significantly, soon after 1800 both men and women adopted costumes very similar to those of their own and their children's youth. Women began to wear simple, white, Empire-styled dresses not unlike the white muslin frocks that little girls had worn for thirty years. Not long after, men adopted long trousers, which had previously been the dress of laborers and middle-class boys. The new costumes were not borrowed from the young. They came out of a changing social and political climate in England and France. The popularity of the life of an English country gentleman, and the upheavals of the French Revolution, for practical and political reasons encouraged the adoption of long trousers for men and simple walking dresses for women. Before 1750, when the fourth and fifth decades of life were prized as the age of ability and power, no one would have desired to adopt any fashion associated with callow youth. After 1800, adults took up new styles regardless of the fact that they had long been worn by adolescents. This by no means represented a worshipping of youth, but it did suggest that childhood was so far accepted that adults no longer shunned things associated with the young. That boys wore long trousers, for example, did not influence men to adopt the style, but it did not stop them, either.

The position of adult women also improved vis-à-vis youngsters after 1770. If children of the early eighteenth century dressed like little women, it was also true that women dressed like grown-up children. With a new lexicon of costumes, artifacts, and hairstyles for children, much of the old feminine idiom became by default the exclusive property of the adult woman, and therefore could be used to express both her gender and her maturity.

Finally, a new interest in the nuclear family appeared in portraiture after 1770. An increasing number of patrons chose to have the whole family portrayed on one canvas (or in a pair of paintings). The new family portraits, while fulfilling the traditional purposes of preserving likenesses and displaying worldly success, stressed the inner life of the family itself. Artists replaced conventional backgrounds of fantastic draperies and baroque gardens with individual domestic interiors. They also tried to portray affection between family members and, to some extent, the nature and individuality of children. The rising demand for such pictures after the Revolution may be said to reflect the growing sense of the family as a unit sufficient and satisfying unto itself, and the increased interest in children as vital members of that unit.

Figure 13. A. R. AND KENNETH LAWRENCE. Yonkers, New York, 1893. (Collection of the author)

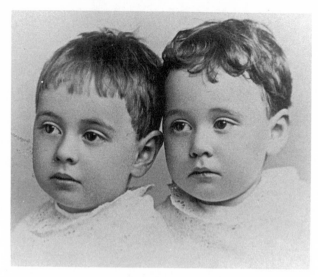

Figure 14. REBECCA RANCK SMITH AND HELEN ROGERS SMITH. Philadelphia, c. 1885. (Collection of the author)

Figure 15. BOY'S TUNIC DRESS. *Godey's Lady's Magazine,* August 1859. (Collection of the author)

Figure 16. PAUL MERLYN CORNELIUS. Reading, Pennsylvania, c. 1900. (Collection of the author)

Figure 17. LITTLE LORD FAUNTLEROY. Frances Hodgson Burnett; *St. Nicholas: An Illustrated Magazine for Young Folks,* July 1886. (Collection of the author)

Figure 18. PROMENADE DRESS FOR THE BOY AND GIRL. *Godey's Lady's Magazine,* December 1860. (Collection of the author)

Figure 19. LITTLE GIRL WITH DOLL. Tintype, c. 1860. (Collection of the author)

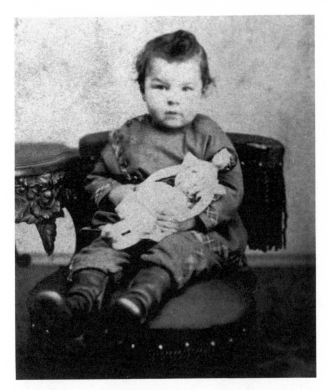

Figure 20. LITTLE BOY WITH CHINA DOLL. Canastota, New York, c. 1865. (Collection of the author)

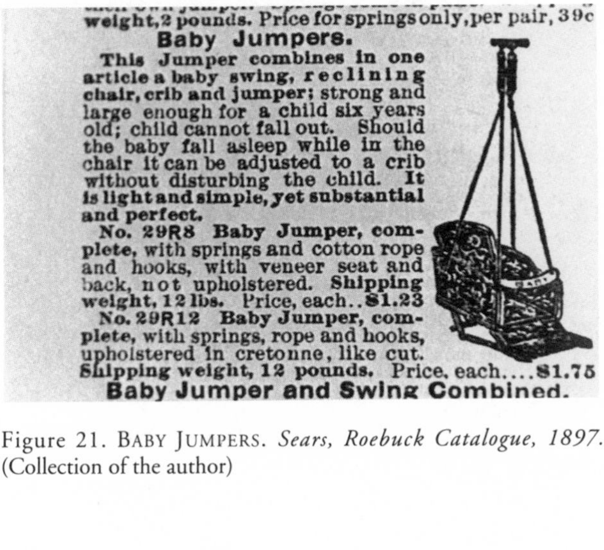

weight, 2 pounds. Price for springs only, per pair, 39c

Baby Jumpers.

This Jumper combines in one article a baby swing, reclining chair, crib and jumper; strong and large enough for a child six years old; child cannot fall out. Should the baby fall asleep while in the chair it can be adjusted to a crib without disturbing the child. It is light and simple, yet substantial and perfect.

No. 29R8 Baby Jumper, complete, with springs and cotton rope and hooks, with veneer seat and back, not upholstered. Shipping weight, 12 lbs. Price, each..$1.23

No. 29R12 Baby Jumper, complete, with springs, rope and hooks, upholstered in cretonne, like cut. Shipping weight, 12 pounds. Price, each....$1.75

Baby Jumper and Swing Combined.

Figure 21. BABY JUMPERS. *Sears, Roebuck Catalogue, 1897.* (Collection of the author)

Figure 22. BABY IN ROMPERS, c. 1910.
(Collection of the author)

Figure 23. THE NEW BABY. *Godey's Lady's Magazine,* August 1845. (Collection of the author)

Figure 24. 1879 CARRIAGE WITH PHAETON-SHAPED BODY. "Beautifully painted, elaborately ornamented, and upholstered in the best manner with plush or silk . . . with dash-rail and lanterns." F. A. Whitney Carriage Company. (Courtesy of the Henry Francis du Pont Winterthur Museum Library, Collection of Printed Books, Winterthur, Delaware)

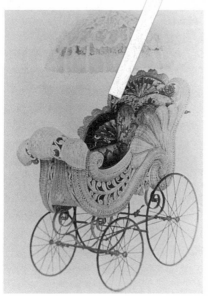

Figure 25. 1902 VARNISHED REED PERAMBULATOR WITH SILK SATIN DAMASK UPHOLSTERY. F. A. Whitney Carriage Company. (Courtesy of the Henry Francis du Pont Winterthur Museum Library, Collection of Printed Books, Winterthur, Delaware)

Figure 26. BABY IN CARRIAGE, c. 1920. (Collection of the author)

PART III
THE INNOCENT CHILD: 1830 TO 1900

5

Androgynous Dress and Gender-Specific Toys

ANDROGYNOUS DRESS

 Throughout the nineteenth century mothers continued to dress their infants in the long baby gowns that had been common since the 1770s. Their infants wore a flannel band around the stomach to protect the navel and to support the back (the last vestige of swaddling), a gauze undershirt, nappies (diapers), and a long flannel petticoat, cotton petticoat, and gown. A christening gown was a very special costume, more elaborate than most, but still similar to the everyday dress of a baby. Infants routinely wore gowns from three-quarters to one and a half yards long, and some gowns were a full two yards long, cascading over the arm of the person carrying the child and falling nearly to the floor (Figure 13).[1] The long gown kept a baby warm, but its appeal was based on more than purely functional considerations. In a society becoming increasingly enamored of babies and young children, the long gown gave the tiny child substance, presence, and grace. While delighting in babies, Victorian society still preferred a rather stately and elongated image for its infants. Baby gowns were almost invariably white, which suggested both a large wardrobe and the services of a laundress to keep all of the little clothes fresh.

Parents made no attempt to visually identify the sex of their infants by dress or color. A rigid adherence to a gender-specific color code developed only in the years before World War II. Nineteenth-century babies wore predominantly white clothing trimmed in white or, occasionally, in whatever color the mother fancied. Twelve-year-old Eliza Ridgely of Baltimore reported in 1841 that her mother had purchased for the new baby, Julia Maria, a cap trimmed in blue and had considered two others, one trimmed in yellow and the other in pink. After deliberation, Mrs. Ridgely "chose the yellow one and the pink one was sent back." Mrs. Merrifield in 1853 suggested that toddlers should not wear yellow and lilac, but that most children looked good in sky blue, pink, and pale green. Forrest Reid reported that when he was four or five in the early 1880s he wore sailor suits in blue, brown, white, and pink.[2] Victorian society viewed infants as infants, and saw no need to differentiate baby girls from baby boys.

In June of 1860, Caroline Richards, a child of eleven from upstate New York, reported in her diary that she and her sister had been invited to visit a neighbor's infant. Caroline was most eager to go and anxious to hold the baby girl and "carry it around the room." Before the young mother would let the girls hold the child, however, she "asked us if we had any pins on us anywhere. She said she had the nurse sew the baby's clothes on every morning so that if [the child] cried she would know whether it was pains or pins."[3] Mothers by the middle of the nineteenth century demonstrated a growing concern with their babies' comfort and happiness, and believed even the youngest infants capable of suffering pain, fear, and distress. Many mothers rejected the use of straight pins to fasten their infants' clothes, relying instead on ties. However, pincushions with "Welcome, Little Stranger" printed out in straight pins remained a popular baby gift throughout the 1800s. Only late in the century did safety pins come into common use, to the great relief of mothers.

Victorian parents were also less inclined to harden their children with cold baths and cold beds. Authorities advised bathing the child in warm water, and maintaining a temperature of about 68° F in the nursery, at least for the first three months; then the temperature could dip as low as 55° without ill effects for the child. Permitting a baby to get overheated, however, was still regarded as a greater risk to the child than being kept too cool. From sleeping in an overly heated room a child "becomes pale, loses appetite, shows symptoms of indegestion, occasionally vomits, stops gaining weight, [and] takes cold readily," warned one physician.[4] On the other hand, another authority warned that "changing under-garments twice per week is quite often enough. Most babies are shirted quite too often. One undershirt is no sooner warmed and dried than another is substituted, thus facilitating colds." He drove home his point by noting that "woodsman wear a new thick woollen shirt *out* without washing, and are remarkably robust."[5] With such conflicting advice, young mothers were left to determine for themselves how best to keep their babies both comfortable (warm) and healthy (cool) at the same time.

Mothers usually put their babies into short coats (dresses) when the children were between six and nine months old, when "they are beginning to learn the use of their limbs, and would be too much confined by . . . long robes, however graceful they may be."[6] The shorter dresses reached just to the ankle and permitted the child some freedom of movement. Babies wore short coats until they were about three years of age, at which point they acquired a very new and different costume consisting of half-length petticoats and pantaloons.

In the early 1840s Joseph and Anna Raymond posed for an unknown artist. In their portrait, both children carried toys—a doll for Anna and a pull toy for Joseph—sported very short, straight haircuts, and wore knee-length frocks with fashionably puffy sleeves over ankle-length white cotton trousers. To modern eyes, the new costume is not all that different from earlier ones for children, but to Americans of the 1830s and 1840s the differences were significant and controversial.

The new costume of half-length petticoat and pantaloons that appeared in America in the 1830s was first worn by young visitors from Europe. As the accepted style in London and Paris, it gained gradual, though sometimes reluctant, acceptance here. Parents had no hesitation in dressing their young sons in the new style, since boys had always worn frocks of one sort or another and had already been wearing trousers for well over fifty years. The new fashion simply combined two types of clothing already commonly worn by boys. Fashionable mothers preferred the new frock to the older skeleton suit that now seemed to transform "the little urchin into the semblance of a monkey in his hand-organ costume." Charles Dickens described the skeleton suit as "one of those straight blue cases in which small boys used to be confined before belts and tunics had come in." Clearly, one generation's reform in dress is another's absurdity. By 1830 "the prettiest, and at the same time the most comfortable and convenient dress . . . for boys from two years old to five, is a loose sacque, girt by a belt, over white linen 'pantaloons,' as the young gentlemen will be apt to call them."[7]

For girls the situation was quite different. They had, of course, always worn frocks, but they had never been permitted to dress in any element of masculine clothing. While to us the white, sometimes lace-trimmed, pant legs demurely peeking from beneath a child's frock look very feminine, no one in 1840 would have mistaken them for anything less than trousers. Both sexes had always worn lace, but only males wore pants. Any form of bifurcated garment was strictly a male prerogative. Until the middle of the nineteenth century, that distinction had been absolute, but the new costume simply broke all the rules.

Young girls who dressed like boys in a short frock and trousers met with severe disapproval when the style was first introduced from Europe. In 1824, Sara Hutchinson wrote upon hearing that her little niece now wore trousers under her skirts, "I am sorry to hear that dear little Good-Good has been breeched—for some . . . opine that it is much better that females should not."[8] From the comfortable perspective of the 1850s, Sarah Hale, editor of *Godey's Lady's Magazine*, recollected that nothing had been "so revolting to the sense of grave people of both sexes as was the first use among us of ladies' pantalettes, which came to us slowly and cautiously about the year 1830." She remembered that the first young girl "who had the hardihood to appear abroad" in pantaloons was the daughter of a British officer. Such unconventional behavior shocked many American observers. "Often we heard the remark in serious circles," Hale recalled, "that it was an abomination unto the Lord to wear men's apparel." The desire to keep up with European fashions proved stronger than the fear of defying tradition, however. "The fashion," continued Hale, "went first to children til it got familiar to the eyes, and then ladies, little by little, followed after."[9] By the 1850s the costume had become standardized as well as accepted. The pantaloons had to be white and the dress must end within a few inches of the knee to pass muster on the schoolyard. Ten-year-old Catherine Havens of New York City confided to her diary in 1849 the case of a stepmother who made her "stepchild wear nankeen [beige cotton] pantalettes, and when she plays in the parade ground, the boys tease her and call her ginger legs and she is very unhappy." As Catherine concluded, "It is a very sad case."[10]

The major objection to girls in pantaloons had been the familiar one that females should not usurp masculine prerogatives. A girl in pants would quickly lose her modesty, critics argued, and become as coarse and wild as any boy. When such a "hoyden" grew to womanhood, culture and refinement would depart from American homes. To some extent, the argument was true. Since girls had never worn any form of underwear beneath their many petticoats, the adoption of pantaloons did indeed give them the opportunity to romp or roll, climb trees, or play leapfrog without undue immodesty. Significantly, girls appropriated jumping rope, which had traditionally been a boys' game, at the same time that they adopted the new pantaloons.[11] Once girls began to play, boys gave up the game.

Americans soon took to calling the new children's trousers "pantaloons," the same name they used for the long pants adopted by men in the 1820s and 1830s. In the latter decade, when the style was new, girls shortened their frocks only a few inches to reveal just a hint of the pantaloons underneath. As the style gained general acceptance, however, girls' skirts gradually crept ever higher until, by the 1840s, they reached just to the knee. Boys and girls at that point were dressed very much alike. Gradually, over the last half of the nineteenth century, while skirts remained at about the same length, pantaloons became frillier and shorter, until they ended above the knee and disappeared from view altogether. No longer visible, they became something intimate and personal. Pantaloons, under the new name of bloomers, had become underwear.

The cagelike hoops supporting the fashionably huge skirts of the 1850s made pantaloons necessary for women of all ages as insurance against the all-too-likely danger of the unruly hoop skirt tipping up to expose their legs to view. The phenomenon of women wearing pantaloons met with no major objections. Girls, after all, had been wearing them for nearly two decades by then. Women simply adopted (or continued to wear) what they themselves had worn as children. The whole thing seemed quite innocent. Yet what had occurred was, in its own way, quite revolutionary. In both 1650 and 1750, all members of a family except adult and adolescent males wore skirts; in 1850, all members of a family except babies wore pants. Bifurcated clothing was no longer strictly privileged attire. Pants still held symbolic meaning for the society (hence the resistance in the first place to permitting little girls to wear them), and only men retained the right to wear pants as their primary outer garment. The combination of frocks and pantaloons worn by women and children suggested, however, that a recognition of their subservience to men was now tempered with a sense of their own importance within the family circle.

Boys and girls between the ages of three and seven now dressed alike. Both wore half-length petticoats and ankle-length pantaloons, which could be plain, scalloped, or lace edged. Plain or elaborate frocks were acceptable for children of both genders, and boys and girls wore the same colors, the same trims and laces, and the same coral necklaces and pins. Any distinctions were blurry at best.

Popular hairstyles furthered the androgynous image of children. Both Joseph and Anna Raymond, like many of their contemporaries, wore their hair cropped severely short above the ears in a style known as the Brutus or Titus cut. In 1835 the widely respected childrearing authority Lydia Child wrote that parents should "keep children's hair cut close until ten or twelve years old; it is better for health and the beauty of the hair."[12] The style was still popular when Rebecca and Helen Smith, two young girls from Pennsylvania, sat for their photograph near the end of the century (Figure 14). In their eagerness to have the fashionable short cut, girls sometimes took matters into their own hands. Sixteen-year-old Caroline Richards recorded in her diary in 1859 that "it is all the fashion for girls to cut off their hair and friz it. Anna and I have cut off ours and Bessie Seymour got me to cut her lovely hair to-day."[13]

On the other hand, many parents kept the hair of their young sons and daughters long and curled. *Godey's* in August of 1859 offered a sketch of a little boy in a tunic dress with a fancy jacket and skirt, lace-trimmed blouse, sash and pantaloons, and ribbons in his long blond curls (Figure 15). About thirty years later, little Paul Merlyn Cornelius posed for his photograph wearing a short frock, large straw hat, and his long curls also pulled off his face with a wide ribbon tied in a big bow (Figure 16).

The ideal little boy of the age was the young hero of Frances Hodgson Burnett's *Little Lord Fauntleroy*. The favorite of mothers in particular, Lord Fauntleroy was "one of the finest and handsomest little fellows" to be seen anywhere. "He had a strong, light, graceful little body and a manly little face . . . and carried himself with a brave air." With his "innocently fearless eyes, he looked as if he had never feared or doubted anything in his life" (Figure 17).[14] Cedric, the little lord in question, first appeared in the pages of the children's periodical *St. Nicholas* in 1886; suddenly the very name Cedric, invented by Sir Walter Scott for a character in *Ivanhoe*, became a popular choice for baby boys born in the decades around the turn of the century. Burnett's Cedric, with his long blond curls, dainty hands and feet, and genteel bearing was the product of a highly propitious genetic combination. His mother was a virtuous middle-class American woman who endowed her son with piety, modesty, a willingness to work, and the egalitarian principles of a republican. His father, the youngest son of a British lord, passed along to Cedric the aristocratic virtues of grace and dignity, honesty and courage. The resulting "Ceddie" was every mother's darling and instantly won the hearts of American mothers, who took to brushing their unenthusiastic sons' hair into long curls and dressing them in velvet suits with Vandyke collars. Young Kenneth Lawrence wore a typical Fauntleroy suit in 1893 when he posed with his little brother for a photograph, though he managed to escape the long curls (Figure 13). For many little boys, their first haircut became as momentous a rite of passage as their first pair of pants.

A young child in half-length petticoat, white pantaloons, and coral jewelry, with long curls or short hair, could be of either gender. An illustration from the December 1860 issue of *Godey's* of a boy and a girl in the common curls, frocks, and pantaloons of the day clearly plays down gender and concentrates on their common youthfulness (Figure 18). There were very few visual clues to gender—boys sometimes wore a skirted suit; girls more often parted their hair in the center, while boys more often parted theirs on the side or wore a curled topknot—but the rules were not absolute. There were girls in very short hair, high boots, and plain clothing, and boys in delicate long curls, lace-trimmed frocks, and thin leather slippers. Ribbons, bows, pink, blue, ruffles, pinafores, boots, pants were all equally acceptable children's attire. Boys were not dressed as girls; girls were not dressed as boys. By combining elements of masculine and feminine clothing, children were quite deliberately dressed as children, and quite deliberately not differentiated as to sex.

By combining masculine and feminine elements in the dress of young children, parents created an image that reinforced the concept of childhood as a separate stage of development. At the same time, they denied (or blurred) the sexual distinctions between boys and girls, or, more precisely, asserted that such distinctions were irrelevant for youngsters. As Doctor Struve explained in *Domestic Education of Children*, if young people were not dressed similarly, then "the attention of children [might] be excited to the differences of the sexes, a circumstance which would deprive them, at an early age, of their innocence and happy ignorance."[15] The new androgynous children's costume became popular not only because it protected a child's ignorance about sex but also because it created an image of innocence that charmed and reassured parents.

A common theme in much of the popular and scholarly literature of the nineteenth century was that of mankind's dual nature—the belief that a single individual could be both good and evil, and that one quality could be hidden beneath the other. In the popular fiction of the day, authors posited the theory that one person could contain within his character the qualities of Jekyll and Hyde or the dark secrets of Dorian Gray or young Goodman Brown, or could learn, like Peer Gynt or Heathcliffe, that man is propelled by forces within himself that he does not understand and cannot always control.[16] Fascination with man's contradictions and complexities, and his propensity for seemingly irrational behavior, dampened much of the previous century's optimism about man's natural and rational perfectibility. The characters created by Robert Louis Stevenson, Oscar Wilde, Nathaniel Hawthorne, Henrik Ibsen, and Emily Brontë articulated the increasingly dark fears about the fundamental nature of man.

Many nineteenth-century parents believed that their children were, like all human beings, a complex and even contradictory combination of good and evil traits. Perhaps because of their emotional investment in their offspring, there was a tendency to exaggerate the intensity of the duality in children's natures, a tendency for parents to view their children as beings of almost celestial goodness who harbored within themselves the seeds of evil and their own corruption. Adults, therefore, viewed parenting as a vital struggle to protect the good and to suppress or control the potential for evil in their offspring. Children were born good; it was their parents' task to keep them that way. With children understood as creatures of vulnerable purity, their innocence made them charming, and their complexity made them intriguing. The combination and contradiction made both children and childhood more interesting to American society than they had ever been in the past. Victorian parents, in fact, were often obsessively concerned about the nature of their children.

A general shift in social and theological attitudes toward children became apparent in the first half of the nineteenth century. Many influential theologians and authors of the period no longer regarded children as tainted by original sin, but more as pure and innocent gifts of God.[17] Popular theology, as expounded in the growing number of journals and periodicals of the day, endowed the very young with a special spirituality. Children, it was argued, entered this world with the innocence and sanctity of heaven still clinging to them. "There is in childhood," explained one contributor to *Godey's* in

1832, "a holy ignorance, a beautiful credulity, a sort of sanctity, that one cannot contemplate without something of the reverential feelings with which one should approach beings of a celestial nature." As products of heaven, youngsters maintained the aura of heavenly beings in mortal form. "The impress of divine nature is, as it were, fresh on the infant spirit—fresh and unsullied by contact with the breathing world."[18] Children were virtually angels reincarnate who, should they die in infancy, would transmute back to their angelic state.

Whereas eighteenth-century minds focused on the natural biological development of children, nineteenth-century romanticism found a special spirituality in the very young. William Wordsworth, in "Ode: Intimations of Immortality from Recollections of Early Childhood," best expressed the classic romantic notion of the celestial nature of infants: "Our birth is but a sleep and a forgetting . . . / But trailing clouds of glory do we come from God, who is our home."[19] Growing older is a process of regression as man's spirit becomes deadened by the struggles of daily existence. On this side of the Atlantic, Ralph Waldo Emerson argued that the revelation of God through a oneness with nature "illuminates only the eye of the man, but shines into the eye and heart of the child."[20] Thus the purity of children gives them understanding no longer possible for adults. But perhaps the ultimate confidence in the spirituality of children belonged to Bronson Alcott, who held conversations about Jesus with the infant scholars at his school, believing that if they recognized the truth of Christ's sayings that was proof positive that Christianity was the true religion.[21]

The near perfection of the infant state made children not only distinct from, but actually superior to, adults, all of whom had inevitably been corrupted by the world. The eighteenth-century concept of human development as unmitigated progress had been stood on its head. Life now began on the pinnacle of sanctified infancy, then slipped steadily downward, the adult, battered by the exigencies of daily life, inevitably succumbing to compromise and corruption. Maturity and wisdom seemed less desirable than innocence and joy. The American artist Thomas Cole very clearly presented the new conception of the life cycle of man in his series of paintings from 1840 entitled "The Voyage of Life." In the four canvases, Cole portrayed life as a journey in earnest, setting his Everyman adrift in a small boat. In infancy, a guardian angel steered the boat down a gently flowing stream edged with meadows of spring flowers, while the new babe delighted in the beauty and ease of life and the security of divine protection. Youth, in its turn, set off on a broader river, steering the boat for itself, while the guardian angel watched from the shore. The grown man endured violent storms and turbulent rapids bereft of any divine aide. Finally, adrift on a dark sea, the old man's hope rekindled as he beheld a distant vision of the guardian angel once more. Cole's sentimental series struck a responsive note with the American public, and prints of the series sold very well for many years.[22] As Cole illustrated, and as many others believed, childhood had come to represent the best, the happiest, the purest stage of human existence. Whatever followed could never quite live up to that early promise. One anonymous poet of the 1840s drew comfort from the hope that when his "life-long toil is o'er" he could dwell in "a bright realm, a child once more."[23]

Where an earlier age had viewed children's development toward adulthood as progress, and had believed the road to salvation opened only to maturer minds who could grasp theological complexities, Victorian parents believed that their children were born in a state of grace from which they themselves had strayed. An adult's reward for perseverance and righteousness was to eventually rediscover his original self—to be a child again. The attainment of maturity now contained within it a new and disquieting sense of loss.

By the 1830s adults had come to perceive children as delightful, endearing, entertaining, and "cunning"—the nineteenth-century equivalent of the modern use of the word "cute."[24] A corollary to the new concept of the joyousness of childhood was the assumption that children were not touched by pain or sorrow. As one father, contemplating the "bright eyes" and "happy faces" of his children commented, "nothing seems to weigh down their buoyant spirits long; misfortune may fall to their lot but the shadows it casts upon their life path are fleeting."[25] Childhood, it was commonly pointed out, was the last age of mankind still resident in the Garden of Eden, where sin and sorrow could not reach—an ironic allusion in itself, since no children dwelt in the biblical Eden; childbearing was a product of the Fall.[26]

Parents savored a new nostalgia for their own lost childhood in the perceived innocence, simplicity, and happiness of their children's lives. In fact, a feeling of loss pervaded America in the nineteenth century, both in the sense of the personal loss of one's own happier past and in the collective loss of the nation's youth, when life seemed simpler and more heroic. The first celebrated American author, Washington Irving, returned to the theme of the lost Eden frequently, but perhaps most vividly in *Diedrich Knickerbocker's History of New-York* of 1809:

> Happy it would have been for New Amsterdam could it always have
> existed in this state of blissful ignorance and lowly simplicity, but alas!
> the days of childhood are too sweet to last! Cities like men, grow out of
> them in time, and are doomed alike to grow into the bustle, the cares,
> and miseries of the world. Let no man congratulate himself, when he
> beholds the child of his bosom increasing in magnitude and impor-
> tance—let the history of his own life teach him the dangers of the one,
> and this excellent little history of Manna-hata convince him of the ca-
> lamities of the other.[27]

A parent's pleasure in his children's joys was tempered with the knowledge
that childhood was too short and the world a dangerous place.

Victorian parents were surrounded by reminders of the specialness of
childhood. Nineteenth-century authors filled books and articles with examples of the ideal child whose innocent nature shown through any adversity.
Such children as Oliver Twist and Little Eva were exemplars of innocence
and sweetness.[28] If such youthful paragons represented the purest examples
of humanity, then it followed that adults could learn from children and benefit from their presence in the home. As one contributor to *Godey's* asked,
"which of us . . . may not stoop to receive instruction and rebuke from the
character of a little child. Which of us, by comparison with its divine simplicity, has not reason to blush for the littleness, the insecurity, the worldli-
ness, the degeneracy of his own."[29] Adults now regarded themselves as suffering from "littleness" and "insecurity" and as in need of "rebuke" and
"instruction" from their own children. Parents were told to look to their
offspring for inspiration. "It is said," commented the author of another article, "that men would be little better than savages but for women. With
equal truth we may assert, both men and women would be hard and selfish
beings but for children [who] refine and soften the best feelings of the parental heart."[30] Dozens of books, periodicals, and temperance tracts contained stories of adults saved by the intercession or example of an innocent
child, including *Ten Nights in a Barroom* by Timothy Arthur, *An Old-Fashioned Girl* by Louisa Alcott, and *Little Lord Fauntleroy* by Frances Hodgson
Burnett. The purest children, such as Little Eva, Carol Bird, and Beth of
Little Women, were too good for this earth and taught their most poignant

lessons on their deathbeds as they returned to their angelic state. So consistent was the pattern in nineteenth-century children's fiction that the introduction of a character as "our little Willie" was as good as a death sentence. One author of children's stories, Kate Douglas Wiggin (who herself had written of the beatific death of the ten-year-old heroine of her novel *The Birds' Christmas Carol*), years later referred to the popular authors of her day as so many "literary Herods who put to death all the young children in their vicinity."[31] Angelic babies, whose short and innocent lives remained a constant source of inspiration to their parents, abounded in nineteenth-century literature. They were children who were so pure that they had never really broken their ties to heaven and could never really belong to this earth—a comforting view, perhaps, to any parent who had lost a young child.

An extreme example of the genre of the innocent child as inspiration appeared in an 1848 short story by Rose Ashley about a girl suffering severe mental retardation. Her mother attempted to teach her various skills without success, and the child remained completely insensible to her surroundings. Upon the mother's death, the young girl was married to a cousin charged with her care. (The author seems oblivious to any ethical questions about a marriage made and consummated without the informed consent of the bride.) A year later she gave birth to a daughter and, with the advent of motherhood, suddenly blossomed into a bright and charming wife and mother. She became completely responsive and "remembered" the lessons her own mother had tried to teach her years before. Suddenly she could write a good hand, paint, play the harp, embroider, and completely manage her house, all without any additional instruction. When the baby daughter died tragically at the age of five, the mother immediately reverted to total idiocy and died the following year.[32] The story is rich with implications concerning a woman's need for childbearing for true fulfillment, and a child's almost miraculous ability to bring light and cheer to any home.

While few stories described such profound improvement, many pressed the idea that adults, especially women, benefited from the very presence of little children. The love of youngsters was "a love which is necessary to a woman's perfect development, as the sunshine and the rain are to the beauty and the health of the flowers."[33] By giving the mother an opportunity to render selfless service and devotion to the helpless babe, and by the example of the innocent child's sweetness and purity, the young one became the parents' heaven-sent blessing. The apotheosis of the child as teacher, savior (of the father from drunkenness or selfishness, the mother from purposelessness, and the home from emptiness), and shining example left little room for the natural foibles of humanity and immaturity. The child as cherub, guiding his parents, was an image that did not always reconcile with the reality of living, breathing children.

If children were angelic, then it followed that they were also asexual and androgynous, innocent of the ways of the flesh. By favoring a costume exclusive to children but inclusive of both boys and girls, parents created an image of childish asexuality that concurred with their image of childlike innocence and purity. A half-length petticoat and pantaloons certainly did little or nothing to maintain a child's ignorance of sexual differences; any youngster familiar with women in crinolines and men in long pants and top hats knew that there were two distinct sexes in the world. What the new style of dress actually did was to bring the visual image of children into accord with social expectations. Parents wanted their children to look like children, that is, to look different from adults. They wanted the physical appearance of their sons and daughters to be in accordance with their belief in the innocent nature of children. A costume that blurred distinctions of gender by dressing both boys and girls in frocks and trousers, with long or cropped hair, reinforced perceptions of androgynous (that is, angelic) innocence.

For centuries, skirts had been as much a part of a boy's dress as hats or shoes. Since his frocks represented his childish state, a great moment in his early life was the day that he gave them up for pants to become a big boy. When men wore knee breeches, boys wore long trousers; after men adopted long pants around the 1830s, boys gradually came to wear short pants or knickers. It was not the length of pants as such that mattered, but maintaining the visual distinction between men and boys. Whether a boy discarded his frocks for long or for short trousers, the move signified advancement. An 1881 story for children, for example, describes a little boy who gives up his red frock for short trousers. This was "a very important day," for he goes from being "Baby Benny" to being a big boy in one fell swoop. His mother sadly observes that now "he will be a noisy, shouting, out-of-doors boy, and not a dear little house-boy any more at all."[34] The image projected by costume was primarily age specific. However, beginning in the 1890s, frocks came to be viewed as something inherently feminine, representing not just the age but also the gender of the wearer. Gradually it began to seem somehow incorrect to dress a boy in what were becoming girls' clothes. In contrast to "Baby Benny," a little boy in an 1895 story ran home crying after being mistaken by another child for a little girl in his pretty dress and pinafore. One mother expressed the changing view when she wondered "why it is that every boy seems to have an inborn instinct that he belongs to the stronger sex, and indignantly resents being mistaken for a girl, long before his mamma thinks he is old enough for short hair and his first trousers."[35] Parents gradually moved away from an androgynous image of angelic children to a more strictly human, and hence gender-specific, image of their young. Mothers and fathers in the second half of the nineteenth century came to see mild forms of disobedience as harmless, even funny, mischief, for "boys will be boys, and we ought more frequently to think it in their nature to be."[36] There seemed less and less reason to dress little boys in frocks as parents came to see in them more boyishness than angelic sweetness. Dresses and long curls became steadily less common for little boys, until the custom died out in the years after World War I. Victorian parents had emphasized the youth and innocence of their children; twentieth-century parents would be more attracted by real or imagined precociousness in their youngsters, dressing their offspring in everything from little three-piece suits and matching mother-daughter dresses to professional-looking baseball uniforms and miniature medical scrub suits.

GENDER-SPECIFIC TOYS

An androgynous image of children was acceptable to Victorian parents only so long as the nature and destiny of each sex seemed unalterable and secure. They knew that their children would become adults in a society with very distinct and rigid social roles for men and women. All of this meant that parents were faced with the somewhat conflicting need both to reassure themselves of their children's asexual innocence and to receive clear indications that any child would be able to fill its proper place in society. Therefore, as costume became more androgynous, toys seemed an ideal means by which to identify and encourage socially correct behavior for boys and girls. Parents preferred toys that they believed fostered the manliness of their sons and the femininity of their daughters. Virtually all types of playthings commercially available in nineteenth-century America were intended for children of one sex or the other. Only a very limited number of toys (including baby rattles and teething rings, the games of grace hoops and battledore and shuttlecock, Noah's Arks, the increasingly popular new board games, and a few animal pull toys) won parental approval for children of both sexes. Babies played with anything available, including a "spoon and rattle and clothespins and string of buttons," gutta-percha teethers, and other such "homely toys."[37] Many infants, in fact, continued to play with the traditional coral and bells that had served so many generations as a toy, teether, and charm.[38] Coral jewelry also remained particularly popular for children. While many mothers purchased coral necklaces and pins for their baby sons and daughters merely because its long-established association with children made coral seem particularly appropriate, others still had faith in its protective powers. "Constance," reported eleven-year-old Catherine Havens in 1851, "wears a string of coral beads, and says she takes cold if she takes them off."[39]

Parents gave their children sexually stereotyped playthings to bring out what was considered to be their inherent nature and because they honestly believed that suitably gender-specific toys would give their children the most pleasure. A short story in *Godey's* of 1850 described the case of a little girl who, when denied a doll by her father (who wished to raise children free of sexual stereotyping), dressed a rabbit in baby clothes and rocked it to sleep. The child was obeying the laws of nature, explained the author, because "each sex has a use in society peculiarly its own." Therefore "the boy takes the hammer, the whip, or any other plaything that is noisy, or calls for the exercise of strength and action; while the girl, as naturally, busies herself with her doll, or her cups and saucers."[40] In language common to the time, a boy "takes" his pleasures, while the girl works (or "busies herself") in imitation of woman's duties. Victorian parents believed that within each child was the inherent nature of the adult man or woman. Androgynous, or at least ambiguous, clothes helped shield the innocence of children, while the correct toys guided their development along the path to their inevitable gender-determined role in society.

Parental attitudes toward toys and play differed in more than just the type of playthings permitted for boys and girls. Parents tended to offer their sons more toys and more types of toys than they offered their daughters. An examination of the portraits of 325 boys under the age of seven painted between 1830 and 1870 revealed that artists portrayed 217, or two-thirds, of the subjects with one or more of fifty-five types of toys. About 8 percent of the boys carried balls, battledores, and other accoutrements of outdoor sports and games. Seventeen percent posed with toys of a military nature, including little swords, guns, military costumes, bugles, drums, cannons, and toy soldiers. Eighteen percent stood by hobbyhorses, wagons, wheelbarrows, hoops, and other large toys that could be ridden on or in, dragged, chased, pulled, and pushed. Sixty-five little boys, or 20 percent of the sample, carried pony whips in their portraits. Some of the whips were as large as the real thing, standing up far taller than the children who held them; some were little more than tiny sticks with bits of string attached. Many whips appeared in paintings in addition to rocking horses or wagons. It is not really surprising that toy whips were the most popular playthings in the portraits of little boys, in genre paintings and prints, and among the actual wares in retail catalogues, for the whip succinctly summed up the approved masculine characteristics of physical courage, control, and dominance. With his whip, the boy could make his imaginary steed or team of horses (or the younger siblings conscripted into the equine role) do his bidding. The whip was a badge of authority. In general, boys' playthings tended to be large enough to climb on or in, to make noise, to require physical exertion and team effort, to be meant for outdoor play, or to encourage competition. Boys were expected to be fond of "skating, sliding, riding, playing, racing, lifting and scuffling" in their "imperious demand for exercise."[41] Most of the toys, not surprisingly, were large and sturdy, capable of rough treatment and active play, and made, for the most part, of wood, metal, or leather. Parents seemed to expect and sanction rough, boisterous group activity for their sons.

By contrast, only 20 percent of the 309 girls under the age of seven sampled carried a toy in their portrait, and only twenty-one types of toys appeared with girls. While less than half the variety found with boys, the figure is still deceptively large, since nearly 80 percent of all the little girls depicted with any sort of toy carried just one type—the doll (Figure 19). The vast majority of other types of toys for girls were doll related, including small-scale "bureaux, beds, bedsteads, chairs, tables, cups and saucers . . . and many other things."[42] Girls' playthings tended to be small, fragile objects (frequently made of porcelain, wax, paper, and papier-mâché), such as a miniature china tea set, a wax doll, or a music box. They required quiet, careful handling and often encouraged solitary play indoors. In fact, many of the finer toys offered to little girls discouraged play altogether, being much too delicate and elegant to withstand much handling. Lucy Larcom remembered hours of play in her New England girlhood with her rag dolls, "absurd creatures of my own invention, limbless and destitute of features." They had enduring appeal because they could withstand being routinely handled, dressed, and carted around, while her beautiful imported wax doll was much too fragile. Her homemade toys were not particularly pretty, but she "loved them, nevertheless, far better than . . . the London doll that lay in waxen state in an upper drawer at home—the fine lady that did not wish to be played with, but only to be looked at and admired."[43] Eliza Ridgely, living in Baltimore in the 1840s, invited friends to her home to admire her dolls, and went to view the dolls of other little girls, but did not actually play with the elegant wax and porcelain ladies. When she wanted to play in earnest, she brought out her collection of paper dolls and their costumes. Eleanor Abbott also preferred "playing on the floor with my paper dolls," as did Mary Ellen Chase growing up in Maine in the 1890s.[44] Many stories for girls in the new children's periodicals dealt specifically with the theme of the careless little girl who broke her ceramic toy or left her wax doll in the sun to melt. No similar stories concerned the need for special care on the part of boys. While boys' play developed physical strength, stamina, dexterity, confidence, and teamwork, girls' toys concentrated on such specific skills as sewing, mothering, developing a sense of fashion, and serving tea—the skills of the future wife, mother, and hostess. Even though girls' toys required very quiet and careful play, and consisted predominantly of playthings for imitating women's work, there still remained a general disapproval of any sort of play for girls as unladylike. Far more little girls stood for their portraits holding flowers, bonnets, or books—traditional feminine articles—than toys of any sort. American society viewed play as necessary and beneficial for boys and encouraged their enthusiastic participation. Parents offered far less encouragement to girls to play at all, preferring them to spend their time in more useful activities such as sewing or minding the baby, or in the quiet pastimes of embroidery or reading. It is not surprising that the nineteenth-century expression "boys will be boys" has no feminine counterpart. Parents still preferred their daughters to behave like little women.

The gender-specific toys that appeared in children's portraits also were displayed on the shelves of stores and in the pages of the increasingly popular retail catalogues. The Montgomery Ward and Sears, Roebuck catalogues of 1893 and 1897, respectively, carried only "boy's" wagons, wheelbarrows, and carts; Ward's also offered three kinds of "boy's" whips with "braided leather lash" and one deluxe model with "a whistle in the handle."[45] Ward's also sold two types of large three-wheeled vehicles—tricycles for boys with a single large wheel in front and a straddle seat, and velocipedes for girls with a small wheel in front and the seat fixed between the two large rear wheels. The distinction adhered to a cardinal rule of childrearing in the nineteenth century that forbade girls to sit straddling any object. Parents were advised not to let their daughters ride hobbyhorses, rocking horses, bicycles, tricycles, or even seesaws, and a true lady always rode real horses sidesaddle. The straddle position, parents believed, threatened the sexual innocence of their young daughters. As the pioneering sex researcher Havelock Ellis warned, "girls in France . . . are fond of riding the . . . hobby horse, because of the sexual excitement thus aroused; and that the sexual emotions play a part in . . . this form of amusement . . . is indicated by the ecstatic faces of the devotees." In fact, the child prostitute astride a rocking horse was a common motif of French pornographic postcards. Ellis went on to charge that "sexual irritation may also be produced by the bicycle in women." Even the humble garden swing came under attack. "Swinging another person may be a source of voluptuous excitement, and one of the 600 forms of sexual pleasure enumerated in De Sade's *Les 120 Journées de Sodome* is to propel a girl vigorously in a swing," Ellis assured his readers.[46] There were even serious concerns about women using a treadle sewing machine, for the same reason.[47]

While childrearing authorities urged parents to expressly forbid their daughters to use anything with a straddle seat, all children were generally discouraged from straying into the preserves of the other sex. "The boys," wrote another medical expert, "must be watched for evidence of a tendency to effeminacy, or a fondness for girlish games, and girls must be influenced against too great an enthusiasm for boyish sports and the danger of being tomboys."[48] Playing the wrong games or using the wrong toys could prematurely awaken sexual feelings in children and destroy their natural purity. Disquieting parental fears lay behind the little stories that dotted children's books urging boys to trundle their hoops and girls to content themselves with their dolls.

While a few authorities, including Lydia Child, approved of girls engaging in active games, most accepted the necessity of separate spheres of play for boys and girls. The children themselves disagreed. When given an opportunity to express an opinion, they revealed a far more eclectic taste in playthings than their elders would have sanctioned. T. R. Crowell conducted a survey of 1,000 girls and 1,000 boys in Massachusetts in 1898, asking each child to list her or his favorite toys. Only about two-thirds (621) of the girls put dolls on their list at all, and less than one-quarter (233) considered them their favorite toy.[49] This trend was borne out in the diaries of little girls. Amid the pages devoted to critical accounts of local fashions, school gossip, daily activities, and long, loving, detailed descriptions of the local candy store's wares, some girls did mention their dolls and make-believe tea parties with their friends. Many, however, made only cursory mention of dolls, being far more interested in other forms of play. The toy most prized by both girls and boys, in fact, seemed to be the hoop. Edward Everett Hale remembered the hoop he rolled as a boy on Boston Common in the 1830s. The hoop was made from the "large hoops of sea going casks" and was named Whitefoot. In the popular game of post office, Hale rolled Whitefoot about the town, depositing "letters" in the crooks of trees or under stones for other boys to retrieve.[50] Ten-year-old Catherine Havens of New York City never mentioned traditional girls' toys, but she regularly recounted her trips to Washington Square to roll her hoop and jump rope during the summer of 1849. Caroline Cowles (Richards) and her sister Anna, ages ten and seven respectively, chose for their birthday presents in 1862 "two rubber balls and two jumping ropes with handles and two hoops and sticks to roll them with, and a bag of lemon drops" from a store in Canandaigua, New York. From then on, rolling the hoop became Caroline's favorite activity before and after school.[51] Twelve-year-old Eliza Ridgely of Baltimore kept a diary in 1841 and 1842. She enjoyed playing with paper dolls, and showed off her baby house to every young visitor (though she never seemed to play with it otherwise), but her true passion was trundling her hoop. For the one month of November 1841, Eliza recorded rolling her hoop on fourteen different occasions — or every time she made an entry in her diary. On fair days, she played with her hoop in the garden or on the school portico until it was too dark to see; when it rained, she rolled it up and down the front hall of the house. Girls did not limit themselves to hoops, however. Eliza also threw snowballs, rode sleds, played catch and King George's troops, and after one morning of paper dolls "walked out with the boys and Aunt Ellen with our bows and arrows." Most surprising was her penchant for wrestling matches. A typical entry on the subject, this one for 26 November 1841, reads: "After dinner I had six fights or wrestlings, three with Isabel Laroque and three with Lizzy

Berny, in all of which I laid them flat and conquered them both."[52] Caroline and Anna Cowles rode their sleds along the roads by hanging on to passing wagons, played jump rope and snap-the-whip, climbed fences and trees, and enjoyed a seesaw and swing in their garden; Anna once sprained an ankle while sliding down the school bannister. At the age of eleven, Caroline developed a passion for mumblety-peg, a game in which one contestant threw a jackknife as deeply as possible into the ground and another player tried to extract it with his or her teeth. One young advocate of the game noted that, after pulling loose a well-placed knife, the player's "nose and mouth invariably looked like a vacant asparagus bed." Caroline was a passionate devotee of the sport, regretting only that her otherwise tolerant "grandmother [with whom she lived] won't give me a knife [of her own] to play with."[53] Typically, little girls quite matter-of-factly interspersed accounts of rough-and-tumble play with descriptions of Bible readings, school studies, sewing lessons, and family events. They rarely concerned themselves with adult reactions to their play, unless those reactions interfered with their preferred activities. The girls were not overtly rebellious, just acting on personal preference. Many simply enjoyed racing a hoop as much as rocking a doll's cradle, sometimes more.

At the same time many little boys counted a doll among their cherished possessions. Dolls did not figure prominently in boys' journals, since, by the time a boy was old enough to keep a diary, he was too old to still play with them. Evidence of doll play exists in numerous photographs of little boys and their dolls and in the memoirs of men looking back on their early childhood. For example, in a photograph from the 1860s one anonymous boy of about three, dressed in boots and a military-style tunic, cradled a china-headed lady doll with leather body (Figure 20). Howard Woodman, of upstate New York, owned a similar lady doll in the 1890s and whiled away long days of recuperating from illness by sewing a patchwork quilt for her.[54] In an autobiography written with the perspective and tolerance of maturity, E. H. Southern recalled the toys of his boyhood in the 1860s as including "many kinds of dolls of both sexes and both black and white, waxen and wooden." He also remembered an encounter with "a small boy of the lower orders [with] a dilapidated doll on his lap."[55] Fiction written for children in the second half of the nineteenth century occasionally refers to little boys with dolls of their own. A story from the periodical *Babyland* in 1881, for example, centered on a little boy with a doll named Joe, while an issue of *Nursery* recounted the adventures of Tommy and his "naughty male doll of African descent, known as Dandy Jim."[56] Such stories invariably described the little boy as owning a male doll; in reality, lady dolls were much more common and were more often owned by boys. For much of the nineteenth century most children's toys were hard and rigid. Toy animals were made of carved wood, wood covered with leather or fur, or with stiff leather bodies stuffed with sawdust. Many of these were attached to wheeled wooden platforms and meant as pull toys for young children. The only really cuddly toys available were rag babies and cloth- and leather-bodied dolls. In a world where nearly everyone was bigger and stronger than the small child, a doll was someone even smaller and weaker who could be protected or bullied according to the mood of the moment. Doll play gave children a pleasant sense of superiority and control in a world that rarely permitted them such feelings. A young boy who craved the comfort of close contact and companionship had little choice but a girl's doll, and many mothers seem to have recognized the need and indulged the child. By the end of the century, when a renewed interest in children's make-believe produced a market for soft stuffed rabbits, bears, Brownies, and Golliwogs, most little boys found satisfactory alternatives to dolls, and their ownership among this group declined markedly.

If some boys had dolls, most girls certainly did—elaborate ones with china, parian, wax, or metal heads, inexpensive penny woodens, "indestructible" gutta-percha dolls of vulcanized rubber, or simple homemade babies of rag or wood. Purchased dolls in particular reveal more about the adults who made and bought them than about the play preferences of little girls. From the founding of the American colonies to the middle of the nineteenth century, the elegant lady doll dominated the market. Such a doll was meant to introduce a young girl to the feminine world of fashion, dressmaking, and entertaining, giving her the opportunity to learn skills that would be necessary later in life when, as Rousseau observes, "in due time she will be her own doll" and live the life she once played.[57] Society's attention focused on the potential adult within the child, grooming girls to become women.

Only after about 1850 did European factories begin producing child dolls, porcelain *bébés* in search of a little mother. Childlike dolls gained rapid popularity in America, where many established residents feared that the influx of eastern and southern European immigrants with large and healthy families would eventually overwhelm the established American culture unless something was done. With declining birthrates among middle-class women, childrearing authorities hoped that early play with baby dolls would discourage later "companionate marriages" and "one-child mothers."[58] Little girls had to be convinced of the joys of motherhood so that they might ensure the survival of their way of life. Doll play had become very serious business. The popularity of the child dolls among adults and children also rested, however, simply on their visual appeal. With their round faces, rosy cheeks, oversized eyes, and long curls, they were the epitome of the Victorian ideal of the beautiful, unspoiled, innocent child.

There was no one plaything that was associated with boys the way the doll came to represent the state of girlhood. If anything prevailed, it was a passion for horses and riding, very similar to the fascination of little boys in the twentieth century with automobiles. Boys enjoyed hobbyhorses, rocking horses, tricycles with replicas of horses' heads attached, little toy horses, sets of small harnesses and reins that could be fastened onto a little brother or sister, pony whips, hoops, and wagons large and small. But horses represented only a small part of the range of playthings for boys. Unlike prescribed girls' toys, which focused their attention on one accepted future role, boys' play developed basic skills and encouraged such socially desirable traits as courage, leadership, teamwork, and competitiveness. Play also simply offered boys outlets for their seemingly boundless energy and enthusiasm. Altogether, boys' play had fewer strings attached.

As the wealth of playthings in children's portraits and photographs and in retail catalogues and toy shops indicated, Victorian parents believed that toys taught important skills, enabled children to develop appropriate role behavior, and encouraged healthful exercise. Play and playthings refreshed the body and mind so that children could return to more serious tasks invigorated.[59] However, play for pure amusement, play without any practical purpose, remained somewhat suspect; it still smacked of idleness, mischief, and self-indulgence. Childrearing authorities argued against playing with very young babies at all, "never until four months, and better not until six months. The less of it at any time the better for the infant." If babies are played with, "they are made nervous and irritable, sleep badly, and suffer in other respects."[60] Older children could be made materialistic and worldly by an overemphasis on toys and games, which might destroy their natural innocence. Toys rarely appeared in nineteenth-century children's novels or short stories, where virtuous children found pleasure and satisfaction in gardening, playing with pets, caring for baby, or romping out-of-doors, since "the more you give to the child the less chance he has to develop his own resources."[61] For much of the century, American adults remained ambivalent toward toys. On the one hand, toys made up an important element in their image of childhood as a special world, carefree and innocent. Yet grown-ups also feared that any overindulgence would spoil the child and destroy that innocence.

6

Furniture for Containment
and Display

FURNITURE FOR CONTAINMENT

Nineteenth-century society was one of self-restraint and control, where appearances counted greatly and ceremony was valued above spontaneity. "We are constantly required to sacrifice comfort to conventionality," authorities on etiquette reminded their readers, "and the discipline is good for us. When we commence to move in the reverse direction, it is impossible to tell where we shall stop."[1] Parents were responsible for teaching their children both the specific rules and the self-discipline necessary to function satisfactorily in polite society, certainly no easy task. Such authorities as Catherine Beecher advised mothers that teaching morals and manners (and the two were definitely linked in Victorian minds) could neither start too young nor be pursued too diligently. "There is no more important duty devolving upon a mother," Beecher warned, "than the cultivation of habits of modesty and propriety in young children. All indecorous words or deportment should be carefully restrained and delicacy and reserve studiously cherished."[2] Civilization depended on standards maintained by everyone, and even "babies must be taught to be decent members of society."[3]

For children too young to have developed a reliable degree of self-discipline, the nineteenth-century mother required external forms of control to ensure that her offspring functioned within the accepted bounds of decorum, at least when anyone was likely to be watching. Control was not as easy as it had once been. The new perception of childish innocence meant that most traditional methods of child control were now considered inappropriate. While physical punishment had been an accepted deterrent in colonial homes, experts now cautioned that the wise mother instructed with loving words and by example, for the innocent nature of children needed only patient nurturing and guidance. "Infantile tenderness becomes calloused, and sweetness soured by scolding; much more by chastisement," warned Orson Fowler.[4] A mother forced to resort to the rod had already failed with her children.

Servants and baby nurses, another useful form of external control over young people, had been an integral part of many households. As the nineteenth century progressed, middle-class mothers continued to employ nurses, but with increasing concern. As fewer and fewer middle-class girls were willing to go into service, parents sought nurses among the working classes and new immigrants. Many mothers and fathers saw a serious risk in permitting children to spend considerable time with women whom they considered their social inferiors, particularly because they believed such nurses were more likely to cling to traditional childrearing methods and because the nurses often held quite different cultural and religious beliefs. Stories abounded of the dangers of trusting children to an untried servant girl. In 1835, Lydia Child described a case where a "farmer and his wife decide to take a trip because travel is so cheap and everyone is doing it." Despite the mother's misgivings, they left their children in the care of a young servant girl. Upon their return, "tired and dusty," having "spent all their money; had a watch stolen from them on the steamboat," and having been "dreadfully sea-sick off Point Judith," they "found the babe sick, because Sally had stood in the door with it, one chilly, damp morning, while she was feeding the chickens; and the eldest girl screaming and screeching at the thought of going to bed, because Sally, in order to bring her under her authority, had told her a frightful 'raw-head-and-bloody-bones' story."[5] Even well-meaning nurses were no longer completely satisfactory, and could be very dangerous.

Mothers who still wanted the services of a nurse could mitigate the possible damage by screening applicants for the position very carefully. A nurse needed to be well spoken, soft spoken, of modest demeanor and habits, patient, conscientious, and dedicated. She should be religious, temperate, and either a virgin or a widow. If finding such a paragon were not hard enough, it was also, counseled Mrs. Dewing in 1882, "no unimportant matter, in choosing a nurse for children, that she should be of pleasing appearance, with an honest, modest, cheerful expression of face; . . . for children copy the expression of those around them unconsciously, till we often see a strong resemblance between children and their nurses." Dewing went on to compound her readers' sense of guilt, should they happen to rely on the services of a nurse, by concluding her advice with the observation that "no children have as refined an expression of face as those who are in the habit of being with their parents."[6] Since no nurse could live up to the ideal completely, and since any compromise presented some risks to the children, mothers who employed nurses lived with a certain amount of anxiety about the permanent effects of their decision. For conscientious parents, any strong influence on their young and impressionable children, other than their own, was cause for some concern.

Mothers and fathers anxious about the potentially harmful consequences of employing a children's nurse could still rely instead on Mogg's Mixture or Godfrey's Cordial to quiet restless infants. In fact, some boarding schools for girls routinely gave their students a dose of calomel if they were in "too robust health" to make them more "languid and listless" and "lady-like." More and more parents, however, were aware of the dangers of giving drugs to children.[7] Physicians and childrearing authorities unanimously denounced giving alcohol or opiates to children. Orson Fowler warned in 1870 against calomel, morphine, paregoric, and opiates of all kinds, which were routinely available in patent medicines designed specifically for use with children. "Soothing syrup," he concluded, "has spoiled and buried millions of babies."[8] Reliance on patent medicines was a common enough occurrence among women and children that, by the end of the century, many women's periodicals regularly carried advertisements on their inside back cover from doctors specializing in drug addictions. Typical was an ad in the very middle-class and wholesome *Godey's Lady's Magazine* in 1892:

> OPIUM – Morphine Habit
> No pay till cured. Ten years established.
> 1,000 cured. State case.
> Dr. Marsh, Quincy, Mich.[9]

As popular opinion swung against the use of addictive drugs, manufacturers were quick to announce the innocent nature of their ingredients. The Sears,

Roebuck catalogue of 1902 declared their patented Baby Syrup to be "a blessing to parents, harmless and effectual in soothing and quieting children of any age. We guarantee it to contain no opium or morphine; [it is] prepared from simple herbs."[10] Of course, like their close kin, the nerve tonics, cough syrups, and elixirs, many soothing syrups continued to be heavily laced with alcohol. Gradually, many nineteenth-century parents came to believe that both servants and drugs could prove of more danger than benefit in the delicate matter of childrearing.

Since physical punishment, drugs, and hired help could all have detrimental effects on young children, and since constant parental supervision was not always practical, many parents turned to specially designed children's furniture as a benign mechanism of external control. The traditional forms of furniture for youngsters had already fallen into disfavor, and they did not function in ways consistent with nineteenth-century perceptions of children and their needs. Old-fashioned baby furniture disappeared, to be replaced by totally new and different forms. The cradle gave way to the crib; the walking stool and standing stool to the swing and jumper; the high chair, rare before 1830, increased in popularity and gained a tray; and the baby carriage appeared, evolving into a prominent element in Victorian homes.

Since the last quarter of the eighteenth century, most parents had no longer insisted that their infants conform as closely as possible to an adult model of behavior. They no longer tried to physically force the soft spot on a baby's head closed, tied an infant's legs straight, or pushed their babies to stand and walk as soon as possible. As parents came to accept the physical limitations of infancy as natural and temporary, those limitations lost many of their negative associations. Infantile behavior seemed less a shortcoming or weakness than a part of babies' winsome nature. While seventeenth-century mothers and fathers saw the infant "mewling and puking in its mothers's arms," nineteenth-century parents regarded their babies as gurgling and cooing charmers, and they were not unaware of how much their perceptions had changed. As one author explained in 1869, "The dragon, the hydra, and the dwarf, which exhaust the descriptive powers of the old poets, have given place to the untouched, all-promising and exquisite child."[11] Parents liked the way babies looked and acted, and they revelled in infant antics to a degree that could drive nonparents to distraction.

When verticality lost its social significance, and infants were no longer forced on their feet by their first birthday, the go-cart and standing stool lost their usefulness. The go-cart, in fact, disappeared from common use in the decades around 1800, for most mothers had come to perceive the risks of a child walking into danger as greater than the benefits of getting toddlers up on their feet. A few versions of the standing stool were still produced in the early 1800s. They were small wooden boxes with a built-in seat and an attached wooden tray. When placed within it, the baby could stand or sit, amusing itself with objects placed on the tray. The primary function of the device was not to encourage early walking, but to enclose and protect the child and to keep it from harm. Such baby containers did not gain significant popularity. Most, if not all, seemed to be homemade affairs, and they generally disappeared from use by about 1850. Most parents seemed to want more from a piece of furniture than simple containment. They were looking for something that would exercise and entertain their babies, as well as keep them out of harm's way. Essentially, they sought a device that could replace the attentions of a nurse.

In the Victorian home by 1850, the swing (or any number of variations on the jumper) had replaced the go-cart and the standing stool as the object of choice for exercising a baby. "To enable a mother who has no servants, to relieve herself at pleasure from carrying her child," one correspondent as early as 1839 recommended the use of a swing "for cleanliness and decency."[12] The swing offered cleanliness since it kept children off the floor, and decency because it prevented them from crawling. Advertisements for swings appeared regularly in catalogues and ladies' magazines, and childrearing manuals extolled their usefulness. "A safety swing may be easily put up in the nursery," noted the *Ladies Home Journal* in 1899, "and furnishes amusement to the children in the winter days when they are so often confined to the house."[13] The most common swing was a simple wooden seat with wooden arms and back suspended from a doorway by four ropes; a bar across the front held the baby in place. A jumper, essentially, was a swing attached to a spring to give it some bounce. Fancier models, like the one offered by Sears in 1897, were more versatile (Figure 21). "This Jumper combines in one article a baby swing, reclining chair, crib and jumper," the caption announced; "should the baby fall asleep while in the chair it can be adjusted to a crib without disturbing the child" by reclining the back and raising the footrest. Sears assured parents that the swing was "strong enough for a child of 6 years."[14] The conscientious mother feared as much for the immediate safety of her toddler as for her baby, and she dared not depend on servants for help. A swing was a satisfactory solution, for it offered children amusement and exercise while protecting them from mishap by tethering them to one spot. Like the walking stool before it, the swing was a simple device, easily made at home or cheaply purchased. The walking stool had forced infants to stand on their own two feet (however unsteady those might be) and had offered a sense of independence, although at the risk of possible injury. The swing, on the other hand, catered to the physical limitations of nonambulatory children; it presented them with a seat, exercise, and amusement. In fact, the swing not only offered a seat but restricted the child to it. As advertisements clearly stated, swings and jumpers could easily hold a child of six years of age, thereby limiting the mobility of the walking child as well as the baby. For children of the nineteenth century, the price of safety could well be the loss of independence.

For the first half of the century, crawling remained suspect. The long gowns worn by most babies certainly made creeping virtually impossible, and one of the appealing aspects of the swing and jumper was that they permitted babies to exercise their legs without allowing them to creep.

Not until the 1870s was American society comfortable enough with the fact that babies naturally crept on all fours as part of the process of learning to walk that illustrators, advertisers, and manufacturers could depict crawling infants and feel secure that their audience would be attracted to the images.[15] In 1871 both Robert J. Clay of New York City and Alfred Vincent Newton of London received patents for mechanical crawling baby dolls that, when wound up and placed on their hands and knees, would crawl rapidly across the floor.[16] Crawling dolls and the ceramic figurines known as piano babies, some of which were also sculpted to resemble a baby on its hands and knees, became popular after about 1875. They, and the creeping babies they were modeled after, were now described as "cunning." Concurrently, the convention of photographing a naked infant lying on its stomach on a fur rug became so popular as to become a visual cliché of the times. Earlier generations would have recoiled at such a patently animalistic presentation of human infants, completely devoid of the trappings of civilization. Nineteenth-century parents adored it. The baby on all fours had become an accepted enough part of babyhood that women's magazines could suggest "a crawling blanket [as] a suitable gift" for an infant. These were simply small, thick blankets to place on the floor in order to give a baby a comfortable place to play.[17] Only after the turn of the century, however, did parents generally discard the fashionable long skirts traditionally worn by babies since 1750. For everyday wear, mothers dressed their little ones in rompers, voluminous one-piece bifurcated garments that left the lower legs unencumbered and made crawling possible (Figure 22). As such, rompers were an early form of play clothes. With their advent, the swing lost favor to both an old favorite and a new device—the go-cart and the playpen. The twentieth-century versions of the go-cart contained a seat that supported a good portion of toddlers' weight as they pushed themselves along. Introduced in the decade after World War I on a commercial scale, the wheeled playpen combined mobility, safety, and the freedom to stand, sit, or crawl within a protected miniature environment. Some mothers also began childproofing their homes by removing anything dangerous or breakable from a child's reach, so that babies could play uninhibited by furniture, with minimal supervision and minimal risk. In either a childproof home or a playpen, infants enjoyed both a choice of activities and the freedom to switch from one activity to another at will, which gave them a new sense of control over their immediate world.

American parents discarded the walking stool for the swing, and the swing for the playpen. The basic form of the high chair, however, although centuries old, only became a common household item after 1830. One of the most important training grounds for both manners and morals was the Victorian family's dining table, where little children were most visible to family and company. English upper- and middle-class children commonly took their meals apart from adults, but the majority of American youngsters appear to have joined their elders at all but the most formal social occasions.[18] Family meals, the authors of childrearing manuals believed, were excellent opportunities for teaching children etiquette and self-restraint. Dining with company revealed to the world how well such lessons had been learned. Successful internalization of the rules of civilized behavior mattered because at stake were the physical well-being and future character of the child, as well as the family's claim to gentility and refinement. "Good conduct at meals," declared one expert in "nursery discipline" early in the nineteenth century,

> is, with children, a fair criterion of manners and meals may be made use of, as favorable opportunities for inculcating propriety of behavior. Children should be taught to sit down, and to rise from the table, at the same time; to wait, whilst others are served, without betraying eager-

ness, or impatience; to avoid noise and conversation, and if they are no longer confined to the nursery, to be able to see delicacies without expecting or asking to partake of them.[19]

Lydia Child described a visit to a friend's house just as the family was about to sit down to the supper table. "A little girl, about four years old, was obliged to be removed, to make room for us. Her mother assured her she should have her supper in a very little while, if she was a good girl." When discipline broke down almost at once as the child cried in protest, the embarrassed mother "led her out of the room and gave orders that she should be put to bed without supper."[20] Age still had its privileges, and it was the youngest who were expected to wait until everyone else had been served or to give way to their elders if there were not enough places for everyone. For the very young, this was a hard rule to accept with grace.

Most authorities firmly held that a child's diet should be simple and wholesome, free of all delicacies and rich foods. Many urged that the most healthful food for the first few years was plain bread and milk.[21] Bland foods, cereals, unsweetened or very lightly sweetened puddings, and plain vegetables were easiest for a child to digest, medical authorities believed, while rich or spicy food would stimulate children and make them restless, sick, or sexually excited. Children had to learn to sit quietly at the table, eating their milk porridge or unsweetened bread pudding, while their elders indulged in meats, sauces, and rich desserts; a hard lesson perhaps, but one many parents accepted as essential to the health of the child. A short story in *Arthur's Ladies Magazine* of 1866 illustrated the seriousness of the message clearly. A young mother had been warned by her husband never to give their year-old son rich foods. After a particularly trying day, the mother gave in to her baby's incessant pleas and permitted him to indulge in food from her plate. When the child became gravely ill that night and nearly died, his mother realized that hers was the lack of self-discipline (and, of course, failure in wifely obedience) that had nearly led to tragedy.[22] Self-restraint at the table ensured health and demonstrated strong character, and parents as well as children were judged on the basis of the child's behavior.

Traditional high chairs raised a small child up to the height of the dining table. Rare before 1830, they became common in American homes within the following twenty years. For the youngster who had yet to master sufficient self-discipline, the Victorian high chair came complete with its own attached tray, which not only held the child securely in place but also separated the young person from direct contact with the dining table. The new tray (or table, as it was first called) successfully restrained the baby, permitting access only to those items that someone else saw fit to place upon the tray's surface. As *The Furniture Gazette* of 1870 advertised, a high chair with a tray promised "well-regulated demeanor at the table."[23] The separation of the young child from the main dining table suppressed or at least isolated any display of bad manners. Babies could not grab what they fancied, disrupt the orderly array of dishes and utensils, or smear sticky fingers on white tablecloths. If a child's baser nature was not yet under firm control, it could at least be restrained and isolated.

By the last quarter of the nineteenth century, two distinct versions of the high chair began to appear in trade catalogues and advertisements. One form, with an attached tray, was called a "high chair" or "child's high chair." The other, frequently larger and without a tray, was a "youth's chair," "youth's table chair," "half high chair," and "youth's or misses' chair."[24] The former type was meant for babies who had not yet mastered the art of dining and needed physical restraint and isolation to preserve the dignity of the meal for the rest of the family; the latter was intended for children old enough to conduct themselves properly at the table but who needed a little extra elevation to reach it comfortably. Youth chairs remained in the dining room, but high chairs gradually moved to other parts of the house. The high chair, with its attached table, separated infants not only from physical contact with the full-sized dining table but also from any real reason for eating with the rest of the family. In fact, it was easier for a mother to feed her baby before the family sat down to dinner, so that she could then enjoy her own meal without having to attend to the child's needs. Gradually, the high chair moved into the kitchen of many homes without servants, or into the nursery of those families that did employ a nurse. Babies kept completely ignorant of adult delicacies would be more likely to remain content with nursery food, and infants fed before the rest of the family could not disrupt the family meal. In some households, the baby only joined the family at dinner when old enough for a youth's chair. Even that carried too much of the stigma of baby furniture for some. Eleanor Hallowell Abbott remembered Thanksgiving Day when she was about four. "Relieved for once of the unspeakable ignominy of a high chair and raised by the aid of a huge Webster's Dictionary to what might at least have been called the corporal heights of my elders, I felt myself for the first and last time in my life, an absolute peer among my peers."[25]

The high chair also served many mothers as a convenient baby tender, a safe place for youngsters to amuse themselves without risk of injury or mischief. Boredom was an inevitable problem in such a confining situation, and mothers sought to fend it off by collecting such simple playthings as wooden spoons, teething rings, and empty wooden spools strung together and tying them to the arms of the high chair so that little children could retrieve for themselves the toys they threw overboard. Some manufacturers catered to this secondary use of the high chair by producing chairs that converted to strollers, rockers, or other forms of baby tenders.

The swing, the jumper, and the high chair served as containers to hold a baby securely in one spot. With nearly every flat surface in a Victorian home, from table to piano to fireplace mantel, covered in hanging lambrequins or paisley shawls and topped with abundant collections of glass, ceramics, and assorted objets d'art, a toddler grabbing at a handy bit of artfully draped fabric for support could easily bring the whole thing crashing down, with serious consequences to both child and knickknacks. Victorian mothers were as concerned with keeping the house safe from the child as the child safe from household injuries. Their solution was to immobilize little children with special furniture whenever they could not be carefully monitored.

The ideal form of protection for both house and child was to give youngsters a space of their own, free of any potentiality for reciprocal damage. Rooms set aside as nurseries, which had begun to appear in a very few homes around the turn of the nineteenth century, gained favor and popularity as the century progressed. Traditionally, children had shared rooms with siblings, servants, and, quite often, their parents. Such sleeping quarters were merely that, and young people did not feel any proprietary rights to the space or spend much time there during the day. The room in which the children frequently gathered with their mother and any female relatives or visitors during the day was the mother's room (the "master bedroom" is a twentieth-century innovation), where they read, sewed, played quiet games, and chatted. Harriet Manigault's schedule was fairly typical for the early 1800s. At the age of nineteen, she spent each morning at her home in Philadelphia reading, translating French, and practicing her music. After a walk in the hall, "Mamma is generally ready . . . for us to assemble in her room" for an afternoon of reading and sewing.[26]

Gradually, as the century progressed, room use shifted. It became "a matter of no small importance, in towns and cities, to have a well regulated nursery for the children," in which they slept, played, and sometimes ate, and to which their mother took her work during the day.[27] One author described a fictional character in 1849 as "so unfashionably fond of her husband's society, that she could illy endure the loneliness of the nursery during the hours which he usually devoted to study."[28]

The nurseries continued to be very simple affairs. "The children's apartment is too frequently one of the least comfortable in the house," complained one mother in 1848, "being either a damp gloomy division of the basement story, or else a narrow room" upstairs at the back of the house.[29] Catherine Havens was annoyed when strangers on their way to the back door "sometimes peek through the window into the basement, which is my nursery," in her home in New York City in 1849.[30] More common was Eliza Ridgely's nursery in Baltimore; at the age of twelve, she shared the second-floor room with her brother Charles, baby sister Julia, her nurse, and, occasionally, her cousin Nicholas. Their nursery was used most of the time simply as a bedroom. While they did play there occasionally, in bad weather they also played in the hall, on the doorstep, and in the parlor on Sunday for quiet games. Most indoor play occurred, however, in the garret.[31] Lucy Larcom agreed that "the garret was the children's castle," and Edward Hale remembered that "the principal part of the attics—or, as we called them, garrets—in every house we lived in was surrendered to us boys."[32] The large, unfinished attic spaces became the playrooms of children. Specific rooms designed and furnished for play did not gain popularity until the turn of the century.

"The articles of furniture [in a nursery] should be few and simple," argued Dr. John Bright of Kentucky, echoing the consensus among experts. The room should have very simple rugs and curtains, a few chairs, simple beds, and "a wardrobe or bureau or two for [the children's] clothing."[33] Not until very late in the nineteenth century did furniture especially designed to aid mothers in the daily care of their infants enter the nursery. Mothers began making and buying special nursery baskets to hold powder, soap, sponge, comb and brush, safety pins, and other infant toiletries. Most were small wicker baskets, but some had "stands available to raise the toilet-basket to convenient height."[34] There were no special changing or bathing tables for infants in the nineteenth century. Beginning at about this time, medical authorities encouraged mothers to change their babies' diapers as soon as they became wet or soiled. To the question "should napkins [diapers] which have been only wet be used a second time without washing?" Emmett Holt offered the standard reply that "it is no doubt better to use only fresh napkins, but there is no serious objection to using them twice unless there is chafing of the skin."[35] Not until after World War I did washing a diaper after every changing become expected practice. The introduction of commercially made rubber goods brought several new products into the nursery by midcentury. Rubber nursery sheeting protected babies' beds, and rubber carriage aprons kept infants dry on outings. Rubber teething rings eventually replaced the old coral and bells, and rubber-lined pants were more effective than heavy felt pants, which had never been too successful at absorbing wetness anyway. Probably the most significant new product for the nursery was the rubber nipple for use with glass baby bottles. Infants of earlier generations had been forced to make do with unyielding pewter nipples or ceramic pap boats that poured a thin gruel into the little mouth. Rubber nipples could be sucked for nourishment in a far more natural and comfortable manner. A popular early design attached flat glass bottles to long rubber tubes with the nipple on the end. Mothers could put the bottle down beside babies, who could then hold the nipple end and nurse at their leisure. Unfortunately, the long rubber tubes were impossible to wash thoroughly and became a breeding ground for bacteria and a serious health hazard for infants.[36] Only at the very end of the century, with the advent of pasteurized milk and short rubber nipples that could withstand the high temperatures necessary for sterilization, did mothers finally have a safe alternative to breast milk at their disposal.

The most important item in the nursery was the child's bed, and those of the nineteenth century were very different from anything babies had slept in before. *Godey's Lady's Magazine* in 1856 observed the revolution in children's sleeping furniture then under way and announced that "there is nothing that has undergone a greater transformation of late years in nursery management, than sleeping arrangements for children." While "in olden times the wooden cradle . . . was thought as indispensable an article of housekeeping as a table or bedstead . . . at present, very many city nurseries have discarded the cradle altogether, and children are accustomed from their birth to sleep in a crib, without the furious rocking . . . that seemed to confuse the infant brains of our grandfathers."[37] The new cribs were plain and simple affairs, occasionally of wood, but more often of white painted metal. The nursery was not one of the public rooms of the house; it was not meant to receive visitors, and it was, in any event, a temporary space maintained only until the youngest child in the family outgrew a need for it. Most people, therefore, did not see any point in putting significant sums of money into children's furniture. Cribs were unornamented, functional, and cheap, ranging in price from $1.40 to $8.75 in the Sears catalogue of 1897. After the Civil War, the crib so completely replaced the cradle that the 1890 volume of *The Upholsterer,* under the unequivocal heading "The Cradle Is No More," asserted that "a cradle is a thing unknown nowadays. Go to the furniture store, and ask for cradles, and they will show you cribs, perambulators, hammocks, and basinettes."[38] Actually, American factories continued to turn out limited quantities of cradles (and still do), but the crib had become the most common form of infants' sleeping furniture in America—and still is.[39] As the cradle lost its primary function to the crib, it gained a new, less tangible ideotechnic one. Beginning with the Centennial celebrations of 1876, Americans discovered a new interest in their own colonial past, now seemingly distant and venerable. They became involved in pursuing genealogies and town histories and in acquiring American antiques. The cradle, which had fallen into such disfavor, now joined a constellation of artifacts, including the open fireplace, the spinning wheel, and the old oaken bucket as tangible symbols of America's simpler, purer, preindustrial past. Over the course of the nineteenth century, changing social patterns had brought new and often disquieting dislocations in daily life. Families felt pulled apart by forces beyond their control. More and more men left the home each day for work; older children went off to school, while younger ones remained sequestered in an upstairs nursery; even women spent more time outside the home tending to shopping and social obligations. The obsolete artifacts came to represent an idyllic past when the entire family had lived and worked together in close harmony, sharing the warmth and light of a single hearth. Many orators, writers, and illustrators of the late nineteenth century maintained a comfortable fiction that things had not really changed all that much in America, that the Victorian babe still slept in a cradle by the warm fireside, because the illusion of continuity helped to soften the anxiety that accompanied rapid social change. Americans continued to cling to the image of the cradle for the sake of its pleasant associations, long after they had pretty much discarded the object itself.[40]

Cribs were originally designed "to be placed, during the night, by the bedside of the mother; and for that purpose, the height of the crib should correspond with that of the large bed, and one of the sides be made to lift out."[41] This made it easy for the mother to tend or nurse her infant without getting out of bed. At the same time, the separate crib protected the baby from being rolled on and suffocated in a bed shared with its mother or nurse. By midcentury, expert advice and common practice had shifted in favor of not only the separate crib but also an individual room for even newborn infants, who slept from their first nights in a separate nursery as plain and functional as their white metal crib.[42]

Parents believed the secluded and controlled environment of the nursery protected children's innocent natures and physical well-being and provided them an enclosed area in which they learned the discipline of regular habits. "It is in the nursery, in a great measure," advised an eminent Philadelphia physician in 1832, "that the habit of early or late rising is generated—this is a matter of much importance, and the greatest regularity should be observed."[43] Orson Fowler was in full agreement forty years later: "Periodicity should be faithfully observed in everything. They should be bathed quickly at one specified hour, . . . put to sleep at regular intervals, and nursed by the clock."[44] Catherine Beecher concurred, favoring putting children, while still awake, into their cribs for scheduled periods, as this would "induce regularity in other habits, which saves trouble. In doing this," she continued, "a child may cry at first, a great deal, but for a healthy child, this use of the lungs does not harm, and tends rather to strengthen, than to injure them."[45] She went on to assure the young mother that the child would soon become accustomed to lie or sit in its crib much of the time, freeing the mother for other activities. Training a child to the clock was a very useful discipline in an industrialized society that valued punctuality and respect for schedules.

The crib was admirably constructed to contain the child who might object to confinement during the process of training. The tall legs and high sides made escape difficult and dangerous, especially when compared to old-fashioned trundle beds, which rested only inches off the floor. The interior dimensions (in feet) of cribs ranged from $2\frac{1}{2} \times 3\frac{1}{2}$ to 3×5, not only large enough to give a baby plenty of room to kick and move about, but ample enough to comfortably accommodate a four-year-old. Like the jumper, the crib could confine the toddler, as well as the infant, until the intricacies of self-discipline were mastered. By 1901 the Acme Company was advertising the "accident-proof crib," with very high sides and tightly spaced spindles to keep even quite large children securely inside.[46] This is not to say, of course, that determined toddlers could not get out of a crib, given sufficient motivation, but only that the crib was *intended* to keep them in even against their will.

Eighteenth-century physicians had encouraged putting small children to bed with older siblings or "some handy reasonable servant."[47] Nineteenth-century childrearing authorities, however, increasingly agreed that children should be separated from others while they slept. "When practicable," advised one physician in 1832, "children should sleep in separate beds; and these should be large for it is injurious to have them cramped together when they sleep, as well as indelicate to crowd opposite sexes together."[48] Catherine Beecher agreed that a mother and child should each have their own beds, and Doctor Bright grudgingly permitted "not more than two" older children to share a bed, so long as they had sufficient room so that they would not touch each other.[49] Near the end of the century, a popular childrearing manual asked, "Should a child sleep in the same bed with its mother or nurse?" and answered, "Under no circumstances if this can be avoided. Nor should older children sleep together."[50] Descriptions of how to arrange the furniture in the nursery were predicated on the assumption that each young child would sleep in a separate crib.[51]

Ideally, once children grew too old for the nursery they moved into rooms of their own. This seems to have been a very American custom; most European cultures were not concerned with assigning each child a space of his or her own. "At a suitable age, a child may be removed from the nursery to a separate sleeping chamber," wrote William Alcott in 1839. "Here, if circumstances permit, it should sleep by itself."[52] "Where your dwelling will admit it," Walter Houghton agreed nearly fifty years later, "give each child a room to himself or herself, or, if there are several children, give two brothers or two sisters a room, and hold them responsible for its appearance."[53] "As children grow older, and are allotted separate bedrooms," concurred Edith Wharton and Ogden Codman in 1897, their rooms should be furnished and decorated in accordance with their sex and interests.[54] The most fervent proponent of a separate room for every child was Orson Fowler. "Especially is it important that every child, and, indeed, permanent members of every family, should have a separate room, exclusively to himself or herself." And again, "sleeping by themselves is also a first-rate plan, both for health, and to prevent their imbibing anything wrong from other children."[55] Experts and parents believed that children given their own rooms would study better without interruptions, take greater pride in their room since it was really their own and so keep it clean and neat, and appreciate a private place to entertain their friends. But it was the second reason Fowler offered, "to prevent their imbibing anything wrong from other[s]," that cut to the quick of many parental fears. If social perceptions of children were predicated on a belief in their perfectly innocent and pure natures, then anything that compromised that innocence destroyed the image and the child. The loss of innocence was nothing less than the loss of childhood, the loss of a state of grace and promise. Mothers and fathers were obsessive in their zeal to protect their children.

The fear that something might compromise the innocence of their little ones was always present, for parents believed there was a darker side to the nature of children. John Neal, writing for *Godey's* in 1849, warned his readers that children have "all the arts and vices and cunning and flirtatiousness and bravado of adults." Neal knew who to blame for childish weaknesses that stemmed from a contamination of innocence. "If it be true," he asked, "that as the twig is bent, the tree's inclined, how much [do] you [parents] have to answer for?"[56] "Children," explained Kate Sutherland, "are all born with certain evil affections, which they inherit from their parents."[57] God and nature meant each child to be a sweet and innocent being, but the intention frequently failed because of the imperfections of parents, which could be inherited by and adversely affect their children. Considerable confusion about the nature of cultural, infectious, and hereditary transmissions from parents to their offspring existed even among the scientific and medical communities, and the general public was bombarded by scores of theories in popular journals. Common belief, reinforced by experts, held that dishonesty, insanity, alcoholism, and lust or sexual frigidity, as well as natural refinement, musical talent, and courage were all equally inheritable. Similarly, the physical and psychological health of the parents at the time of conception, the mother's emotional state during pregnancy, and even a father's youthful excesses before marriage could all affect the offspring of the union. Alexander Walker, in a treatise on marriage written in 1839, declared that according to "one of the newly-discovered laws of nature . . . one parent gives to the progeny the forehead and organs of sense" and digestion, "while the other parent gives the backhead and cerebral or organ of will together with" the general physique. Therefore, no match should ever be entered into without first considering the possible hereditary combinations implied. Like most of his contemporaries, Walker also accepted the theory of the inheritability of acquired characteristics, noting a remarkable difference in the capacities of children for learning, which is connected with the education of the parents; "the children of educated parents taking easily to their studies," while "the natural dullness of children born of uneducated parents was proverbial." On the other hand, he also warned that women "who exercise the mental organs severely and continually are in most cases barren, . . . because they carry all their powers towards the brain, and deprive the sexual organs of their natural energy."[58] Apparently, an educated father enhanced his child's development, while an educated mother put her child's very existence in jeopardy. In this fashion, Walker spent hundreds of pages in his scholarly treatises detailing the hazards of heredity and assuring his readers that parents were directly responsible for any weaknesses or flaws in their children.

Orson Fowler, the famous phrenologist and champion of the octagon house, also emphasized the significance of acquired over congenital characteristics. All of a mother's thoughts and emotions directly affected the child she carried. "Her merely temporary states during pregnancy are also written right into the original qualities, mental and physical, of her offspring." A woman's distaste for (or intemperate enjoyment of) the sexual act at the moment of conception, as well as her anxieties about her approaching travail, would each appear in exaggerated form in the character of the child. Even if both parents were perfectly healthy and scrupulously guarded their actions, thoughts, and emotions, they could not protect their unborn child from all contamination. Fowler described the case of "two virtuous parents" who produced a mulatto child. Convinced of his wife's innocence, the husband visited his ancestral home in France "and found his fifth ancestor was an African, yet that no intermediate descendant was thus marked." Any form of influence, tendency, contamination, or corruption could remain hidden within the inheritable nature of a family for generations, only to appear again without warning.[59] Another popular authority on the mechanics of heredity reiterated Fowler's position: "No family blood is so noble that it is not in a measure contaminated by the legacy of some ancestor, more or less remote, . . . and a failure to recognize this is to admit one's self a fool or demigod." Every child was born "with good and bad propensities, for health and disease, for morality or vice" predetermined by its parents.[60] God had intended all children to enter the world unsullied, but the weaknesses of men and women over many generations inevitably contaminated the unborn child. If this were so, then any failure on the part of the child automatically reflected back on the family. As Fowler declared, "Willing or unwilling, you are compelled to predetermine [your child's] future virtues or vices, talents or foolishnesses, happiness or misery."[61] The nineteenth-century family perceived itself as a close biological unit, the sum of each member's thoughts and actions permanently affecting future progeny and tightly linking them all together. The deficiency or deformity of any one member announced to the world the secret weaknesses shared by the whole family. This, then, was the era when parents hid retarded, deformed, demented, and handicapped children in attics and cellars; this was why the revelation of an imperfect child could destroy wedding prospects for a healthy sibling. A single child's deficiency became the entire family's guilt and shame.

Many scientists of the nineteenth century were less than sanguine about America's future. They found ample evidence of children inheriting the vices and deficiencies of previous generations, but much less indication that positive qualities were as frequently transmitted. Study after study concluded that great men rarely produced great sons, but that weak and corrupt men habitually sired tainted offspring.[62] With the vices of humanity believed to be accumulating generation upon generation, the inevitable degeneration of mankind seemed a fearful but very real possibility. Each generation seemed to produce fewer geniuses and heroes than the one before. "It is a curious fact that, in the present time, we have none of those precious prodigies so numerous in the olden time," wrote another contributor to *Godey's*. "It seems to have been one of the peculiar privileges of the wisdom of our ancestors to produce those infant miracles of learning and science, the 'admirable Chrichtons' of the nursery, who studied in cradles, and lectured from go-carts."[63] Great deeds and even great children seemed all in the past.

Americans themselves felt that they were squandering their precious inheritance. Toward the end of the century the popular cartoonist Charles Dana Gibson drew a series of pictures of strong, handsome young American women, the products of good pioneer stock, who married decrepit, debauched old men for wealth, social position, or European title. Such unions, in Gibson's cartoons, resulted in bleak, childless marriages or in weak, sickly offspring—unworthy heirs of a great nation. Through everything from popular cartoons to the doll play of little girls, Americans tried to guard against the feared moral, physical, and numerical decline of future generations.

As each adult marked the process of degeneration within his or her own life from the full promise of childhood to the realities of maturity, so there seemed a literal degeneration in the very nature of Western society. Nineteenth-century men and women compared themselves to earlier generations and found themselves wanting. The concept of degeneration captivated authors and readers, and it appeared in scientific articles and contemporary literature, including Zola's novels of the Rougon family, Ibsen's *Ghosts,* and Poe's "Fall of the House of Usher." In Harriet Beecher Stowe's *Oldtown Folks* of 1869, a young student brooded over "the fearful law of existence by which the sins of the parents who themselves often escape punishment are visited on the heads of innocent children, as a law which seems made specifically to protect the existence of vice and disorder from generation to generation."[64]

Where Americans in the years after the Revolution had looked forward to the ultimate perfection of mankind and had seen their own children as part of the process, mid-nineteenth-century parents feared the cumulative corruption that surrounded them and strove to protect their children from its influence. Like their seventeenth-century forebears, they perceived youngsters as vulnerable creatures. Victorian parents sought to preserve the natural sweetness of their children, all the while conscious that their offspring might already be tainted with inherited weakness or vice. There was a new serpent in the Garden of Eden—although fewer people believed that babies were burdened with original sin, many still believed that children carried within them the sins of their fathers.

Yet there was hope that children could escape an unfavorable heredity. "Environment is the cooperating and to us vitally important factor," wrote Dr. D. K. Shute in the *New England Medical Journal* in 1897, "inasmuch as it may supplement and thus reinforce the hereditary tendencies . . . or it may turn them into new channels, correcting the evil or vitiating the good."[65] Parents had a second chance, as it were, to suppress the weaknesses and cultivate the virtues inherent in their children's nature, but they needed to start early. "Success may more confidently be looked for in the upbuilding of character and physique if the child is early sent in the right direction, and his virtues will overcome his hereditary weaknesses," an authority in heredity studies assured his readers.[66] The insurance against weak character was proper training and discipline, combined with careful protection from any further contamination.

Parents could do only so much to compensate for any ill effects they may have had on their youngsters, and it was frustrating and terrifying to know that their children's shortcomings were their fault. They therefore tended to focus on protecting their young from any outside contamination. Within each young Dr. Jekyll was a Mr. Hyde eager to get out, and it was the duty of parents to see that this did not happen. The wrong knowledge was dangerous; ignorance was innocence and virginity was purity. Behind the movement for separate rooms for children and individual beds for each child was an almost hysterical fear of masturbation and of the physical and mental deterioration thought to emanate from the practice. Masturbation gave parents something to blame for their children's defects or shortcomings besides themselves. It focused all of their fears for their children, and helped them redirect their own sense of guilt, helplessness, and anger, by supplying them with a Mr. Hyde to blame and fight. Children were pure and innocent unless corrupted by the secret vice; stop that practice and they remained safe. Authorities warned parents that masturbation caused or contributed to more than a hundred "morbid conditions," including everything from insanity, epilepsy, eye disease, asthma, cardiac murmurs, deafness, and sterility to acne and warts on the hands.[67] If the practice continued, the child would eventually die "amidst delirium and convulsions."[68] Doctors believed that children almost invariably learned about masturbation from someone else, and that they were most at risk in the privacy of their own beds. "[Boarding] schools generally have the credit of germinating this enervating fascination," warned Orson Fowler, "but it also is acquired from servants, relations, and others with whom [children] sleep."[69]

While doctors explained the nature of the contamination and its transmission with clinical bluntness, many other childrearing authorities only alluded to the real nature of their concerns. Lydia Child, for example, warned parents in 1835 that "it is a bad plan for young girls to sleep with nursery maids, unless you have the utmost confidence in the good principles and modesty of your domestics," who were, after all, given to "talking on forbidden subjects" and other vulgar practices.[70] Fowler, on the other hand, minced no words as he presented case after case of lost innocence:

> A minister and his wife brought their darling daughter of eighteen, who had yet no signs of womanhood, whom they desired to fit for teaching,

to ascertain why she was too weakly to study. When told "masturbation from childhood," they were first confounded, then enraged. When appealed to for the actual truth, she confessed, and told what servant-girl had taught her but who had not been in their family since this girl was six years old.[71]

While in the household, the maid had shared a bed with the young girl. Another typical pattern in the case histories involved an older brother or sister teaching masturbation to younger ones. Children had to be separated from adults, from servants, and from each other for their own protection. Victorian parents feared masturbation as vicious, insidious, deadly, and nearly omnipresent. Fowler claimed to have found the practice among boys as young as six and girls of four.[72] "What are the most common bad habits of children?" asked E. L. Holt in 1894; he answered "thumb-sucking, nail-biting, bed-wetting, and masturbation."[73] The German physician Oskar Berger declared in 1876 that "99 percent of young men and women masturbate, while the hundredth conceals the truth"; Dr. D. C. Townsend, in a paper entitled "Thigh-friction in Children under One Year," presented to the American Pediatric Society in 1896, found masturbation among healthy infants.[74] Clearly, no child was safe. All the doctors' reports, however, found the vice rampant, even universal, in the younger generation, but never commented on the habits of their own youth. The problem was always presented as a new epidemic.

The best protection from the vice of masturbation was isolation from any potential source of contamination. Very young children might share a nursery, but the nurse, if there was one, should have a room to herself, and each child should sleep in a separate crib. Older children should have rooms of their own if possible and "should never be allowed to remain in bed longer than requisite."[75] About 1850, the first "night-dress with feet" appeared on the American market. Popularly called Dr. Denton's after their most enthusiastic advocate, the new pajamas protected a child from both cold and accidental or deliberate sexual stimulation better than the traditional nightshirt. Often, in fact, Dr. Denton's came complete "with cuffs to roll down over the hands and [fasten with] a draw cord" that simultaneously discouraged thumb sucking and masturbation.[76]

Experts also warned of stimulation outside of bed that might unwittingly awaken a child's sexual nature. "Ignorant mothers know not how frightful those habits are which they first teach by tickling," cautioned Alexander Walker. Permitting children to sit with the knees crossed, ride upon hobby-horses, or bounce on a paternal knee all could lead to "degrading sexuality."[77] Wise parents saw to it that their children avoided rich and spicy foods, red meats, overly warm beds or sleeping rooms, inadvertent genital stimulation from clothing, toys, or games, and intimate contact with servants or previously contaminated children. Such homely items as the crib, the high chair, bread pudding, and footed pajamas were really weapons in a defensive arsenal against contamination from both the outside world and the child's own internal weaknesses. At jeopardy, Victorian parents feared, was the innocent nature and future happiness of their children.

Common furniture in use before 1750 pushed the child forward into contact with adults and the adult world. The sharing of beds with grown-ups, the use of leading strings and go-carts to place children in the midst of adult activities, and other practices all derived from a worldview that saw development from the imperfect infant to the civilized adult as a natural and desirable progression. Victorian children's furniture, on the other hand, served to contain and isolate the child, to pull it back from contact with all but the intimate family. The jumper or swing, the high chair, and the crib held children safely in one spot so that they could not wander into trouble, and the isolated nursery offered sanctuary or exile.

FURNITURE FOR DISPLAY

Not all furniture designed for children was primarily defensive, however. While the swing, high chair, and crib safeguarded children, a second constellation of artifacts, including the bassinet and perambulator, enhanced the ideal image of the purity of infancy.

The bassinet, a wicker basket fitted with a small mattress, originally served as a portable bed. "It is very useful for carrying about, and may be set upon table, sofa, or bed, or taken in a carriage, or even upon the lap with little inconvenience."[78] While occasionally described in American periodicals, the portable bassinet never really gained favor on this side of the Atlantic. Americans preferred a more elaborate version made "of wicker, fastened to a firm wicker stand and having a projecting rod to hold a canopy."[79] Most of the exterior of the basket and stand was hidden under a many-layered skirt festooned with ribbons, swags, lace, and ruffles (Figure 23). The end result was not a portable bed, but an elaborate presentation vehicle in which the newborn infant could be viewed by friends and family.

As a piece of presentation furniture, the bassinet usually resided in the master bedroom, parlor, or wherever the new mother received guests. Families who desired even grander settings for the introduction of the young heir could purchase elaborate wooden hanging cradles (or swinging cots), which hung suspended from a wooden frame. Whether first introduced to the world in the pomp and circumstance of a walnut swinging cradle or in a ruffled wicker bassinet, most babies were whisked away at night to the plain and inexpensive but functional crib within the seclusion of the nursery. In its appearance, costliness, and ceremonial nature, the bassinet closely resembled the elaborate white wedding gown that became popular at just about the same time. Both the white gown and the white bed were sacramental artifacts, used for brief ceremonies consecrating the creation of family and celebrating the fact that the strength of the family lay in the innocence and purity of its components, particularly the virgin bride and the innocent babe.

The most expensive and by far the grandest piece of late nineteenth-century children's furniture was the perambulator, a device that went from very modest beginnings to lavish, overwrought splendor in little more than a decade. Before 1865 few babies rode in any form of carriage of their own, but rather took the air in the arms of an attendant.[80] An account of the latest in children's fashion for 1853 described "an infant's walking dress—if we may be allowed the expression, while the little thing is still borne in the arms of the nurse."[81] Even in 1870, carriages were rarities in most places, as one woman remembered from her childhood in Illinois. As her family walked home from church, she recalled, "father was carrying the baby; perambulators hadn't come into use yet."[82] The few carriages that were in use in antebellum America were simple wooden wagons with plain wooden seats pulled along over bumpy roads. They were modest affairs of simple convenience to carry a child out into the fresh air (or to transport any other cargo, for that matter). They were really nothing more than a child's toy wagon with a seat for baby.

In 1857, American landscape architect Frederick Law Olmsted began construction of New York City's Central Park. His designs for the 840 acres of open meadow, tree-shaded walks, and artistically bridged ponds brought a new standard of graciousness and beauty to American cities. By the end of the century, many American towns and cities had parks in the Olmsted manner. At the same time, the extension of streetcar lines from city centers out into the surrounding countryside encouraged the development of new suburbs where each house sat well back on its own lawn and branching elms and paved sidewalks lined the streets.[83] In such charming surroundings, Americans rediscovered an old European tradition, the promenade. On summer evenings and Sunday afternoons, families strolled along residential streets and through local parks and cemeteries to enjoy the view and meet acquaintances—to see and be seen. With the cultivated landscape, smooth sidewalks, and new social rituals, the baby's airing took on new form. The promenade made possible the perambulator. No longer solely an object of convenience, the baby carriage became a showcase for the family's youngest member. During the 1870s the simple, optional baby wagon gave way to the ornate and expensive pram, a new necessity in style-conscious Victorian homes.

Elaborate baby carriages began to appear in the late 1860s (Figure 24). They were expensive affairs made of leather and fabric and styled after phaetons, surreys, victorias, and buggies—miniature versions of adult carriages. Like an adult-sized carriage, a baby carriage was meant to be drawn by a wooden tongue attached at the front. By the 1870s carriages were no longer designed to be pulled, but pushed. At the same time, the carriage became considerably more elaborate, more stylish, and more expensive. The transition is clearly evident in the 1868 catalogue of the Colby Brothers Company of Waterbury, Vermont. The carriages depicted ranged from a two-wheeled vehicle with a wooden body and a draw tongue for $8.50 to a four-wheeled suspension carriage with collapsible leather hood, silver-plated trim, and oil-burning side lamps for $52.00. Significantly, the more elaborate models were meant to be pushed, placed up front where they could be seen, while the cheaper ones were pulled and trailed along after the attendant. Gradually catalogues dropped most of the simple, earlier forms and concentrated on the new push-style prams. In 1876 the catalogue of the F. A. Whitney Carriage Company of Leominster, Massachusetts, listed fifty-four models of carriages whose wholesale prices ranged from $6.50 to $80.00. The extensive number of models available and the relatively high prices people were willing to pay attested to the considerable importance Victorian parents placed on being seen with the right pram. The Sears catalogue of 1897, for example, carried a total of eight models of children's beds, ranging in price from $1.40 to $8.75, compared to twenty-two models of perambulators, which cost from

$2.45 to $33.00 Clearly, nineteenth-century parents were willing to invest considerably more in a baby carriage than in a crib tucked away in the back space of the nursery. A pram was public and ceremonial, out front where it could be seen and admired, as could its occupant.

The 1881 catalogue of the Peabody and Whitney Company of Boston contained a second stylistic shift, as prams ceased imitating adult buggies and developed a look uniquely their own. Half of the twenty-eight Peabody carriages were modeled after adult carriages, and half were newer wicker-work fantasies, called parlor carriages, which were described as suitable for either indoor or outdoor use. By the 1890s, the transition was complete, and the Montgomery Ward catalogue of 1893, the Sears catalogues of 1897 and 1902, and the Acme Company catalogue of 1901 offered only wicker-bodied carriages. Late nineteenth-century society considered the perambulator such an important piece of public furniture that it deserved the most fantastic and elaborate vocabulary of ornamentation that could be devised (Figure 25). A stylistic vocabulary borrowed from adult carriages was no longer adequate.

By the 1890s all but the very cheapest prams were topped off with silk parasols, and most models came with plush upholstery, Brussels carpets, and plated wheels. A typical turn-of-the-century perambulator was the F. A. Whitney Carriage Company's No. 257. The pram had an elaborately serpentine varnished reed body, deeply tufted silk satin damask upholstery, a silk satin parasol covered with lace ruffles and lined in satin, rubber-tire wheels, and enamel-finished gears, axles, and springs. Obviously, most of the elaborate appointments of the pram (and most of the expense) were not directly for the baby's benefit. The child would appreciate the springs, the upholstered seat, and the shade provided by the parasol, but it was not the comfort of the ride, but the looks of the thing that was stressed in the advertisement. In the Ward's catalogue of 1893, forty varieties of carriages were offered, with prices from $1.35 to $27.00. All but the cheapest of them had parasols, and all but the cheapest parasols came with lace. Only on the more expensive models, beginning at a price of $10.80, were springs of any sort included. In fact, parasols, lace, Brussels carpets, large wheels, and plated wheels were all more popular options than any form of improved suspension. Visual effect was everything.

The pram was meant to be seen and admired, and to have that admiration extended to its young passenger, either as the child was wheeled into the parlor to meet guests or on a Sunday promenade in the park. The baby was the ultimate symbol of the family, the culminating product of the "cult of domesticity," the center of familial and cultural expectations. The pram was designed to draw attention to its occupant and show the baby off to best advantage, like a bright jewel on a dark velvet tray. Most baby carriages were upholstered in the rich colors of cardinal red, wine, bronze, peacock blue, and emerald green, a perfect foil to set off the pristine whiteness of baby clothes. Most prams were also large, and the roomy interior made children appear even smaller and more precious.

Carriages were ideal for keeping babies on their best behavior during the viewing. The pleasure in the ride and the passing scenery entertained the children, while the body of the carriage, and the seat belt included after about 1880, kept them out of mischief and danger. Much like swings, high chairs, and cribs, Victorian prams were sized to hold a child of five or six as easily as a baby. Many models, usually called go-carts, permitted the child to ride sitting up, wheeled along like a young pasha riding in state. The physical nature of the carriage discouraged any undesirable behavior, while enhancing the qualities of sweetness and childlike innocence, thus playing nicely on the sentimental expectations of Victorian society. Like a well-designed theatrical set, the pram focused the attention of the audience on the figure at center stage.

After World War I, when Victorian pomp and sentimentalization had gone out of favor, carriages became much plainer. Still made of wicker or leather, they lost their fantastic shapes, their tufted upholstery, plush carpets, and silk parasols. At the same time, comparably more attention was given to rain protection for the baby and to a quality suspension for the carriage. Manufacturers also turned the pram around so that the child faced the mother as she pushed it along (Figure 26). With the baby facing backward now, and shielded from view by the carriage hood, the new style gave priority to reassuring eye contact between mother and child, rather than to the presentation of the baby to the world.

Since it was commonly held that a couple became a family only through the arrival of a child, the baby, as an object in and of itself, served important ideotechnic functions for the Victorian family. An infant legitimized and gave purpose to its parents' union and enhanced its mother's social position, power, and sense of self-worth. To some extent, womanhood was idealized and sentimentalized because of its close relationship with and responsibility for the innocence of childhood. Parents were caught up in the centrality of children in both their personal goals and social expectations. "The cradle is the only undisturbed throne today," wrote one parent in 1869. "Philip my King is undisputed monarch on the mother's breast."[84] Parents fancied themselves ruled and dominated by their infants. The sweet kitten, pet, lamb, or chick of the first half of the century had become "King Baby," "the little emperor," "l'enfant terrible," and "the little tyrant" by the latter half.[85] "There is an emperor in our house—Emperor Frank the First. He rules us all, but not exactly with a rod of iron. . . . Emperor Frank is not quite a year and a half old . . . and he rules us with smiles."[86] Seventeenth-century parents had ruled their children; their late nineteenth-century counterparts made their infants their ruling passion. Colonial young people had to conform to an adult model of correct behavior. Nineteenth-century children had to conform to an ideal of the cherub-child, and failure to do so stigmatized not only the children but their parents and family as well. The parents were guilty either of transmitting the flaw to their children or of failing to guard against external corruption. The children's faults were the parents' fault. Unfortunately, infants are notoriously unreliable actors who cannot be counted on to play their roles as scripted. Colonial parents used clothing and furniture to mold their children in the ideal image of an adult and to push them into the world. Victorian parents used clothing and furniture to mold their children in their ideal image of a child and to protect them from contact with the world.

Conclusion

Parents do not merely raise their children; they define them. More precisely, they accept certain definitions concerning the nature and needs of children current in their culture, and then try their best to bring their youngsters into line with the accepted patterns. Parents dress their children to look the part expected of them and may favor clothing that encourages desired and restrains unacceptable behavior. They adopt furniture forms and childrearing devices to coerce or cajole their children into acting in ways deemed appropriate by accepted standards. As those standards change, old artifacts may be jettisoned in favor of new forms that better express the new perception of children or that produce newly desirable forms of behavior. Such major shifts in culturally accepted notions have occurred at least twice in America between the founding of the European colonies and the beginning of the twentieth century. The process was a long and gradual one, with some groups in society proceeding more slowly than others. However, rough periodization is possible, and the periods of change are characterized by a rejection of previously common forms of costume, furniture, toys, books, and other paraphernalia of childrearing. Such a change occurred around the last quarter of the eighteenth century and again in the second quarter of the nineteenth century. The result is a series of three very distinct approaches to childrearing among middle-class Americans before the beginning of the twentieth century.

Colonial children lived precarious lives. In the late seventeenth century, the New England divine Cotton Mather enjoyed the blessings of a large family. His first wife bore him ten children before her death at the age of thirty-six. His second wife gave him an additional six children before her death, while his third was past her childbearing years when she married Mather. He wrote with affection about his children in his journal, describing their antics, their progress with their studies and religious instruction, and his concerns for them. He also wrote of his grief and loss when any of his children died. Ten of them died before their fifth birthday—nine in their first year and one at the age of four. Three daughters and one son died while in their early twenties. Altogether, Cotton Mather saw fourteen of his sixteen children die before his own death at the age of sixty-four. Mather's family is not particularly demographically typical of colonial families in general; no one family could be. At the most, its size and his longevity were fairly common in seventeenth-century New England. It may, however, offer some insight into the mind-set of colonial parents. The first five years of life were by far the most vulnerable. Children died before, during, and soon after birth, and subsequently from childhood illnesses, accidents, and lack of sufficient nourishment. If a boy survived his first five years, he had a good chance of living to a healthy old age, barring accidents, of course—Mather's twenty-one-year-old son was lost at sea. Girls who survived infancy faced a second and much longer period of vulnerability when they reached their own child-bearing years—Mather lost two wives and three daughters to the effects of pregnancy.[1]

Infancy represented such a precarious existence that parents regarded it as essentially a state of illness, rather the way pregnancy was understood in the first half of the twentieth century. Babies needed to be protected assiduously from light and drafts, dosed with medicines and tonics through their first few months, and then pushed beyond infancy as quickly as possible. Growing up meant growing strong and gaining sufficient autonomy to be able to take care of oneself.

Adults in the colonial period did not look back to their own youth, but forward to their prime in the fourth and fifth decades of life, before the decline into old age. Then, if all had gone well, they would enjoy the prestige, comfort, and security for which they had worked so hard throughout their youth. For women, life became decidedly easier once they passed their child-bearing years and their children required less attention and began to offer more help. As David Hackett Fischer has pointed out in *Growing Old in*

America, colonists admired the mature adult. Gentlemen cultivated a noticeable paunch and stocky figure and powdered their hair a fashionable gray. Mature men and women were honored, respected, and envied for the position they had attained. By comparison, the trials of youth held no charm, and infancy was best forgotten.[2]

Loving parents wanted to see their children out of the dangers and miseries of infancy and safely on their way to secure positions in the world. Furniture that would hasten the process—devices that got infants up and walking as quickly as possible—had great appeal. Autonomy and self-sufficiency were considered better for both the children themselves and their overworked parents.

Martha Custis bore four children and buried two before she married George Washington. Years later, she undertook to raise two young grandchildren. By then, however, the world had changed. In the decades around the turn of the eighteenth century, there was a growing confidence in the rationality of nature and in the ability of the young of any species, including our own, to grow into healthy adults if the natural process was not interfered with. Parents began to attribute infant deaths to too much, rather than too little, coddling. If children got sick, it was because their parents had weakened them by treating them as invalids. Mothers and fathers who embraced the new ideas rejected the confining devices of earlier generations, such as swaddling bands, standing stools, and tiny corsets. If infancy had formerly been viewed as a kind of illness, it came now to promise robust health. Children were best off unfettered, uncovered, and uncoddled. Light clothes, thin blankets, and cold baths would best ensure the health and happiness of the next generation.

Although the same sorts of changes were happening in England and in parts of Europe, youth took on special meaning in America. Americans of the Revolutionary era and of the new republic had become accustomed to a new political rhetoric in which America was the child colony or the young country, as opposed to the overbearing mother country and the old European monarchies distrusted as decadent and dying. The advantage lay with youth and vigor. Men's fashions matched the changing political climate. From the 1760s onward, the fashionable male silhouette slimmed to a youthful, athletic line as the clothes became more form fitting and the full skirt of the frock coat shrank back into narrow tails. Gradually, men gave up wigs and powder, appearing in their own natural hair. It is quite remarkable to view in chronological order the portraits of someone such as Thomas Jefferson, who had several painted over the course of his lifetime, and watch him get progressively younger as gray hair gives way to red. The new attitude toward youth could not help but to improve the image of youth and childhood. This is not to say that parents loved their children more, but that they found more to appreciate about the state their children were in. Childhood had its good points.

As childhood became more a period of essential preparation for life and less one of vulnerability, more the healthy natural state of freedom before the constraints of civilization, parents took greater delight in their children's childishness. Gradually, the duration of childhood increased. Instead of wishing their children through it, parents wanted their youngsters to get as much as possible out of their childhood years that they might be fully prepared for their roles as future citizens of the new country. Childhood had become a valued part of human development.

Godey's Lady's Magazine is filled with stories and poems, from the 1830s on, of a parent mourning the death of a small child and taking comfort in the fact that the little one has merely been called back to heaven, where it will be spared the harshness and wickedness of earthly life. Nineteenth-century Americans were preoccupied with the concept of loss. Mourning pictures, tragic love stories, and fears of the gradual decline of the human species were common fare. Childhood fit nicely into this romantic pattern; it was something bright and fleeting to be cherished while it lasted. Maturity, in the new schema, was a corrupting process from which no one emerged unscathed. It served to make childhood seem more precious, a time free of guilt, regret, or care. Parents tried to build a separate world for their children, far away from the harsher realities of the adult sphere.

At the same time, childhood was imbued with an almost sacred character. Children were pure and innocent beings, descended from heaven and unsullied by worldly corruption. The loss of this childish innocence was akin to the loss of virginity, and the inevitable loss of childhood itself was a kind of expulsion from the Garden of Eden.

It was the parents' duty to protect the happy innocence of their children, and they did so by isolating their offspring from adult society. Contact risked contamination. The separate nursery was a safe haven, and the newly available high chairs, jumpers, and prams imprisoned the innocent to protect them from the guilty. Freedom had become dangerous, but containment was possible and practical in the nineteenth-century middle-class world.

In the last half of the twentieth century, that is no longer the case. We have had to abandon the idea that children are best served by isolating them from the realities of the surrounding world so that they might remain care-free and innocent as long as possible. Such isolation is simply no longer possible. More akin to the views of their colonial counterparts, late twenti-eth-century parents see their youngsters surrounded by dangers from which there is no safe haven. In a world of latchkey children, illicit drugs, terrifying new illnesses, and the horrors of child molestation, innocence has become vulnerability. The uninformed child is the child at risk. The protected child is once again the child who can cope successfully in the adult world.

In an environment in which children need to be sophisticated and on their guard, it is not surprising that they no longer dress in clothes designed to stress their youth but, like their colonial predecessors, dress more often like little adults. Young people today wear jogging suits, bomber jackets, and miniature medical scrub suits, and they are eschewing childish forms of play at a far younger age than did their more sheltered Victorian counterparts. Perhaps the Victorian childhood will prove to be a fluke, a somewhat claus-trophobic idyll in the more common pattern of integrating children into family and community life; or perhaps it is the postmodern childhood that is the aberration. It is still too early to tell.

Throughout our history, there were endless variations within and outside each model of a given society's concept of the nature of childhood. In every era there have been parents who did things quite differently. The real point is that the first dozen years of life can be and have been perceived and interpreted in radically different, even diametrically opposed, paradigms by different generations. Childhood is not an unchanging, natural phenomenon or a steady progression from a dismal past to an enlightened present. The question is not whether a given society at a given time had a concept of childhood, but rather what that concept was and the nature of its advantages and disadvantages. Infancy, with its very special needs, is an undeniable state of existence, and the maturation of the human being is a slow and gradual process continuing long after infancy ends; the concept of childhood, how-ever, is very much a social invention, one reinvented by every society and age. It is the natural malleability of the young (or perhaps of the species) that enables children to make themselves into whatever is expected of them.

Notes

INTRODUCTION

1. Philip Greven, *The Protestant Temperament.*
2. Caroline Cowles Richards, *Village Life in America.*
3. A photograph of Patty Polk's sampler is reproduced in Ethel S. Bottome and Eva J. Cove, *American Samplers,* 96.
4. Kenneth Ames, "Material Culture as Verbal Communication."
5. Karin Calvert, "The Image of Childhood in America: 1670 to 1870," unpublished master's thesis, 1979.
6. Lucy Larcom, *A New England Girlhood,* 118.
7. Philippe Ariès, *Centuries of Childhood.*
8. Edward Shorter, *The Making of the Modern Family;* David Hunt, *Parents and Children in History;* and Lloyd deMause, ed., *The History of Childhood.*
9. Ross W. Beales, Jr., "In Search of the Historical Child"; and Daniel Blake Smith, *Inside the Great House.*
10. Linda Pollock, *Forgotten Children,* 268.
11. John Demos, *A Little Commonwealth;* Michael Zuckerman, "An Amusement in This Silent Country."
12. Ariès, *Centuries of Childhood,* 58; and Hunt, *Parents and Children in History.*

CHAPTER 1

1. William Buchan, *Advice to Mothers,* 44. In the passage quoted, Buchan was describing practices common in his youth in the 1740s.
2. Paulus Bagellardus, *Ad Illustrissimum Principam Dominum Nicola* (Padua, 1472), reprinted in London in 1603 and 1642, and in John Ruhrah, ed., *Pediatrics of the Past,* 34. Buchan, *Advice to Mothers,* 46.
3. An American Matron, *The Maternal Physician,* 132.
4. For example, several photographs taken by Jacob Riis in the tenements of

New York City in the early years of the twentieth century include tightly swaddled infants among the images of immigrant families.

5. Bagellardus, *Ad Illustrissimum,* 34.

6. Felix Wurtz, *An Experimental Treatise of Surgerie in Four Parts* (London: Gartrude Dawson, 1656), reprinted in Ruhrah, *Pediatrics,* 211–15.

7. Francis Glisson, *De Rachitide Sire Marbo Puerili* (London: George S. Bates, 1650), reprinted in Ruhrah, *Pediatrics,* 283.

8. Sir Richard Steele, *The Tatler,* 43.

9. For further information on childbearing, see Catherine M. Scholten, *Childbearing in American Society.*

10. Sir Walter Raleigh, *The History of the World,* Book I, p. 31. A similar image of the infant can be found in Henry Cuff, *The Differences of the Ages,* 117–20.

11. Bartholamaeus Metlinger, *Wann Noch Anschung Gotlicher und Menschlicher Ordenung* (Augsburg: Gunther Zainer, 1473), reprinted in Ruhrah, *Pediatrics,* 77.

12. David Hunt, *Parents and Children in History,* 110.

13. François Mauriceau, *Traite des Maladies des Femmes Grosses, et de Celles qui sont Nouvellement Accouchees* (Paris: Gerard, 1675), quoted by Hunt, *Parents and Children in History,* 130.

14. For a classic discussion of the development of the concept of the chain of being, see Arthur O. Lovejoy, *The Great Chain of Being.*

15. Georges-Louis Leclerc, Comte de Buffon, *Histoire naturelle, générale et particulière* (Paris, 1778), quoted by Buchan, *Advice to Mothers,* 75.

16. Edmund Spenser, *The Faerie Queene* (London: H. Hills, 1678), Book 6, Canticle 4, Stanza 11.

17. For an in-depth study of wild men, see Timothy Husband, *The Wild Man.*

18. Quoted by Ross W. Beales, Jr., "In Search of the Historical Child," 386.

19. Husband, *The Wild Man,* 3.

20. Raleigh, *The History of the World,* Book I, 31.

21. Wurtz, *Treatise of Surgerie,* 202.

22. Peter C. Hoffer and N. E. H. Hull, *Murdering Mothers;* and Scholten, *Childbearing in American Society,* 34.

23. Wurtz, *Treatise of Surgerie,* 202–12.

24. Glisson, *De Rachitide,* 283.

25. Ibid.; and Metlinger, *Gotlicher und Menschlicher,* 77.

26. Wurtz, *Treatise of Surgerie,* 205.

27. Ibid.

28. Metlinger, *Gotlicher und Menschlicher,* 77.

29. Glisson, *De Rachitide,* 284.

30. Ibid., 284–88.

31. The Victoria and Albert Museum owns an early eighteenth-century pair of boned stays made for an infant. Lists of the contents of an infant's layette frequently included stays. Mary Thresher of London composed a list of necessary baby clothes in 1698 that included "8 fine long stays" (reprinted in Pamela Clayburn, "My Small Child Bed Linning [*sic*]," *Costume: The Journal of the Costume Society* 13 [1979]: 38–40). Mention of "5 short stays" for a baby also appears in a record of the "chil-

dren's linen and plate" for 1718 in the Brudenell family accounts (*Brudenells of Deene*, ed. J. Wake [London: Fletcher, 1953], 85). In America, the author of *The Maternal Physician*, 132, also comments on the stays worn by babies of her grandparents' generation, which would have been mid–eighteenth century.

32. Mauriceau, *Traite des Maladies des Femmes*, 130.

33. Buchan, *Advice to Mothers*, 75.

34. William Alcott, *The Young Mother*, 232.

35. Glisson, *De Rachitide*, 273; Wurtz, *Treatise of Surgerie*, 219.

36. Descriptions of several homemade versions of the standing stool appear in *An Encyclopaedia of Cottage, Farm & Villa Architecture*, 351. A surviving pole standing stool is in the collection of the Cambridge Folklife Museum, Cambridge, England.

37. Wurtz, *Treatise of Surgerie*, 219–20.

38. Ibid.

39. Joseph E. Illick, "Child-rearing in Seventeenth-Century England," 303–51; and Scholten, *Childbearing in American Society*, 8–31.

40. William Cadogan, *An Essay Upon Nursing and the Management of Children* (reprinted as an appendix to Buchan, *Advice to Mothers*, 123–24).

41. Ibid.

42. J. T. Smith, *Nollekins and His Times*, 9.

43. Wurtz, *Treatise of Surgerie*, 220.

44. American Matron, *The Maternal Physician*, 132.

45. For a discussion of sleeping arrangements in colonial America, see David H. Fletcher, *Privacy in Colonial New England*.

46. Probate inventory of Walter Smith, Calvert County, 1711, Maryland Hall of Records, Inventories and Accounts, pp. 50–52, 133–34.

47. Philip Alexander Bruce, *Economic History of Virginia in the Seventeenth Century*, 184.

CHAPTER 2

1. The use of European prints by American artists has been most thoroughly researched by Waldron Phoenix Belknap, Jr., *American Colonial Painting*. For a quantitative study of children's portraits in America, see Karin Calvert, "Children in American Portraiture, 1670 to 1810."

2. Anne Buck, *Dress in Eighteenth-Century England;* and C. Willett and Phillis Cunnington, *A Picture History of English Costume*, 52–90.

3. Nicholas Noyes, "Reasons Against Wearing Periwigs," *Publications of the Colonial Society of Massachusetts* 20 (1971): 120–28.

4. Examples of boys wearing petticoats from portraits painted between 1750 and 1770 are Jeremiah Theus's "Charles Cochran" (c. 1754, Maryland), Museum of Early Southern Decorative Arts, Winston-Salem, N.C., and Charles Wilson Peale's "Child with Toy Horse" (1768, Pennsylvania), Museum of Fine Arts, Houston, Tex. Portraits of little girls of the period 1750 to 1770 include John Wollaston's "Mrs. Perry and Her Daughter Anne" (c. 1758, Pennsylvania), Philadelphia Museum of

Art; Theus's "Sarah White" (1753, Maryland), Mrs. John Campbell White Collection; John Singleton Copley's "Two Sisters of Christopher Gore" (c. 1755, Massachusetts), Gore Place, Waltham, Mass.; Copley's "Mary and Elizabeth Royall" (1758, Massachusetts), Museum of Fine Arts, Boston; John Durand's "Catherine Beekman" (c. 1768, New York), New-York Historical Society, New York, Beekman Family Association; Jeremiah Theus's "Peggy Warner" (c. 1750, South Carolina), Telfair Academy of Arts and Sciences, Savannah, Ga.; and Joseph Blackburn's "Four Children of Governor Saltonstall" (1762, Connecticut), New Haven Historical Society, New Haven, Conn.

5. Portraits of young girls of the period ending in 1750 include [artist unknown], "Alice Mason" (1670, Massachusetts), Adams National Historic Site, Braintree, Mass.; [artist unknown], "Elizabeth Eggington" (c. 1680, Connecticut), Wadsworth Atheneum, Hartford, Conn.; [artist unknown], "Margaret Gibbs" (1670, Massachusetts), Collection of Mrs. Alexander Quarrier Smith; [artist unknown], "Christina Ten Broek" (1720, New York), Mrs. Ledyard Cogswell Collection; Justus Kuhn's "Eleanor Darnall" (1710, Maryland), Maryland Historical Society, Baltimore; [artist unknown], "Girl of the Schuyler Family" (c. 1730, New York), Collection of Mrs. W. Leland Thompson; attributed to John Smibert, "Joanna and Elizabeth Perkins" (1749, Massachusetts), Paul M. Hamlen Collection; and [artist unknown], "Catherine Van Alstyne" (1732, New York), Albany Institute of History and Art, Albany, N.Y.

6. Other portraits of young boys in petticoats before 1750 include [artist unknown], "Henry Gibbs" (1670, Massachusetts), Collection of Mrs. David M. Gilttiman; [artist unknown], "The Barclay Children" (c. 1700, New York), Ten Eyck Powell Collection; Justus Kuhn's "Frank Child" (misidentified as Elizabeth Frank) (c. 1710, Maryland), Milwaukee Art Center, Milwaukee, Wis.; Kuhn's "Ignatius Diggs" (1710, Maryland), Philip Carroll Collection; Francis Berkeley, from John Smibert's "Dean Berkeley and His Entourage" (1730, Massachusetts), Yale University Art Gallery, New Haven, Conn.; [artist unknown], "Mrs. Mann Page and Her Son" (c. 1745, Virginia), College of William and Mary, Williamsburg, Va.; and Charles Bridge's "Mann Page" (c. 1738, Virginia), College of William and Mary, Williamsburg, Va.

7. Other examples of boys wearing robes from portraits before 1750 are [artist unknown], "Boy with Fawn" (c. 1700, New York), Collection of Edgar William and Bernice Chrysler Garbisch; [artist unknown], "The Barclay Children" (c. 1700, New York), Ten Eyck Powell Collection; and Frederick Tellschaw's "Thomas Lodge" (1745, New York), New-York Historical Society, New York.

8. Philippe Ariès, *Centuries of Childhood,* 55–60.

9. The distinction between adult and youth is ably demonstrated through conventional documentary sources by Ross W. Beales, Jr., "In Search of the Historical Child."

10. Portraits painted before 1750 of breeched boys holding feminine or childish props include the following paintings by unknown artists: "Pau de Wandelaer" (c. 1725, New York), Albany Institute of History and Art, Albany, N.Y., flowers; "Edward Jacquelin" (c. 1722, Virginia), Virginia Museum of Fine Arts, Richmond, Va.,

pets and drapery; "Johnathon Benham" (c. 1710, region unknown), Garbisch Collection, pet and flower; "Edward Broadnax" (c. 1720, Massachusetts), Virginia Museum of Fine Arts, pet; "Matthew Ten Eyck" (1733, New York), Collection of Mrs. Frank H. Nowaczek, flower; "Adam Winnie" (c. 1710, New York), Winterthur Museum, Winterthur, Del., fruit; "John Van Cortlandt" (c. 1730, New York), Brooklyn Museum, N.Y., pet; and "Two Boys with Pets" (c. 1730, region unknown), Garbisch Collection, pets, fruit, and flowers.

11. For a description of the doll's town "Mon Plaisir" of 1716 in the Schlosemuseum at Arnstadt, see Karl Ewald Fritzsch and Manfred Bachmann, *An Illustrated History of German Toys.*

12. William Shakespeare, *A Midsummer Night's Dream,* V.i.3., "I never may believe these antick folkes, nor their fairy toyes"; John Milton, *Paradise Lost,* IX, 1034, "So said he and forbore not glance or toy, / of amorous intent, well understood / of Eve"; Bishop Robert Sanderson, *Works of Robert Sanderson* (London: Joseph Richards, 1660), "One would have a grave pavana, another a nimble gallierd, a third some striking toy or jig"; and Captain John Smith, *Virginia,* I.3., "We presented him with divers toys, which he kindly accepted."

13. Francis Sylvius, *Of Children's Diseases* (London, 1682), reprinted in John Ruhrah, ed., *Pediatrics of the Past,* 304–5.

14. Ibid., 310; and Robert Pernell, *A Treatise of the Diseases of Children* (London: F. Lagett, 1653), reprinted in Ruhrah, *Pediatrics,* 293.

15. Thomas Phaer, *Boke of Children* (London: William How, 1584), reprinted in Ruhrah, *Pediatrics,* 174; Pernell, *Diseases of Children,* 293; and Sylvius, *Children's Diseases,* 305.

16. Phaer, *Boke of Children,* 174.

17. Bernard Mergen, "Toys and American Culture."

18. "Plus ori les fouette mieux il vent," taken from a series of seventeenth-century emblems depicting the four ages of man, entitled "De Tout Cote Peine"; reproduced in Samuel C. Chew, *The Pilgrimage of Life,* 159.

19. Southern portraits of boys with bows and arrows include Charles Bridges's "Boys of the Grymes Family" (c. 1735–38, Virginia), privately owned; William Dering's "George Booth" (c. 1740–45, Virginia), Colonial Williamsburg Foundation, Williamsburg, Va.; and Justus Kuhn's "Henry Darnall" (c. 1710, Maryland), Maryland Historical Society, Baltimore.

20. Constance Eileen King, *The Collector's History of Dolls,* 63–64.

21. Mergen, "Toys and American Culture," notes that toys are made by adults to sell to other adults.

22. Peter Wagner, "Literary Evidence of Sport in Colonial New England: The American Puritan Jeremiad," *Stadion* 2 (1976): 236.

23. Cotton Mather, *Being the Wonders of the Invisible World* (London: R. Brown, 1693), 35.

CHAPTER 3

1. Representative of the men who contributed to the growing perception of a logical and orderly universe were Sir Isaac Newton, *Philosophiae Naturalis Principia*

Mathematica (London: H. Woodfall, 1687); Francis Bacon, *Historia Naturalis* (London: I. Hauiland, 1622); René Descartes, *Discourse on Method* (Paris: Haefner, 1649); Karl von Linnaeus, *Species Plantarum* (Laurentii Salvii, 1753); and Edward Gibbon, *Decline and Fall of the Roman Empire* (London: W. Strahan, 1790).

2. Marquis de Condorcet, *Outline of an Historical View of the Progress of the Human Mind,* 367.

3. For a thorough discussion of the theory of acquired characteristics, see Conway Zirkle, "The Early History of the Idea of Inheritance of Acquired Characteristics and Pangenesis," 94–95.

4. Ibid., 105–23.

5. Oliver Goldsmith, *The History of the Earth and Animal Nature* (1774; reprint London: T. J. Wilson, 1928), 234–35.

6. Condorcet, *Progress of the Human Mind,* 114–15.

7. Ibid., 115.

8. Jean-Jacques Rousseau, *Emile, or on Education,* 10.

9. References to or borrowings from Locke appear in An American Matron, *The Maternal Physician;* [author unknown] *Hints for the Improvement of Early Education and Nursery Discipline;* D. D. Hitchcock, *Memories of the Bloomsgrove Family;* William P. Dewees, *A Treatise on the Physical and Medical Treatment of Children;* and John Eberle, *A Treatise on the Diseases and Physical Education of Children.*

10. William Cadogan, *An Essay Upon Nursing and the Management of Children.*

11. Among those relying on the works of William Buchan were the authors of *The Maternal Physician* and *Hints for the Improvement;* Hitchcock, *Bloomsgrove Family;* Dewees, *Physical and Medical Treatment;* and Eberle, *Physical Education of Children.*

12. John Locke, *Some Thoughts Concerning Education,* 50.

13. Hitchcock, *Bloomsgrove Family,* 83.

14. Rousseau, *Emile,* 6.

15. Mary Rowsell, *Life of Ch. de la Tremoille, Countess of Derby* (London: John D. Bates, 1905), 76; Felix Wurtz, *An Experimental Treatise of Surgerie in Four Parts* (London: Gartrude Dawson, 1656), reprinted in John Ruhrah, ed., *Pediatrics of the Past,* 212; Pamela Clayburn, "My Small Child Bed Linning [*sic*]," *Costume: The Journal of the Costume Society* 13 (1979): 38–40.

16. Locke, *Thoughts Concerning Education,* 15–16.

17. Samuel Richardson, *Pamela,* 97.

18. William Buchan, *Advice to Mothers,* 41–42.

19. American Matron, *The Maternal Physician,* 132.

20. Buchan, *Advice to Mothers,* 48.

21. Ibid.

22. Ann E. Porter, "Cousin Helen's Baby," *Godey's Lady's Magazine* 38 (March 1849), 237.

23. Locke, *Thoughts Concerning Education,* 10.

24. Ibid.

25. Cadogan, *The Management of Children,* 111.

26. Ibid.

27. Locke, *Thoughts Concerning Education*, 20; Buchan, *Advice to Mothers*, 38–39; American Matron, *The Maternal Physician*, 21.

28. William Alcott, *The Young Mother*, 225.

29. Cadogan, *The Management of Children*, 124.

30. Van Swietne as quoted by Buchan, *Advice to Mothers*, 71.

31. Ibid.

32. Ibid., 71, 95.

33. W. Alcott, *The Young Mother*, 225.

34. Ibid., 36, 274; Buchan, *Advice to Mothers*, 35; and *The Servant's Guide and Family Manual*, 119.

35. Dewees, *Physical and Medical Treatment*, 108.

36. W. Alcott, *The Young Mother*, 108, 36.

37. Philip Vickers Fithian, *Philip Vickers Fithian*, 129.

38. Buchan, *Advice to Mothers*, 35, 79–80.

39. Harriet Manigault, *The Diary of Harriet Manigault, 1813–1816*, 51.

40. Ibid., 79.

41. Buchan, *Advice to Mothers*, 69.

42. W. Alcott, *The Young Mother*, 232.

43. American Matron, *The Maternal Physician*, 129.

44. Ibid., 128.

45. Buchan, *Advice to Mothers*, 70.

46. Ibid., 67–70.

47. American Matron, *The Maternal Physician*, 129.

48. Eberle, *Physical Education of Children*, 59–60; Buchan, *Advice to Mothers*, 93–94.

49. "Fashions," *Godey's* 74 (March 1867), 271–72, and "Some Italian Babies," *Babyland* 9 (September 1885), 76.

50. W. Alcott, *The Young Mother*, 336.

51. Manigault, *Diary*, 117.

52. Ibid., 51.

53. Edward Channing, "The Life of William Ellery," 89.

54. American Matron, *The Maternal Physician*, 7.

55. Hitchcock, *Bloomsgrove Family*, 83.

56. Cadogan, *The Management of Children*, 120.

57. Lucy Larcom, *A New England Girlhood*, 199.

58. Locke, *Thoughts Concerning Education*, 52.

59. Hitchcock, *Bloomsgrove Family*, 143.

60. For a thorough discussion of the steady decline in close social contact between members of different socioeconomic classes, see Paul E. Johnson, *A Shopkeeper's Millennium*, and Sam Bass Warner, Jr., *The Private City*.

61. American Matron, *The Maternal Physician*, 158.

62. Landon Carter, *The Diary of Colonel Landon Carter of Sabine Hall, 1752–1778*, Vol. I, 511, entry for 14 October 1770. By 1790 D. D. Hitchcock noted that "comparatively few mothers were so unnatural" as to ignore the very real dangers inherent in putting a child out to nurse. Hitchcock, *Bloomsgrove Family*, 81.

63. Mrs. T. W. Dewing, *Beauty in the Household,* 166.
64. Locke, *Thoughts Concerning Education,* 19–20.
65. Porter, "Cousin Helen's Baby," 237.
66. W. Alcott, *The Young Mother,* 227.
67. Lydia Child, *The American Frugal Housewife,* 29; and American Matron, *The Maternal Physician,* 148–49, 178–79, 206.

CHAPTER 4

1. Toys and other childish artifacts are very rare in English portraits before 1750. Occasionally a portrait of an aristocratic or royal child contained a toy, an elaborate piece of children's furniture, or a fancy-dress costume, but such anomalies had little or no effect on provincial portraiture and did not reflect popular views regarding the appropriate presentation of children. American portraits of children with toys of the period 1750 to 1770 include John Wollaston's "Mrs. Perry and Her Daughter Anne," (1758, Pennsylvania), Philadelphia Museum of Art, rattle; John Singleton Copley's "Master Hancock[?]" (1758–59, Massachusetts), Fuller Collection, battledore and shuttlecock; Joseph Badger's "Two Children" (c. 1752, Massachusetts), Abbey Aldrich Rockefeller Folk Art Collection, Williamsburg, Va., rattle; Badger's "John Joy, Jr." (c. 1758, Massachusetts), Munson-Williams-Proctor Institute, Utica, N.Y., battledore and shuttlecock; Wollaston's "Rebecca Calvert" (1754, Maryland), Baltimore Museum of Art, doll; and John Hesselius's "Charles Calvert" (1761, Maryland), Baltimore Museum of Art, toy drum.
2. John Locke, *Some Thoughts Concerning Education,* 120, 95.
3. Mary Cable, *The Little Darlings,* 34.
4. Philippe Ariès, *Centuries of Childhood,* 98–99.
5. Lucy Larcom, *A New England Girlhood,* 109.
6. Constance Eileen King, *The Collector's History of Dolls,* 89.
7. Ibid., 66, and D. D. Hitchcock, *Memories of the Bloomsgrove Family,* 146.
8. Philip Vickers Fithian, *Philip Vickers Fithian,* 251, 257.
9. Ibid., 145; Barrows Mussey, ed., *Yankee Life by Those Who Lived It,* 19; Larcom, *A New England Girlhood,* 109; and Monica May Kiefer, *American Children through Their Books, 1700–1835,* 203, 217.
10. Portraits of small boys in frocks dated after 1770 include Charles Wilson Peale's "James Gittings Family" (c. 1773, Maryland), Maryland Historical Society; Matthew Pratt's "William Randolph" (1773, Virginia), Colonial Williamsburg Foundation; C. W. Peale's "Mrs. Richard Tilghman and Sons" (1789, Maryland), Maryland Historical Society; Joseph Wright's "Self-Portrait of Artist and Family" (1793, Pennsylvania), Pennsylvania Academy of Fine Arts; Ralph Earl's "Mrs. William Taylor and Son" (1790, Connecticut), Albright-Knox Art Gallery, Buffalo, N.Y.; James Earl's "Charlotte Rhoda and Moses Brown" (1795, Rhode Island), Collection of Mr. and Mrs. R. H. Ives Goddard; and John Brewster, Jr.'s "Francis O. Watts with Bird" (1805, New York or New England), New York State Historical Association, Cooperstown.
11. Locke, *Thoughts Concerning Education,* 16.

12. Hitchcock, *Bloomsgrove Family*, 86.

13. *The History of Little Goody Twoshoes*, 19.

14. John Neal, "The Early Years in Maine," in Mussey, *Yankee Life*, 18.

15. Charles Lamb, "Going into Britches," 21.

16. Elizabeth Ham, *Elizabeth Ham: 1783–1820*, 25.

17. William Buchan, *Advice to Mothers*, 48.

18. Larcom, *A New England Girlhood*, 166.

19. Ibid. For insightful studies of feminine maturation as a loss of freedom, see Nancy F. Cott, *The Bonds of Womanhood*, and Anne MacLeod, "The Caddie Woodlawn Syndrome," 87–120.

20. Among them, in addition to John Smibert, were John Wollaston, Roger Blackburn, and John Greenwood.

21. Some portraits of grandparents and grandchildren do exist. The most striking exception to the general form of nuclear portrait, however, is "The Peale Family Portrait" of 1773 in the New-York Historical Society, in which Charles Wilson Peale has included himself, his wife and children, two brothers, his mother, and the children's nurse. Such a large group would have been very rare as a commissioned piece, due to the considerable expense incurred with each additional subject.

22. Other portraits painted after 1770 that depict an affectionate relationship between the father and young son are Charles Wilson Peale's "Goldsmith Family" (1789, Pennsylvania), Baltimore Museum of Art; Ralph Earl's "Family Portrait" (1804, Connecticut), Garbisch Collection; and [artist unknown], "The Colden Family" (1795, region unknown), Abbey Aldrich Rockefeller Folk Art Collection, Williamsburg, Va. Portraits of fathers posed with young daughters include James Peale's "Paul Ambrose Oliver and Daughter" (c. 1800, Pennsylvania), Collection of Mrs. Elizabeth Brownell, and C. W. Peale's "Edward Lloyd Family" (1771, Maryland), Winterthur Museum, Winterthur, Del. For the best study of the relationship between husbands and wives as presented in portraiture of this era, see Margaretta Lovell, "Reading Eighteenth-Century American Family Portraits."

23. Other portraits of boys in transitional costumes include Joseph Badger's "Master Stephen Crossfield" (1775, Connecticut), Metropolitan Museum of Art, New York, N.Y.; William Wilkie's "Nathaniel Hawley and Family" (1801, New York), Albany Institute of History and Art, Albany, N.Y.; J. S. Copley's "Daniel Verplanck" (1771, Massachusetts), Metropolitan Museum of Art, New York, N.Y.; C. W. Peale's "Johnson Brothers" (c. 1774, Maryland), Maryland Historical Society, Baltimore; Winthrop Chandler's "John Paine" (c. 1780, Massachusetts), Worcester Art Museum, Worcester, Mass.; C. W. Peale's "Mrs. Isaac Hite and James Madison Hite, Jr." (1799, Maryland), Maryland Historical Society, Baltimore; and Ralph Earl's "William Carpenter" (1779, Connecticut), Worcester Art Museum, Worcester, Mass.

24. Examples of portraits by unknown artists containing girls in transitional costumes include "Phoebe Denison" (1792, region unknown), National Gallery of Art, Washington, D.C.; and "Matilda Denison" (1792, region unknown), Collection of Descendants.

CHAPTER 5

1. "How to Cut and Contrive Children's Clothes," *Godey's* 55 (July 1857), 73; "The Nursery," *Godey's* 49 (October 1854), 381; Louisa May Alcott, *An Old-Fashioned Girl,* 209; and J. West Roosevelt, "Hygiene in the Home," 284.

2. Eliza Ridgely, "Journal of Eliza Ridgely of Hampton, Maryland, 1841–42," Waldron Phoenix Belknap Memorial Library, Winterthur Museum, Ph1134, p. 3; Forrest Reid, "Looking Backward Through Time," in *When I Was a Child,* ed. Edward Wagenknecht, 403; and Mrs. Merrifeld, "Some Thoughts on Children's Dress," *Godey's* 46 (June 1853), 541.

3. Caroline Cowles Richards, *Village Life in America,* 121.

4. Emmett L. Holt, *The Care and Feeding of Children,* 15–16.

5. Orson S. Fowler, *Creative and Sexual Science,* 857.

6. "Fashions," *Godey's* 41 (July 1850), 54.

7. Phillis Cunnington and Anne Buck, *Children's Costume in England,* 172; "Chitchat upon Philadelphia's Fashions for Juveniles," *Godey's* 48 (February 1854), 283.

8. Sara Hutchinson, *Letters of Sara Hutchinson,* 270.

9. "Fashion," *Godey's* 53 (July 1856), 256.

10. Catherine Elizabeth Havens, *Diary of a Little Girl in Old New York,* 35.

11. Mary Cable, *The Little Darlings,* 109; Monica May Kiefer, *American Children,* 217.

12. Lydia Child, *The American Frugal Housewife,* 88.

13. Richards, *Village Life,* 107.

14. Frances Hodgson Burnett, *Little Lord Fauntleroy.*

15. R. Struve, M.D., *The Domestic Education of Children,* 37.

16. R. L. Stevenson, *Dr. Jekyll and Mr. Hyde;* Oscar Wilde, *The Picture of Dorian Gray;* Nathaniel Hawthorne, "Young Goodman Brown," *New England Magazine* (April 1835); Henrik Ibsen, *Peer Gynt* (New York: Blocks, 1902); and Emily Brontë, *Wuthering Heights* (London: J. Wyndell, 1847).

17. D. D. Hitchcock, *Memories of the Bloomsgrove Family,* 83.

18. "Childhood," *Godey's* 4 (June 1832), 268. Similar sentiments appear in dozens of other articles, including "Children," *Godey's* 58 (December 1859), 506; "Purity," *Godey's* 35 (September 1847), i; "To a Child Dancing," *Godey's* 28 (January 1844), 1; "To a Child," *Godey's* 32 (January 1846), 4; "The Shadow of Children," *Godey's* 54 (June 1857), 524; "Children," *Godey's* 64 (January 1862), 91; and "Childhood," *Godey's* 21 (December 1840), 280, to name but a few. While *Godey's* was by far the most popular women's periodical in mid-nineteenth-century America, other journals carried similar articles and stories extolling with considerable reverence the holy nature of childhood.

19. William Wordsworth, "Ode: Intimations of Immortality from Recollections of Early Childhood," in *The Literature of England,* ed. George Anderson and William E. Buckler (Glenview, Ill.: Scott, Foresman, 1966), 206.

20. Ralph Waldo Emerson, *Nature: Address and Lectures,* 14–15.

21. Amos Bronson Alcott, "Conversations with Children on the Gospels," in *The Transcendentalists,* ed. Perry Miller, 152.

22. Richard McLanathan, *The American Tradition in the Arts,* 246.

23. "To a Child," *Godey's* 32 (January 1846), 4.

24. Inevitably, there was also a backlash of articles and stories protesting the often saccharine nature of the attention given children. Among the best are "A New Baby," *Godey's* 58 (June 1859), 537–41; Patience Perkins, "My Baby," *Godey's* 51 (November 1855), 404–7; and "Miss Prymm on Babies," *Godey's* 84 (July 1872), 46.

25. "The Shadow of Children," *Godey's* 54 (June 1857), 524.

26. "Children," *Godey's* 64 (January 1862), 9; "Childhood," *Godey's* 21 (December 1840), 280.

27. Washington Irving, *Diedrich Knickerbocker's History of New-York,* 118.

28. Charles Dickens, *Oliver Twist* (1838; reprint Philadelphia: Henry Altemus, 1900); Harriet Beecher Stowe, *Uncle Tom's Cabin.*

29. "Childhood," *Godey's* 4 (June 1832), 268.

30. "Children," *Godey's* 58 (December 1859), 506.

31. Daniel Foley, *Christmas in the Good Old Days: A Victorian Album of Stories, Poems, and Pictures of the Personalities Who Rediscovered Christmas* (Philadelphia: Chilton, 1961), 151; and Mrs. A. M. Diaz, "Willie Wee," in *Christmas Carols and Midsummer Songs by American Poets* (Boston: D. Lothrop, 1881), 26–28.

32. Rose Ashley, "The Idiot: A Psychological Story," *Godey's* 37 (December 1848), 376–82.

33. "Children," *Godey's* 60 (March 1860), 272.

34. "What Happened to Benny," *Babyland* 5 (1881), 27.

35. *Our Boys and Girls at Home,* 10.

36. Lewis Gaylord Clark, "Gossip About Children: In a Familiar Epistle to the Editor," *Godey's* 40 (June 1850), 377.

37. Mrs. A. D. T. Whitney, *Hitherto,* 67.

38. Ridgely, "Journal," 27.

39. Havens, *Diary,* 129.

40. "Playing Mother," *Godey's* 40 (June 1850), 304.

41. Fowler, *Creative and Sexual Science,* 859.

42. A Father, *The Play-house and Workshop,* 38–39.

43. Lucy Larcom, *A New England Girlhood,* 29.

44. Ridgely, "Journal," 24, 45–46; Eleanor Hallowell Abbott, "Being Little in Cambridge," and Mary Ellen Chase, "The Lord's Day in the Nineties," in Wagenknecht, *When I Was a Child,* 169, 314.

45. *Sears, Roebuck Catalogue of 1897,* 143; *Montgomery Ward Catalogue: World's Fair Edition, 1893,* 476.

46. Havelock Ellis, *Studies in the Psychology of Sex,* 174–78.

47. Langdon Down, "Sexuality and Children," *British Medical Journal* (January 1867), as quoted in Ellis, *Psychology of Sex,* 175.

48. James Foster Scott, *The Sexual Instinct,* 64.

49. T. R. Crowell, "Amusements of Worcester School Children," *Pedagogical Seminary* 22 (Spring 1899), 47.

50. Barrows Mussey, ed., *Yankee Life by Those Who Lived It,* 31–32.

51. Havens, *Diary,* 62; Richards, *Village Life,* 5, 24.

52. Ridgely, "Journal," 8, 11–14, 16, 18, 20–22, 26–27, 30, 39, 44, 45, 47.

53. Richards, *Village Life,* 8, 23, 33, 40, 47, 61, 77, 111; J. M. Bailey, "The Danbury News," in Mussey, *Yankee Life,* 48–49.

54. As related to me by Howard Woodman, Hamilton, New York, regarding his childhood in the 1890s.

55. E. H. Southern, "Me," in Wagenknecht, *When I Was a Child,* 343.

56. "Pictures to Draw," *Babyland* 5 (October 1881), 4; "The Little Recruit," *Nursery* 21 (April 1877), 107. Other examples include "Jinx's Wheelbarrow," *Nursery* 18 (June 1875), 179; "The Little Hands," *Godey's* 62 (April 1861), 439; and S. Annie Frost, "Dolly: A Christmas Story," *Godey's* 77 (December 1868), 529.

57. Jean-Jacques Rousseau, *Emile, or on Education,* 202.

58. Bernard Mergen, "Toys and American Culture."

59. Lydia Child, *The Mother's Book,* 57; "Little Girls," *Godey's* 63 (December 1861), 533; and Fowler, *Creative and Sexual Science,* 859.

60. Holt, *Care and Feeding of Children,* 749.

61. Kiefer, *American Children,* 191–200; Kate Douglas Wiggin, "The Training of Children," in *The House and Home,* 327.

CHAPTER 6

1. Mrs. Charles Harcourt, *Good Form for Women,* 83.

2. Catherine E. Beecher, *A Treatise on Domestic Economy,* 233.

3. J. E. Panton, *From Kitchen to Garret,* 231.

4. Orson S. Fowler, *Creative and Sexual Science,* 844.

5. Lydia Child, *The American Frugal Housewife,* 100–101.

6. Mrs. T. W. Dewing, *Beauty in the Household,* 166.

7. "That Blessed Baby," *Godey's* 53 (August 1856), 245; "A Few Words About Delicate Women," *Godey's* 48 (May 1854), 446–48.

8. Fowler, *Creative and Sexual Science,* 844.

9. "Opium," *Godey's* 104 (February 1892), ii.

10. *Sears, Roebuck Catalogue of 1902,* 454.

11. "Children in Modern Literature," *Appleton's* 6 (April 1869), 32.

12. *An Encyclopaedia of Cottage, Farm & Villa Architecture,* 350.

13. "Children's Corner," *Ladies Home Journal* 21 (February 1899), 142.

14. *Sears, Roebuck Catalogue of 1897,* 142.

15. "A Morning Calls," *Nursery* 20 (January 1876), 29; "Bob and Baby," *Nursery* 19 (March 1875), 83; and "Baby's Exploits," *Nursery* 22 (December 1877), 173–76.

16. Gwen White, *European and American Dolls,* 254.

17. "A Baby's Gift," *Godey's* 98 (April 1879), 70.

18. Richard G. Wells, A.M., *Manners, Culture and Dress of the Best American Society,* 423.

19. *Hints for the Improvement of Early Education and Nursery Discipline,* 83.

20. Lydia Child, *The Mother's Book,* 49.

21. An American Matron, *The Maternal Physician,* 141; Beecher, *Domestic Econ-*

omy, 232; Dr. Emile Spurzheim, "About the Food of Children," *Godey's* 46 (March 1853), 214.

22. "Just a Taste," *Arthur's Ladies Magazine* 28 (July–December 1866), 176–78.

23. *Furniture Gazette* 14 (September 1870), 43.

24. *Ludwig Bauman & Co. Catalogue,* 362; *Montgomery Ward Catalogue, 1887,* 645; Gustav Stickley, *Craftsman Homes,* 181.

25. Eleanor Hallowell Abbott, "Being Little in Cambridge," in *When I Was a Child,* ed. Edward Wagenknecht, 167.

26. Harriet Manigault, *The Diary of Harriet Manigault, 1813–1816,* 5.

27. John W. Bright, *The Mother's Medical Guide,* 249.

28. Uncle Thomas, *Christmas Blossoms, and New Year's Wreath for 1849,* 130.

29. Miss Leslie, *The House Book,* 323.

30. Catherine Elizabeth Havens, *Diary of a Little Girl in Old New York,* 12.

31. Eliza Ridgely, "Journal of Eliza Ridgely of Hampton, Maryland, 1841–42," 9–10, 15–16, 18–19.

32. Lucy Larcom, *A New England Girlhood,* 147; and Barrows Mussey, ed., *Yankee Life by Those Who Lived It,* 30.

33. Bright, *Mother's Medical Guide,* 249.

34. "Toilet Basket," *Ladies Home Journal* 41 (April 1899), 42.

35. Emmett L. Holt, *The Care and Feeding of Children,* 12, 15.

36. *Montgomery Ward Catalogue, 1884,* 81.

37. "The Crib and the Cradle," *Godey's* 52 (May 1856), 478.

38. *The Upholsterer* 6 (Fall 1890), 72.

39. Catalogues that continued to carry some cradles included *C. N. Arnold & Co. Catalogue* (1893), *Ludwig Bauman & Co. Catalogue* (1890s), and *Acme Co. Catalogue* (1901).

40. Cradles were not the only obsolete objects valued for their historic associations during the Colonial Revival. For an excellent study of the phenomenon, see Christopher Monkhouse, "The Spinning Wheel as Artifact, Symbol, and Source of Design," *Victorian Furniture: Nineteenth Century* 8, no. 3 (1982): 153–72.

41. *Encyclopaedia of Cottage Architecture,* 35.

42. Authorities who favored separate nurseries for children included Bright, *Mother's Medical Guide,* 249; Miss Leslie, *The House Book,* 323; Walter R. Houghton, *American Etiquette and Rules of Politeness,* 51; "Children's Rooms," *Ladies Home Journal* 21 (January 1899), 26; Edith Wharton and Ogden Codman, Jr., *The Decoration of Houses,* 182; Fowler, *Creative and Sexual Science,* 64; J. West Roosevelt, "Hygiene in the Home," in *House and Home,* 283; and Alice M. Kellogg, *Home Furnishing—Practical and Artistic,* 83.

43. William P. Dewees, *A Treatise on the Physical and Medical Treatment of Children,* 11.

44. Fowler, *Creative and Sexual Science,* 847.

45. Beecher, *Domestic Economy,* 219.

46. *Acme Co. Catalogue* (1901).

47. William Cadogan, *An Essay Upon Nursing and the Management of Children,* 219.

48. Dewees, *Physical and Medical Treatment,* 110.

49. Beecher, *Domestic Economy,* 218; Bright, *Mother's Medical Guide,* 249.

50. Holt, *Care and Feeding of Children,* 110.

51. Dewing, *Beauty in the Household,* 164.

52. W. Alcott, *The Young Mother,* 272.

53. Houghton, *American Etiquette,* 51.

54. Wharton and Codman, *The Decoration of Houses,* 182.

55. Orson S. Fowler, *A Home for All,* 62–63.

56. John Neal, "Children—What Are They?" *Godey's* 39 (October 1849), 260–62.

57. Kate Sutherland, "The Young Mother," *Godey's* 37 (November 1848), 254.

58. Alexander Walker, *Intermarriage,* 163, 354.

59. Fowler, *Creative and Sexual Science,* 76, 79, 764, 795, 808, 981.

60. James Foster Scott, *The Sexual Instinct,* 428.

61. Fowler, *Creative and Sexual Science,* 817.

62. "Are We Womanizing?" *Appleton's Journal of Literature, Science and Art* 2 (31 July 1868), 563–64; "Table Talk," *Appleton's* 3 (September 1869), 122; "Popular Fallacies Concerning Hygiene," *Appleton's* 2 (14 August 1869), 625; "Marriage Between Cousins," *Godey's* 66 (April 1863), 397–98; "Hints About Health," *Godey's* 74 (June 1867), 558; and Fowler, *Creative and Sexual Science,* 76.

63. "Wonderful Children," *Godey's* 51 (September 1855), 209.

64. Harriet Beecher Stowe, *Oldtown Folks,* 437.

65. D. K. Shute, M.D., "Heredity with Variation," *New England Medical Journal* 32 (11 September 1897): 46.

66. Scott, *The Sexual Instinct,* 429.

67. Havelock Ellis, *Studies in the Psychology of Sex,* 249.

68. Walker, *Intermarriage,* 89–90.

69. Fowler, *Creative and Sexual Science,* 891–92.

70. Child, *American Frugal Housewife,* 153.

71. Fowler, *Creative and Sexual Science,* 896.

72. Ibid., 892–97.

73. Holt, *Care and Feeding of Children,* 64.

74. Ellis, *Psychology of Sex,* 181, 235–38.

75. Dewing, *Beauty in the Household,* 164; Walker, *Intermarriage,* 73, 77.

76. "Fashions," *Godey's* 56 (June 1858), 552; "Fashions," *Godey's* 88 (June 1873), 548; *Sears, Roebuck Catalogue of 1902,* 998; Walker, *Intermarriage,* 73.

77. Walker, *Intermarriage,* 74–75.

78. *The Workwoman's Guide,* 41.

79. "A Bassinet," *Ladies Home Journal* 21 (February 1899), 41.

80. American Matron, *The Maternal Physician,* 148; William Buchan, *Advice to Mothers,* 35; Bright, *Mother's Medical Guide,* 252.

81. "Fashion," *Godey's* 46 (May 1853), 381.

82. Mary Austin, "The Walnut Tree," in Wagenknecht, *When I Was a Child,* 386.

83. Sam Bass Warner, Jr., *Streetcar Suburbs: The Process of Growth in Boston, 1870–1900* (Cambridge, Mass.: Harvard University Press, 1962).

84. "Babies," *Appleton's* 2 (April 1869), 12.

85. Panton, *From Kitchen to Garret,* 192; Roosevelt, "Hygiene in the Home," 282; *The Upholsterer* (Fall 1890), 116.

86. "Good Night Papa," *Nursery* 25 (March 1879).

CONCLUSION

1. Cotton Mather, "Diary of Cotton Mather," *Massachusetts Historical Society Collections,* 7:8.

2. David Hackett Fischer, *Growing Old in America* (New York: Oxford University Press, 1977).

Bibliography

PRIMARY SOURCES

Acme Company. *General Catalogue No. 3: Everything in Furniture*. Chicago: Acme Co., 1901.

Adams, Charles, ed. *Memoirs of John Quincy Adams*. Philadelphia: J. B. Lippincott, 1874.

Alcott, Louisa May. *An Old-Fashioned Girl*. New York: A. L. Burt, 1912.

Alcott, William. *The Young Mother or Management of Children in Regard to Health*. Boston: George W. Light, 1839.

An American Matron. *The Maternal Physician: A Treatise on the Nurture and Management of Infants From Birth Until Two Years Old*. 2d ed. Philadelphia: Clark & Roser, 1818.

C. N. Arnold & Co. *Illustrated Catalogue of Chairs*. Poughkeepsie, N.Y.: C. N. Arnold, 1880.

Arthur, Timothy Shay. *Ten Nights in a Barroom, and What I Saw*. Boston: L. P. Crown, 1854; reprinted Cambridge, Mass.: Harvard University Press, 1964.

Artistic Homes or How to Furnish with Taste. London: Ward, 1881.

B. A. Atkinson & Co. *Special Catalogue of Parlor Furniture*. Boston, c. 1870.

Bailey, Abigail. *Memoirs of Mrs. Abigail Bailey*. Boston: Samuel Armstrong, 1815.

Bayard, Martha. *The Journal of Martha Bayard*. Edited by S. Dodd. New York: Dodd & Mead, 1894.

Beale, Edward Bates. *The Diary of Edward Bates Beale*. Edited by Howard Beale. Washington, D.C.: U.S. Government Printing Office, 1933.

Beecher, Catherine E. *A Treatise on Domestic Economy*. New York: Harper & Bros., 1848.

Book of Cuts, Designed for the Amusement and Instruction of Young People. New York: Mahlon Day, 1826.

Bottome, Ethel S., and Eva J. Cove. *American Samplers*. Boston: Massachusetts Society of Colonial Dames of America, 1921.

L. C. Boyington, Manufacturer. *Illustrated Catalogue of Boyington's Automatic and Chiffonier Folding Beds.* Chicago, 1885.

Bright, John W. *The Mother's Medical Guide: A Plain, Practical Treatise on Midwifery, and the Diseases of Women and Children in Seven Parts.* Louisville, Ky., 1844.

Bruce, Philip Alexander. *Economic History of Virginia in the Seventeenth Century.* New York: Macmillan, 1896.

Bub & Kipp's New Illustrated Catalogue of Upholstered Furniture. Milwaukee, Wis., 1887.

Buchan, William. *Advice to Mothers, on the Subject of Their Own Health; and of the Means of Promoting the Health, Strength, and Beauty of Their Offspring.* Philadelphia: Joseph Bumstead, 1809. Reprinted in *The Physician and Child-Rearing: Two Guides, 1809–1894.* Edited by Charles E. Rosenberg. New York: Arno Press, 1972.

Burnett, Frances Hodgson. *Little Lord Fauntleroy.* Serialized in *St. Nicholas: An Illustrated Magazine for Young Folks,* vols. 12 and 13, 1886. New York: Charles Scribner's Sons, 1889.

Butterfield, L. H., ed. *The Book of Abigail and John: Selected Letters of the Adams Family, 1762–1784.* Cambridge, Mass.: Harvard University Press, 1975.

Byron, Joseph. *Photographs of New York Interiors at the Turn of the Century.* New York: Dover, 1976.

Cadogan, William. *An Essay Upon Nursing and the Management of Children, From Their Birth to Three Years of Age.* London: Robert Horsfield, 1769.

Carter, Landon. *The Diary of Colonel Landon Carter of Sabine Hall, 1752–1778, Vol. I and II.* Edited by Jack Green. Charlottesville: The University Press of Virginia, 1965.

Channing, Edward. "The Life of William Ellery," in *The Library of American Biography: The Lives of William Pinkney, William Ellery, and Cotton Mather.* Edited by Jared Sparks. Boston: Hilliard, Gray, 1836.

Chastellux, Marquis de. *Travels in North America in the Years 1780, 1781, and 1782.* Translated by Howard Rice. Chapel Hill: University of North Carolina Press, 1963.

Cheney, Ednah, ed. *Life, Letters and Journals of Louisa May Alcott.* Boston: Roberts Brothers, 1889.

Chesterfield, Earl of. *Letters to His Son on the Fine Art of Becoming a Man of the World and a Gentleman.* 1774; reprint New York: Tudor Pub., 1954.

Child, Lydia. *The American Frugal Housewife.* Boston: Carter, Hendee & Co., 1835.
———. *The Mother's Book.* Boston: Carter & Hendee, 1831.

Condorcet, Marquis de. *Outline of an Historical View of the Progress of the Human Mind.* Paris, 1795.

Cooper, H. J. *The Art of Furnishing on Rational and Aesthetic Principles.* New York: Henry Holt, 1881.

Crane, Ross. *The Ross Crane Book of Home Furnishings and Decoration.* New York, c. 1880.

Cuff, Henry. *The Differences of the Ages of Man's Life: Together with the Original Causes, Progresse and End Thereof.* London: T. Harper, 1640.

Dewees, William P. *A Treatise on the Physical and Medical Treatment of Children.* Philadelphia: Carey & Lea, 1832.

Dewing, Mrs. T. W. *Beauty in the Household.* New York: Harper & Brothers, 1882.

Drinker, Elizabeth. *Extracts from the Journal of Elizabeth Drinker.* Edited by Henry Beale. Philadelphia: J. B. Lippincott, 1889.

Eberle, John. *A Treatise on the Diseases and Physical Education of Children.* Cincinnati, Ohio: Corey and Fairbank, 1834.

Edis, Robert W. *Decoration and Furniture of Town Houses.* London: C. Kegan Paul, 1881.

Edwards, Ralph. *Early Conversation Pictures from the Middle Ages to About 1730.* London: Country Life Ltd., 1954.

Ellis, Havelock. *Studies in the Psychology of Sex. Vol. 1, The Evolution of Modesty; The Phenomena of Sexual Periodicity.* Philadelphia: F. A. Davis, 1924.

Emerson, Ralph Waldo. *Nature: Address and Lectures.* Boston: Houghton, Mifflin and Co., 1885.

An Encyclopaedia of Cottage, Farm & Villa Architecture. London: A. Spottiswoode, 1839.

Fairfax, Sally. "Diary of a Little Colonial Girl." *Virginia Magazine of History and Biography* (vol. 11), 212–14.

A Father. *The Play-house and Workshop.* New York: Edward Kearney, 1839.

Fithian, Philip Vickers. *Philip Vickers Fithian: Journal and Letters, 1767–1774.* Edited by John Rogers Williams. Princeton, N.J.: Princeton University Library, 1900.

Foegne, Marion, and John Anderson. *Child Care and Training.* Minneapolis: University of Minnesota Press, 1929.

Forrester, Francis [Rev. Daniel Wise]. *Minnie's Playroom: or How to Practice Calisthenics.* Boston: Geo. C. Rand, 1854.

Fowler, Orson S. *Creative and Sexual Science: or Manhood, Womanhood, and Their Mutual Interrelations; Love, Its Laws, Powers, etc.; A Mutual Adaptation: Courtship, Married Life, and Perfect Children.* Philadelphia: The National Publishing Co., 1870.

―――. *A Home for All, or the Gravel Wall and Octagon Mode of Building.* New York: Fowler & Wells, 1853.

Froebel, Friederick. *Mother-Play and Nursery Songs, Translated from the German.* Boston: Lee and Sheppard, 1878.

Frohne, Henry, and Alice and Bettina Jackson. *Color Schemes for the Home and Model Interiors.* Philadelphia: J. B. Lippincott, 1919.

Ham, Elizabeth. *Elizabeth Ham: 1783–1820.* London: G. Bredon, 1945.

Hamilton, Alexander. *Gentleman's Progress: The Itinerarium of Dr. Alexander Hamilton.* Edited by Carl Bridenbaugh. Westport, Conn.: Greenwood Press, 1973.

Harcourt, Mrs. Charles. *Good Form for Women.* Philadelphia: John C. Winston, 1907.

Harland, Marion. *Common Sense in the Nursery.* New York: Charles Scribner's Sons, 1885.

Havens, Catherine Elizabeth. *Diary of a Little Girl in Old New York.* New York: Henry Collins Brown, 1920.

Hints for the Improvement of Early Education and Nursery Discipline. Philadelphia: John H. Putnam, 1826.

The History of Little Goody Twoshoes. London, 1765; reprinted London: G. K. Hall, 1969 (first published in America in 1775).

Hitchcock, D. D. *Memories of the Bloomsgrove Family.* Boston: Thomas & Andrews, 1790.

Holland, J. G. *Arthur Bonnicastle; An American Novel.* New York: Scribner, 1873.

Holloway, Edward Stratton. *The Practical Book of Furnishing the Small House and Apartment.* Philadelphia: J. B. Lippincott Co., 1922.

Holt, Emmett L. *The Care and Feeding of Children.* New York: D. Appleton, 1894. Reprinted in *The Physician and Child-Rearing: Two Guides, 1809–1894.* Edited by Charles E. Rosenberg. New York: Arno Press, 1972.

Hone, Philip. *The Diary of Philip Hone.* New York: Library Editions, 1970.

Houghton, Walter R. *American Etiquette and Rules of Politeness.* New York: Standard Publishing Co., 1883.

Hutchinson, Sara. *Letters of Sara Hutchinson.* Edited by Kathleen Coburn. Toronto: University of Toronto Press, 1954.

Irving, Washington. *Diedrich Knickerbocker's History of New-York.* 1809; reprinted New York: Heritage Press, 1940.

Jennings, H. J. *Our Homes and How to Beautify Them.* London: Harrison & Sons, 1902.

Jones, Mrs. C. S., and Henry T. Williams. *Beautiful Homes—How to Make Them.* New York: Henry Allen, 1885.

Kellogg, Alice M. *Home Furnishing—Practical and Artistic.* New York: Frederick A. Stokes, 1904.

Lamb, Charles [Mrs. Leicester, pseud.]. "Going into Britches," in *Mrs. Leicester's School.* London: Juvenile Library, 1809.

Larcom, Lucy. *A New England Girlhood.* 1889; reprinted Boston: Houghton Mifflin, 1924.

Miss Leslie. *The House Book: A Manual of Domestic Economy for Town and Country.* Philadelphia: Carey & Hart, 1848.

Locke, John. *Some Thoughts Concerning Education.* London, 1693; reprinted New York: P. F. Collier, 1910.

Ludwig Bauman & Co. Catalogue. New York: Ludwig Bauman, 1890s.

Manigault, Harriet. *The Diary of Harriet Manigault, 1813–1816.* Rockland, Maine: Maine Coast Printers, 1976.

Mrs. Moberly. *The Art of Conversation.* New York: Wilson & Co., 1902.

Montgomery Ward Catalogue: World's Fair Edition, 1893. Chicago: Montgomery Ward, 1893.

Mussey, Barrows, ed. *Yankee Life by Those Who Lived It.* New York: Alfred A. Knopf, 1947.

Nivelson, François. *Rudiments of Genteel Behavior.* London, 1737.

Our Boys and Girls at Home: Stories and Poems and Pictures For Young Readers. New York: W. B. Conkey, 1895.

Panton, J. E. *From Kitchen to Garret.* London: Ward & Downey, 1893.

Peabody and Whitney Annual Catalogue of Children's Carriages. Boston, 1894.

The Poetic Gift or Alphabet in Rhyme. New Haven, Conn.: S. Babcock, 1828.

Raleigh, Sir Walter. *The History of the World in Five Books.* London: T. Basset, 1694.

Read, Mary. *The Mothercraft Manual.* Boston: Little, Brown & Co., 1916.

Richards, Caroline Cowles. *Village Life in America.* New York: Henry Holt & Co., 1913.

Richardson, Samuel. *Pamela: or Virtue Rewarded.* London: F. Newbury, 1769.

Rolfe, Amy. *Interior Decoration for the Small Home.* New York: Macmillan, 1926.

Roosevelt, J. West. "Hygiene in the Home," in *The House and Home.* New York: Charles Scribner's Sons, 1894.

Rousseau, Jean-Jacques. *Emile, or on Education.* Translated by Barbara Fowley. London: J. M. Dent, 1911 (first published in 1762).

Ruhrah, John, ed. *Pediatrics of the Past.* New York: Paul B. Hoeber, 1925.

Scott, James Foster. *The Sexual Instinct: Its Use and Dangers as Affecting Heredity and Morals.* New York: E. B. Treat, 1899.

Sears, Roebuck Catalogue of 1897. Edited by Fred L. Israel. New York: Chelsea House, 1968.

Sears, Roebuck Catalogue of 1902. Chicago: Sears, Roebuck, 1902.

The Servant's Guide and Family Manual. London: John Lumbird, 1830.

Smith, J. T. *Nollekins and His Times.* London: Windle, 1828.

Spenser, Edmund. *The Faerie Queene.* London: H. Hills, 1678.

Starr, Louis. *Hygiene in the Nursery.* 1871; 7th ed. Philadelphia: P. Blakiston's Sons, 1906.

Steele, Sir Richard. *The Tatler.* London: Johns Hopkins, 1710.

Stevenson, Robert Louis. *Dr. Jekyll and Mr. Hyde.* London: Collins, 1886.

Stickley, Gustav. *Craftsman Homes.* New York: Craftsman Publishing, 1909.

Stowe, Harriet Beecher. *Oldtown Folks.* Boston: Osgood & Co., 1869.

———. *Uncle Tom's Cabin.* London: Clarke & Co., 1852.

Struve, R., M.D. *The Domestic Education of Children.* Philadelphia, 1802.

Throop, Lucy Abbott. *Furnishing the Home of Good Taste.* New York: Robert McBride, 1920.

Uncle Thomas. *Christmas Blossoms, and New Year's Wreath for 1849.* Philadelphia: E. H. Butler, 1849.

Wagenknecht, Edward, ed. *When I Was a Child.* New York: E. P. Dutton, 1946.

Walker, Alexander. *Intermarriage, or the Mode in Which, and the Causes Why, Beauty, Health, and Intellect, Result from Certain Unions, and Deformity, Disease and Insanity from Others.* New York: J. & H. G. Langley, 1839.

Wells, Richard G., A.M. *Manners, Culture and Dress of the Best American Society.* Springfield, Mass.: King, Richardson, 1890.

West, Mrs. Max. *Prenatal Care.* Washington, D.C.: U.S. Government Printing Office, for the U.S. Department of Labor, Children's Bureau, 1915.

Wharton, Edith, and Ogden Codman, Jr. *The Decoration of Houses.* 1897; New York: Charles Scribner's Sons, 1919.

Whitney, Mrs. A. D. T. *Hitherto: A Story of Yesterdays.* Boston: Loring, 1869.

———. *Real Folks.* Boston: James R. Osgood, 1872.

F. A. Whitney Carriage Co.: F. A. Whitney Go-Carts and Baby Carriages. Leominster, Mass.; F. A. Whitney, 1902.

Wiggin, Kate Douglas. "The Training of Children," in *The House and Home.* New York: Charles Scribner's Sons, 1894.

Wilde, Oscar. *The Picture of Dorian Gray.* London: Ward & Locke, 1891.

The Workwoman's Guide. London: Simpkin, Marshall, 1840.

Wright, Richardson. *Inside the House of Good Taste.* New York: Robert McBride, 1918.

MANUSCRIPTS

Byrd, William. Diary. University of North Carolina, Davis Library, Chapel Hill.

Carter, Landon. Diary. University of Virginia Library, Charlottesville.

Pemberton, John. Diary. Historical Society of Pennsylvania, Philadelphia.

Ridgely, Eliza. Journal. Waldron Phoenix Belknap Memorial Library, H. F. du Pont Winterthur Museum, Winterthur, Del.

Young Lady of Virginia. Journal. Waldron Phoenix Belknap Memorial Library, H. F. du Pont Winterthur Museum, Winterthur, Del.

NINETEENTH-CENTURY PERIODICALS

American Cabinet Makers and Upholsterers. New York.

Appleton's Journal of Literature, Science and Art. New York: D. Appleton & Co.

The Atlantic Monthly: A Magazine of Literature, Arts, and Politics. Boston: Phillips, Sampson & Co.

Babyland. Boston: D. Lothrop & Co.

Craftsman Magazine. Syracuse, N.Y.: Craftsman Publishers.

The Delineator: A Journal of Fashion, Culture and Fine Arts. New York: Butterick Publishing Co.

Godey's Lady's Magazine. Philadelphia: Godey Publishing Co.

Good Housekeeping. New York: Good Housekeeping Co.

Harper's New Monthly Magazine. New York: Harper & Co.

House Beautiful. New York: House Beautiful Co.

Ladies Home Journal. Philadelphia: Ladies Home Journal Co.

The Nursery: A Monthly Magazine for Youngest Readers. Boston: John L. Shorey.

Peterson's Ladies National Magazine. Philadelphia: Charles Peterson.

St. Nicholas: An Illustrated Magazine for Young Folks. New York: The Century Co.

The Upholsterer. New York.

SECONDARY SOURCES

Ames, Kenneth. "Material Culture as Verbal Communication: A Historical Case Study." *Journal of American Culture* 3 (Winter 1980): 619–41.

Ariès, Philippe. *Centuries of Childhood: A Social History of Family Life.* Translated by Robert Baldick. New York: Vintage Books, 1962.

Avery, Gillian. *Nineteenth-Century Children Heroes and Heroines in English Children's Stories, 1780–1900.* New York: Hodder & Stoughton, 1965.

Axtell, James. *The School Upon the Hill: Education and Society in Colonial New England.* New Haven, Conn.: Yale University Press, 1974.

Beales, Ross W., Jr. "In Search of the Historical Child: Miniature Adulthood and Youth in Colonial New England." *American Quarterly* 27: 379–98.

Belknap, Waldron Phoenix, Jr. *American Colonial Painting: Materials for a History.* Cambridge, Mass.: Harvard University Press, 1959.

Benes, Peter. *Family and Children: Annual Proceedings of the Dublin Seminar for New England Folklife.* Boston: Boston University Press, 1986.

Bourdieu, Pierre. *Distinction: A Social Critique of the Judgement of Taste.* Translated by Richard Nice. Cambridge, Mass.: Harvard University Press, 1984.

Bremner, Robert. *Children and Youth in America.* Cambridge, Mass.: Harvard University Press, 1970.

Brobeck, Stephen. "Images of the Family: Portrait Paintings as Indices of American Family Culture, Structure, and Behavior, 1730–1860." *Journal of Psychohistory* 5: 81–106.

Brooke, Iris. *English Children's Costume since 1775.* London: A & C Black, 1930.

Buck, Anne. *Dress in Eighteenth-Century England.* London: B. T. Batsford, 1979.

Cable, Mary. *The Little Darlings: A History of Childrearing in America.* New York: Charles Scribner's Sons, 1975.

Calvert, Karin. "Children in American Portraiture, 1670 to 1810." *William and Mary Quarterly* 39: 33–63.

———. "Cradle to Crib: The Revolution in Children's Furniture." In *A Century of Childhood, 1820–1920.* Rochester, N.Y.: Margaret Woodbury Strong Museum, 1984.

Carter, Jan, ed. *The Maltreated Child.* London: Priory Press, 1974.

Chew, Samuel C. *The Pilgrimage of Life.* New Haven, Conn.: Yale University Press, 1962.

Clegg, Alec, and Barbara Megson. *Children in Distress.* Harmondsworth: Penguin Books, 1968.

Cleverly, J., and I. Phillips. *From Locke to Spock.* Melbourne: Melbourne University Press, 1976.

Cott, Nancy F. *The Bonds of Womanhood: "Women's Sphere" in New England, 1780–1835.* New Haven, Conn.: Yale University Press, 1978.

Cunnington, Phillis, and Anne Buck. *Children's Costume in England: 1300 to 1900.* New York: Barnes & Noble, 1965.

Darton, F. J. Harvey. *Children's Books in England.* Cambridge: Cambridge University Press, 1960.

Davis, Glen. *Childhood and History in America.* New York: The Psychohistory Press, 1976.

deMause, Lloyd. "The Evolution of Childhood." In *The History of Childhood,* edited by Lloyd deMause. London: Souvenir Press, 1976.

Demos, John. *A Little Commonwealth: Family Life in Plymouth Colony.* New York: Oxford University Press, 1970.

————. *Remarkable Providences: 1600–1760.* New York: George Braziller, 1972.

Donegan, Jane. *Hydropathic Highway to Health: Women and Water-Cure in Antebellum America.* New York: Greenwood Press, 1986.

Earle, Alice Morse. *Child Life in Colonial Days.* New York: Macmillan, 1899.

————. *Two Centuries of Costume in America.* New York: Macmillan, 1903.

Erikson, Erik. *Childhood and Society.* New York: W. W. Norton, 1963.

Finley, Ruth. *The Lady of "Godey's": Sarah Josepha Hale.* Philadelphia: Lippincott, 1931.

Fletcher, David H. *Privacy in Colonial New England.* Charlottesville: University Press of Virginia, 1972.

Forsyth, Irene. "Children in Early Medieval Art: Ninth through Twelfth Centuries." *Journal of Psychohistory* 4, no. 1: 31–79.

Fritzsch, Karl Ewald, and Manfred Bachmann. *An Illustrated History of German Toys.* New York: Hastings House, 1978.

Gloagg, John. *Victorian Comfort — A Social History of Design from 1830–1900.* London: Adam & Charles Black, 1961.

Greven, Philip. *Four Generations: Population, Land, and Family in Colonial Andover, Mass.* Ithaca, N.Y.: Cornell University Press, 1970.

————. *The Protestant Temperament: Patterns of Child-Rearing, Religious Experience, and the Self in Early America.* New York: Meridian, 1979.

Hanawalt, Barbara. "Childrearing among the Lower Classes of Late Medieval England." *Journal of Interdisciplinary History* 8, no. 1: 1–22.

Hareven, Tamara. "The History of the Family as an Interdisciplinary Field." In *The Family in History,* edited by Theodore Rabb and Robert Rotberg. New York: Harper & Row, 1973.

Hartman, Mary S. "Child Abuse and Self-Abuse: Two Victorian Cases." *History of Childhood Quarterly: The Journal of Psychohistory* 2, no. 2: 221–49.

Helmoltz, R. H. "Infanticide in the Province of Canterbury during the Fifteenth Century." *History of Childhood Quarterly: The Journal of Psychohistory* 2, no. 2: 379–90.

Hoffer, Peter C., and N. E. H. Hull. *Murdering Mothers: Infanticide in England and New England.* New York: New York University Press, 1981.

Hoffert, Sylvia. *Private Matters: American Attitudes toward Childbearing and Infant Nurture in the Urban North, 1800–1860.* New York: Oxford University Press, 1989.

Hoyles, Martin. "Childhood in Historical Perspective." In *Changing Childhood,* edited by Martin Hoyles, 16–29. London: Writers and Readers Publishing Cooperative, 1981.

Hunt, David. *Parents and Children in History: The Psychology of Family Life in Early Modern France.* New York: Basic Books, 1970.

Husband, Timothy. *The Wild Man: Medieval Myth and Symbolism.* New York: Metropolitan Museum of Art, 1980.

Illick, Joseph E. "Child-rearing in Seventeenth-Century England and America." In *The History of Childhood,* edited by Lloyd deMause. London: Souvenir Press, 1976.

Johnson, Paul E. *A Shopkeeper's Millennium: Society and Revivals in Rochester, New York, 1815–1837.* New York: Hill and Wang, 1978.

Kern, Stephen. "Explosive Intimacy: Psychodynamics in the Victorian Family." *History of Childhood Quarterly: The Journal of Psychohistory* 1, no. 3: 437–63.

Kett, Joseph. *Rites of Passage: Adolescence in America, 1790 to the Present.* New York: Basic Books, 1977.

Kiefer, Monica. *American Children through Their Books, 1700–1835.* Philadelphia: University of Pennsylvania Press, 1948.

King, Constance Eileen. *The Collector's History of Dolls.* New York: Bonanza Books, 1977.

Kunicov, Robert. *Mr. Godey's Ladies.* Princeton, N.J.: Pyne Press, 1971.

Laslett, Peter. *The World We Have Lost.* London: Souvenir Press, 1971.

Laslett, Peter, and Richard Wall, eds. *Household and Family in Past Time.* New York: Cambridge University Press, 1972.

Lovejoy, Arthur O. *The Great Chain of Being: A Study of the History of an Idea.* Rev. ed. Cambridge, Mass.: Harvard University Press, 1966.

Lovell, Margaretta. "Reading Eighteenth-Century American Family Portraits: Social Images and Self Images." *Winterthur Quarterly* 22 (1988): 243–64.

MacLeod, Anne. "The Caddie Woodlawn Syndrome: American Girlhood in the Nineteenth Century." In *A Century of Childhood, 1820–1920.* Rochester, N.Y.: Margaret Woodbury Strong Museum, 1984.

———. *A Moral Tale: Children's Fiction and American Culture, 1820–1860.* Hamden, Conn.: Archon Press, 1975.

McClintock, Inez and Marshall. *Toys in America.* Washington, D.C.: Public Affairs Press, 1961.

McClinton, Katherine Morrison. *Antiques of American Childhood.* New York: Clarkson Potter, 1970.

McLanathan, Richard. *The American Tradition in the Arts.* New York: Harcourt, Brace & World, 1966.

McLaughlin, Mary. "Survivors and Surrogates: Children and Parents from the Ninth to the Thirteenth Centuries." In *The History of Childhood,* edited by Lloyd deMause. London: Souvenir Press, 1976.

Marvick, Elizabeth. "The Character of Louis XIII: The Role of His Physician in Its Formation." *Journal of Interdisciplinary History* 4, no. 3: 347–74.

Mergen, Bernard. "The Discovery of Children's Play." *American Quarterly* 26, no. 4: 399–421.

———. "Toys and American Culture: Objects as Hypotheses." *Journal of American Culture* 3, no. 4: 743–51.

Miller, Perry, ed. *The Transcendentalists.* Cambridge, Mass.: Harvard University Press, 1950.

Morgan, Edmund. *The Puritan Family: Religion and Domestic Relations in the Seventeenth Century.* Boston: Trustees of the Public Library, 1944.

Muir, Percy. *English Children's Books, 1600 to 1900.* London: B. T. Batford, 1954.

Pinchbeck, I., and M. Hewitt. *Children in English Society.* London: Routledge & Kegan Paul, 1969.

Plumb, J. H. "The New World of Children in Eighteenth-Century England." *Past and Present* 67: 64–93.

Pollock, Linda. *Forgotten Children: Parent-Child Relations from 1500 to 1900.* Cambridge: Cambridge University Press, 1983.

Rabb, Theodore, and Robert Rotberg, eds. *The Family in History.* New York: Harper & Row, 1973.

Robertson, Priscilla. "Home as a Nest: Middle-Class Childhood in Nineteenth-Century Europe." In *The History of Childhood,* edited by Lloyd deMause. London: Souvenir Press, 1976.

Rosenberg, Charles E. *The Family in History.* Philadelphia: University of Pennsylvania Press, 1975.

———, ed. *The Physician and Child-Rearing: Two Guides, 1809–1894.* New York: Arno Press, 1972.

Rothman, David. "Documents in Search of a Historian: Toward a History of Childhood and Youth in America." In *The Family in History,* edited by Theodore Rabb and Robert Rotberg. New York: Harper & Row, 1973.

Schnucker, R. V. "The English Puritans and Pregnancy, Delivery, and breastfeeding." *The History of Childhood Quarterly* 1: 637–58.

Scholten, Catherine M. *Childbearing in American Society: 1650–1850.* New York: New York University Press, 1985.

Shorter, Edward. *The Making of the Modern Family.* London: William Collins, 1976.

Slater, Peter Gregg. *Children in the New England Mind in Death and in Life.* Hamden, Conn.: Archon Books, 1977.

Smith, Daniel Blake. *Inside the Great House: Planter Family Life in Eighteenth-Century Chesapeake Society.* Charlottesville: University Press of Virginia, 1980.

Stannard, David. "Death and the Puritan Child." *American Quarterly* 26: 456–76.

Stone, Lawrence. *The Family, Sex, and Marriage in England, 1500–1800.* London: Weidenfeld & Nicholson, 1977.

Sutton-Smith, Brian. "Toys for Object and Role Mastery." In *Educational Toys in America: 1800 to the Present,* edited by Karen Hewitt and Louise Roomet. Burlington, Vt.: Robert Hull Fleming Museum, 1979.

Trumbach, Randolph. *The Rise of the Egalitarian Family.* New York: Academic Press, 1978.

Tuan, Yi-Fu. *Segmented Worlds and Self: Group Life and Individual Consciousness.* Minneapolis: University of Minnesota Press, 1982.

Warner, Sam Bass, Jr. *The Private City: Philadelphia in Three Periods of Its Growth.* Philadelphia: University of Pennsylvania Press, 1968.

White, Gwen. *European and American Dolls.* New York: Crescent Books, 1966.

Willett, C., and Phillis Cunnington. *A Picture History of English Costume.* London: Vista Books, 1969.

Wilson, Adrian. "The Infancy of the History of Childhood: An Appraisal of Philippe Ariès." *History and Theory* 19: 132–54.

Wishy, Bernard. *The Child and the Republic: The Dawn of Modern American Child Nurture.* Philadelphia: University of Pennsylvania Press, 1968.

Wrigley, E. A. "Reflections on the History of the Family." *Daedalus* 106: 71–85.

Zirkle, Conway. "The Early History of the Idea of Inheritance of Acquired Characteristics and Pangenesis." *Transactions of the American Philosophical Society* 35
(January 1946): 91–151.

Zuckerman, Michael. "An Amusement in This Silent Country: The Family Life of
William Byrd." Unpublished manuscript, 1979.

———. *Peaceable Kingdoms: New England Towns in the Eighteenth Century.* New
York: Random House, 1970.

Index